25

W9-BQW-533

Being and Belonging

Being and Belonging

Muslims in the United States Since 9/11

Katherine Pratt Ewing, editor

Russell Sage Foundation
New York

The Russell Sage Foundation

The Russell Sage Foundation, one of the oldest of America's general purpose foundations, was established in 1907 by Mrs. Margaret Olivia Sage for "the improvement of social and living conditions in the United States." The Foundation seeks to fulfill this mandate by fostering the development and dissemination of knowledge about the country's political, social, and economic problems. While the Foundation endeavors to assure the accuracy and objectivity of each book it publishes, the conclusions and interpretations in Russell Sage Foundation publications are those of the authors and not of the Foundation, its Trustees, or its staff. Publication by Russell Sage, therefore, does not imply Foundation endorsement.

Library of Congress Cataloging-in-Publication Data

Being and belonging : Muslims in the United States since 9/11 / Katherine Pratt Ewing, editor.
    p. cm.
  ISBN 978-0-87154-328-8
  1. Muslims—United States. 2. United States—Ethnic relations. 3. Islam—United States. I. Ewing, Katherine Pratt.

E184.M88B45 2008
305.6'97073—dc22

                                    2008000344

Text design by Suzanne Nichols.

RUSSELL SAGE FOUNDATION
112 East 64th Street, New York, New York 10021
10 9 8 7 6 5 4 3 2 1

CONTENTS

ABOUT THE AUTHORS

KATHERINE PRATT EWING is associate professor of cultural anthropology and religion at Duke University.

MELISSA J. K. HOWE is a doctoral candidate in sociology at the University of Chicago and a contributor to the Islamic Adaptations Project.

SALLY HOWELL is assistant professor of history at the University of Michigan, Dearborn.

MARGUERITE HOYLER is a cultural anthropology major at Duke University.

AMANEY JAMAL is assistant professor of politics at Princeton University.

CRAIG M. JOSEPH is a postdoctoral research associate in the Department of Psychology at Northwestern University and an associate of the Department of Comparative Human Development at the University of Chicago.

SUNAINA MAIRA is associate professor of Asian American studies at the University of California, Davis.

BILL MAURER is professor and chair of the Department of Anthropology at the University of California, Irvine.

JEN'NAN GHAZAL READ is associate professor of sociology at the University of California, Irvine, and a Carnegie Scholar working on Muslim American political integration.

ABOUT THE AUTHORS

BARNABY RIEDEL is a researcher on the Islamic Adaptations Project and a Ph.D. candidate in the Department of Comparative Human Development at the University of Chicago.

ANDREW SHRYOCK is Arthur F. Thurnau Professor of Anthropology at the University of Michigan.

RICHARD A. SHWEDER is the William Claude Reavis Distinguished Service Professor in the Department of Comparative Human Development at the University of Chicago.

CHARLOTTE VAN DEN HOUT is a Ph.D. student in psychiatric anthropology at the University of California, San Diego.

CHAPTER 1

INTRODUCTION

KATHERINE PRATT EWING

THE ATTACKS on the World Trade Center and the Pentagon on September 11, 2001, had a dramatic, immediate effect on Muslims in the United States. Both the magnitude of the destruction within the borders of the United States and the ensuing war on terror have brought the issue of Muslims living in the United States into public awareness in an unprecedented way. Islam and terrorism were already closely associated in public discourse: Immediately after the Oklahoma City bombing in 1995, for example, public officials and the media had speculated that Muslims were responsible. This error led reporters to be more careful on the morning of September 11 when they made their initial assessments. But once the involvement of al Qaeda became clear, the association between Islam and terrorism moved to the center of public awareness, foreign policy, and domestic politics, where it has remained. In the days following the attacks, some members of the American public, including a few radio talk show hosts and Christian leaders, quickly generalized and racialized this threat to include anyone who might look Muslim or Arab. This public talk created a sense of panic in some circles and triggered a backlash of violence, harassment, and insult that was widely reported in the media. As a result, Muslims and those who looked Middle Eastern feared for their safety. The Bush administration made public statements that distinguished terrorism from the activities of most Muslims and from Islam. Nevertheless, al Qaeda and its possible sleeper cells of terrorists who might be hiding within the United States, ready to strike at any moment, posed the powerful threat of an ethnicized, racialized enemy within that the United States public had not experienced since World War II.[1] Parallels to the imagined threat posed by Japanese Americans during World War II have frequently been drawn. For many American Muslims, the possibility of a similarly strong response to the al Qaeda threat, generalized to include all who had immigrated from Muslim-majority countries, was an unavoidable part of the post 9/11 experience. Muslims had suddenly become highly visible outsiders.

The government's responses to the threat of Islamic terrorism included the passage of the USA PATRIOT Act, the suspension of certain civil rights, the detention of many Muslims, and the launching of the war on terror. Though not as drastic as the internment of Japanese Americans, these policies, as well as media coverage and local politics, have affected the lives of Muslims in the United States, as well as the lives of non-Muslim Arabs, South Asians, and others who fell under suspicion in the wake of 9/11. The racial crystallization of the category of Arab-Muslim legitimized a distinction between an American Us to be protected through homeland security measures and the dangerous immigrant Other who came under intense surveillance. Even those who had considered themselves American suddenly found themselves excluded from the sphere of those who were to be protected.

Not only has this complex aftermath of 9/11 altered everyday environments; it has also shaped possibilities and strategies for belonging, cultural citizenship, and identity, though not always in ways that might have been expected. In addition to the effects of the events of 9/11 on specific communities of immigrants from Muslim-majority countries, this volume examines how local Muslim responses have evolved in the years since 2001. In her comprehensive 2003 overview of existing scholarship on Muslims in the United States, Karen Leonard cautioned that research on the impact of 9/11 might have the effect of obscuring continuities in the history and development of Muslim communities in the United States (2003, 139). This book looks at both disruptions and continuities: chapters in part I highlight how Muslims have experienced and been shaped by the events and aftermath of 9/11, and those in part II foreground how preexisting trends in the development of Muslim communities and Islamic institutions have continued and even intensified despite the disruptions and displacements created by the effects of 9/11 and the war on terror. With their emphasis on local communities, these essays as a collection question and consider the ideas of citizenship and belonging when an entire immigrant minority is abruptly reinscribed as a stigmatized Other.

The papers gathered here were first developed as part of a Russell Sage initiative to document and analyze how Muslims have managed the stresses associated with the effects of 9/11. They are based on several research projects, funded by the foundation, that were developed by scholars who had already been working at their research sites before the events of 9/11. These scholars, representing a range of disciplines, had thus already built relationships of trust that other researchers initiating projects since 9/11 have found difficult to establish, due to an atmosphere of increased suspicion.[2] The result is a collection that explores what Andrew Shryock in the epilogue has called disciplinary inclusion, an ambivalent process of belonging that is constrained by public discourse. In the

United States after 9/11, this discourse inevitably locates Muslims as poised between the choice of being either the assimilable "good Muslim" or the supporter of Islamic terrorism (see Mamdani 2004).

MUSLIMS, ARABS, AND SOUTH ASIANS IN THE UNITED STATES: CROSS-CUTTING CATEGORIES

Estimating the number of Muslims in the United States has been a difficult and often politically charged project.[3] The U.S. Census Bureau does not collect data on religious identification, in part because of the principle of church-state separation.[4] Because Muslims represent a quite a small percentage of the American population, figures drawn from general surveys tend to be unreliable. There are, therefore, widely varying estimates of the number of Muslims in the United States, ranging from 0.4 percent to 2 percent of the total population, with most agreeing on a figure of 0.5 percent. According to one survey, the Muslim population nearly doubled between 1990 and 2001.[5] More recently, a 2007 study by the Pew Research Center that focused specifically on Muslim Americans concluded that Muslims constitute 0.6 percent of the United States population, or a total population of 2.35 million (Pew Research Center 2007, 9). Of these, 65 percent were born outside the United States (Pew Research Center 2007, 15), yet 77 percent of all Muslim Americans are now citizens (Pew Research Center 2007, 16).

Some 26 percent of the Muslims in the United States self-identify as black (Pew Research Center 2007, 17), and most of these are African American. African American Muslims have played a key role in the emergence of Islam as a visible presence in the United States, but there has been considerable tension within the various black Islamic movements about whether to focus inward on local community building or outward on building ties with the transnational ummah (community) of Muslims. Most groups focused on African American empowerment and drew sharp boundaries between themselves and immigrant Muslim groups. Until the mid-1970s, there was thus little contact between African American and immigrant Muslims, even among Sunni Muslim groups. The Nation of Islam, founded in 1930, was at one time the largest Islamic movement among African Americans and played a prominent role in the civil rights movement of the 1960s. This movement, which also had an urgent political and economic agenda, rested on a separatist ideology. It adhered to beliefs and practices that were quite distinct from (and even ran counter to) the principles of Sunni Islam. Members had few ties to the broader Muslim world. The Nation of Islam changed direction dramatically in 1975, when Warith Dean Mohammed became the imam, renamed the organization, and moved its doctrines and practices toward Sunni Islam.[6] As African American Muslims have focused increasingly on participation in a global community of Muslims and a universal Islam, ties between African American and immigrant Muslim communities have begun to develop in the United States, especially with the establishment and growth of Islamic institutions such as schools, advocacy groups, and national organizations. Nevertheless, many mosques continue to be dominated by a single ethnic group (for an account of this divide in the Iranian Muslim community in the late 1980s, see, for example, Fischer and Abedi 1990).

Of Muslims born outside the United States, approximately 37 percent are from Arabic-speaking countries and 27 percent are from South Asia (Pew Research Center 2007, 15). There are also significant populations from Iran (12 percent), Europe (8 percent), and sub-Saharan Africa (6 percent) (Pew Research Center 2007, 15). The largest immigrant groups of Muslims are thus Arab and South Asian, and most of the authors in this volume focus on these two populations. The histories and public perceptions of the two ethnic groups, Arab and South Asian, are very different, however (for a useful overview of the development of Muslim communities in the United States, see Leonard 2003).

Some public responses to the al Qaeda attacks indicate popular confusions surrounding the categories of Arab, Muslim, and terrorist (see chapter 5, this volume). Stereotypical representations tend to equate the Arab and the Muslim, even though in the United States it is likely that fewer than a third of those of Arab descent are actually Muslim (see chapter 3, this volume). Many early Arab immigrants were Christian immigrants who left the Ottoman Empire and, later, Palestine and Lebanon. Reflecting the nature of national identity politics in the Middle East earlier in the twentieth century, Arab Muslims and Christians stressed their specific national identity or, in the effort to establish national organizations in the United States to facilitate integration, a common ethnic identity as Arab. They were among the many populations gradually integrating into the mainstream. The percentage of Muslim Arabs began increasing after the Immigration and Naturalization Act of 1965, which opened the United States to skilled, highly educated immigrants from non-European countries. In the 1980s, leaders began organizing as Muslims and founded national organizations such as the Muslim Students Association (MSA) and the Islamic Society of North America (ISNA) that focused on the maintenance of Islamic practices rather than on a common ethnicity. Today, many Americans would be surprised to learn that most Arabs in the United States are not Muslim.

The South Asian population in the United States has been growing steadily for nearly half a century, with large numbers after 1965. They came from India, Pakistan, and, later, from Bangladesh and Afghanistan. Many first came in the 1970s and 1980s to pursue undergraduate and graduate studies. Since this influx, the South Asian subpopulation has been characterized by upward mobility, a cultural emphasis on education and notable professional success. South Asian Americans have the highest socioeconomic achievement indicators of all Asian American groups. Sixty-four percent of adults of Indian background, for example, have bachelor's degrees (versus 25 percent of white Americans), and 12 percent earn law, medical or graduate degrees (versus 3 percent).[7] About 12 percent of those from India are Muslim (Leonard 2003, 13), as are virtually all of those from the other South Asian countries.

In contrast to the equation of Arab and Muslim in the American public imagination, India is usually associated with Hinduism, and South Asia has little visibility.[8] Historically, there has been virtually no general awareness in the United States of the significant proportion of Muslims in India and other parts of South Asia. This awareness, however, has sharpened since 9/11, given the presence of al Qaeda and Osama bin Laden in Afghanistan and the importance of neighboring Pakistan in the war on terror. Pakistan has gained sustained media visibility as a training ground for Taliban and al Qaeda-linked Islamic fundamentalists. This new visibility has had an impact on Pakistani Americans, who had often been recognized as Indian in an earlier era.

THE BACKLASH AND ITS EFFECTS

Part I describes significant discursive shifts in the United States in response to 9/11, shifts in which the media and government policies played a prominent role. There was a crystallization of the racialized category of Arab–Middle Easterner–Muslim, with racial profiling perhaps most vividly enacted at airport security checkpoints, but felt even more dramatically within many Muslim communities in the less visible processes of detention and deportation. One direct result of government policy was a constraint on the mobility of those associated with Islam and the Middle East. It became more difficult to cross national borders, so that every trip abroad carried with it the uncertainty about being able to return, even among those of the business class. Such constraints affect transnational practices and ties, and also emphasize in an immediate and personal way the extent to which the individual being hindered has suddenly been defined as Other. More pervasively, even Muslims who did not personally experience surveillance and detention were aware that it could happen to them or to someone close to them.

On the basis of research conducted among South Asian Muslim youth in a small New England city, Sunaina Maira examines how immigration and homeland security policies have affected these young people's sense of belonging and their understandings of cultural citizenship (see chapter 2, this volume). She argues that the experience of being Muslim after 9/11 must be understood in terms of the multiple contexts of everyday life and demonstrates that these youth manifest multiple modes of citizenship, which she characterizes as "flexible," "polycultural," and "dissenting," proposing the concept of polycultural rather than multicultural citizenship to characterize how these youth manage a complex set of political affiliations that cannot be described as discrete cultures. Her research targeted a population of working class, recent (in some cases illegal) immigrants who are more vulnerable to dislocation and marginalization than are professional South Asian families who have constituted a model minority in the United States (and are the focus of the chapter by Ewing and Hoyler). She points out that labor itself contributes to this marginalization, because it dictates the time that these youth have available to pursue other aspects of the American Dream. Such forms of marginalization have been exacerbated by the increased "disciplining technology of the state" in the wake of 9/11, experienced acutely within this community in the form of arrests and deportations for visa violations.

Chapter 3 focuses on Arab integration in the Detroit-Dearborn area, which has the most concentrated and long-established Arab communities in the country. Sally Howell and Amaney Jamal examine the post 9/11 backlash in light of two contradictory assumptions: that the post-9/11 experiences of Detroit Arab communities were representative of Muslim communities in other parts of the United States, and that they were exceptional with respect to national patterns because of the high visibility of Arabs and Muslims in this area and the public's resulting perception of their concentrated Otherness. Howell and Jamal note a contrast between national responses and local ones, between, on the one hand, national-level phenomena such as the Patriot Act, humiliation at airports and immigration points, detention and deportation without legal counsel, and unprecedented surveillance and, on the other hand, local-level experiences, in which Arabs in Detroit generally felt safer from retaliation and discrimination than Arabs in other parts of the country did. They argue that Arab Detroit was exceptional because of the established position of Muslims and people of Arab descent in local institutions such as various social services, law enforcement, and the media. They also note Arab political influence and voice at the local level due to the well-established Arab and Muslim institutions. In contrast, parallel efforts to protect the civil rights of those under suspicion by organizing at the national level have been blocked.

In chapter 4, Katherine Ewing and Marguerite Hoyler focus their research on youth from professional South Asian Muslim families living in the Raleigh-Durham area of North Carolina. They found that, especially for those who actively participate in local mosque or Muslim student groups, the aftermath of 9/11 intensified their struggles over identity articulation. A recurrent theme in interviews was the sense of an unnecessary tension between American and Muslim identities generated by the humiliating treatment of Muslims that had directly affected family members, reports of attacks on Muslims both locally and nationally, and the frequent projection in the media of the idea that Muslims are enemies of the United States. Despite being from middle class, professional families, these well-integrated college-bound youth nevertheless found themselves questioning their futures as they sensed the increasing difficulties of being Muslim in the United States following 9/11. Such youth have in increasing numbers intensified their commitment to Islam, taking up an orientation purified of what they consider the cultural contaminations of their parents' homeland. Paradoxically, turning to what they regard as a purified Islam works as an integration strategy in which Islamic practice is experienced as compatible with most aspects of American culture. The sudden public focus on Muslims has thus changed the significance of being Muslim for many people. There were some who sought to hide their Muslim identity or distance themselves from it. But others were moved to reconsider their relationship to Islam and became more closely tied to or active in the Muslim community as a result.

THE CHANGING SHAPE OF COMMUNITIES AND INSTITUTIONS

Despite all of the changes precipitated by 9/11 and the war on terror, most Muslims in the United States have gone on with their lives, often participating in institutions such as mosques, schools, and Islamic banks that have been established to meet their needs as Muslims. These institutions play a critical role in fostering a sense of fully belonging to American society, especially at a time when this sense has been challenged by homeland security measures and stigmatization. The chapters in part II consider if and how the changes in the situation of Muslims have affected such institutions.

The impact of 9/11 on specific institutions is not always predictable or what might be expected. Thus, for example, the demand for spokespersons to represent and explain Islam to government bodies and to the public in the media has given Muslims increased political presence in the national arena. Yet, as Leonard has pointed out, the people who have been tapped as spokespersons have not always been established leaders within Muslim communities and institutions. They tended to be, not the leaders of national organizations, but rather those who were outsiders or marginal to them (Leonard 2003, 26). As a result, new prominence has come to certain leaders to serve as spokespersons for Muslims in the United States, sometimes at the expense of others. Such shifts can change the center and balance of power within a community or organization.

One government action that had an immediate impact on Muslim communities and on a number of Islamic institutions was the freezing of the assets of several Islamic charities that funneled charitable donations overseas. This led to a precipitous shift in patterns of Muslim charitable giving, a shift that has had identifiable institutional effects. Charitable giving is a central aspect of Muslim practice, one of the five pillars of Islam, along with belief in the oneness of God, regular prayer, fasting during the month of Ramadan, and the pilgrimage to Mecca. When channels of giving to transnational organizations were blocked, many Muslims in the United States increased local giving. One effect has been an acceleration in the construction and expansion of mosques and Islamic schools, a phenomenon noted by several contributors.

Mosques have also been affected in other ways. For example, a part of the long-term Americanization of Islam has been the tendency for mosques to function more as community centers (on the model of churches) than in the countries of origin. These functions intensified after 9/11, because Muslims felt a sense of threat and turned inward for support from other members of the Muslim community.

In chapter 5, Jen'nan Read assesses the impact of September 11 on Arab American identity and finds that the shifts in public discourse have affected intraethnic relations among Arabs, making religious difference more salient than it had been. Based on ethnographic, interview, and survey data at an Arab mosque and an Arab Christian church in Houston, Read asks whether and how the consequences of 9/11 have differed for Muslims and Christians. She asks what it means to be an Arab in America today and how this varies by religious affiliation. She also considers what ethnic options are available to Muslims and Christians and to what extent these are contingent on sociodemographic characteristics such as national origin, generational status and social class. She concludes that the events of September 11 created a cultural wedge that factionalized the Arab American community along religious lines. Christian Arabs have emphasized cultural aspects of Arabic identity but downplay political aspects that might be threatening in American society. Muslim Arabs also have strong attachments to American identity but, being more recent immigrants, they have even stronger ties to homelands and also have a sharper religious, ethnic, and racial status as outsiders.

The authors of chapters 6 and 7 are members of a research team working in the community of Bridgeview, Illinois, a suburb southwest of Chicago. Chapter 6 traces the immediate and more long-term impacts of 9/11 and its aftermath in Bridgeview. It finds that this Muslim community, though strongly affected, has demonstrated remarkable resilience in the face of events such as a large demonstration against the mosque on the day after the World Trade Center attacks, smaller acts of intimidation, some painfully negative press coverage, and investigations of Islamic charities based in Bridgeview. The authors emphasize that, though there have been acts of violence and anti-Muslim rhetoric that manifest a xenophobic fear of the alien Other within, there has also been a public discourse of tolerance and a drive to learn more about Islam and Muslims. Their work critiques a mainstream discourse that posits an incompatibility between American values and the demands of Islam, a discourse that perpetuates mainstream American fears about whether Muslims can fully belong to American society. They find that, despite a lingering undercurrent of anxiety and resentment over ongoing surveillance, as well as fear of mainstream bigotry and assimilation pressure, life has generally returned to normal for most of the community.

Chapter 7 offers a portrait of the Universal School, which has served as a model for other Islamic schools across the United States. Craig Joseph and Barnaby Riedel examine how it strives to socialize students to be both good Americans and good Muslims. They point out that a central concern of Islamic schools had been to adapt the secular public school curriculum to Islam. The authors identify a shift of focus toward a greater emphasis on developing an Islamic environment that will shape the moral character of students. In the face of Muslims of a diversity of backgrounds, the Universal School has sought to inculcate what are identified as principles of a common Islam to instill in students an authentic Islamic personality that is simultaneously consistent with authentic Americanness in its universal values and virtues. They point out the recent surge in the establishment of private Islamic schools, a growth that parallels the growth in the Muslim population and is similar to the ways that other immigrant groups who came from places where religion was an important educational component, such as Catholics and Jews a century earlier, established parochial schools in their new communities. With the rising flow of charitable giving into local organizations since 9/11, this growth has accelerated.

In chapter 8, Bill Maurer notes how Islamic banking was thrust into the spotlight when Islamic charities were suspected in the financing of the 9/11 plotters. But this did not lead Muslim Americans who had been using Islamic financial alternatives to transfer assets to more conventional banking institutions. Maurer finds instead a continued development of Islamic financial institutions after 9/11. The events of 9/11 did have a noticeable impact, he argues, but this had less to do with Islam and more to do with banking, finance and American ideas of law and bureaucratic formality. In reaction to the financial shocks of 9/11, Americans in general, including Muslims, took their money out of the stock market and invested in real estate. Muslims also withdrew money from charities under government scrutiny. Maurer suggests that one response to Muslims and Middle Easterners being stigmatized was a desire to increase claims of national belonging by owning one's home, a small piece of America. Analyzing the demographic characteristics of the applicants for mortgages at two rival Islamic banking companies, which use different forms of Islamic financing, he concludes that the choice of one over the other was based, not on an assessment of the financial products themselves and their conformity with Islamic law as determined by Islamic scholars, but on assessments that reveal concerns consistent with contemporary bureaucratic practices and legal consciousness in the United States. He argues that the choices people make reveal the changing status and durability of Islamic legal traditions and practices as they become fully embedded in the United States.

The book concludes with an epilogue by Andrew Shryock, who draws out what he sees as a central theme running through all the contributions to this volume: a trend toward more assertive expressions of American identity and belonging among Muslims, Arabs, and others who were positioned as Other in the wake of 9/11. Although the process of what he calls disciplinary exclusion in the form of hate crimes, surveillance, and stigmatization is readily apparent at this juncture, Shryock calls for a closer examination of the inverse process of disciplinary inclusion. Drawing on the groundwork laid by contributors to this volume, he considers various aspects of citizenship discourse to develop a nuanced characterization of how inclusion, as both policy and desire, is reshaping Arab, South Asian, and Muslim American communities in the post-9/11 era.

Taken together, these essays suggest that in the wake of 9/11, Muslims in the United States have, perhaps paradoxically, developed a growing sense of political assertiveness and confidence in their communities and institutions. The sudden public focus on them as a threatening other exacerbated cleavages within populations with common ethnic identities, such as Arab Christians and Muslims and South Asian Muslims and Hindus, making religious difference more salient than common ethnicity. Although some individuals chose to downplay their identity as Muslims, many others became more self-conscious in asserting it. Simultaneously, Islamic institutions, already developing along with Muslim communities, experienced a growth spurt. Yet these moves toward more public articulations of Islam have been accompanied by assertions of American identity that are consistent with their understandings of Islam and by a growing accommodation of Islamic practices and institutions to the American context.

NOTES

1. The discursive construction of the communist as internal enemy in the 1950s no doubt plays a role in shaping the perception of Islam as an analogous global threat to freedom and democracy, but within the United States, this enemy was not primarily racialized.
2. The researchers include sociologists, anthropologists, political scientists, and scholars of American studies, Asian American studies, and human development. Contributors to this volume first came together at a conference organized by Stephanie Platz on April 1, 2005. Other participants included Louise Cainkar and Nadine Naber.
3. Some Muslim groups, for example, have expressed concern that some researchers have minimized their numbers and significance (for a discussion of surveys that estimate the Muslim population and issues connected with process, see Smith 2001).
4. This has been an issue at least since 1790 (Good 1959, 4). Demographers have periodically pushed to include questions about religion on the census, drawing on surveys to demonstrate that most people are willing to answer such questions. But resistance to their inclusion has been based on the principle of church-state separation and concerns with government infringement on the right of privacy, especially in the wake of the Holocaust (9).

10

5. The CUNY-sponsored ARIS surveys, conducted in 1990 and 2001, indicate that there were 527,000 Muslims in the United States in 1990 and 1,082,000 (0.5 percent of the total population) in 2001 (Kosmin, Mayer, and Keysar 2001).
6. Louis Farrakhan subsequently split with Imam Mohammed and reestablished the Nation of Islam and its original teachings as a splinter group (for an overview of African American Islam, see McCloud 1995).
7. Percentages were calculated from U.S. Census 2000 Demographic Profile Highlights: Selected Population Group: Asian Indian Alone and White Alone (U.S. Census Bureau 2000).
8. When I tell people that I worked in South Asia, most hear Southeast Asia and think of places like Vietnam.

REFERENCES

Fischer, Michael M. J., and Mehdi Abedi. 1990. *Debating Muslims: Cultural Dialogues in Postmodernity and Tradition.* Madison, Wisc.: University of Wisconsin Press.

Good, Dorothy. 1959. "Questions on Religion in the United States Census." *Population Index* 25(1): 3–16.

Kosmin, Barry A., Egon Mayer, and Ariela Keysar. 2001. *American Religious Identification Survey (ARIS).* New York: The Graduate Center of the City of New York.

Leonard, Karen. 2003. *Muslims in the United States: The State of Research.* New York: Russell Sage Foundation.

Mamdani, Mahmood. 2004. *Good Muslim, Bad Muslim: America, the Cold War, and the Roots of Terror.* New York: Pantheon Books.

McCloud, Aminah Beverly. 1995. *African American Islam.* New York: Routledge.

Pew Research Center. 2007. *Muslim Americans: Middle Class and Mostly Mainstream.* Washington: Pew Research Center. Accessed at http://pewresearch.org/assets/pdf/muslim-americans.pdf.

Smith, Tom W. 2001. "Estimating the Muslim Population in the United States." Chicago, Ill.: National Opinion Research Center. Accessed at http://cloud9.norc.uchicago.edu/dlib/muslm.htm.

U.S. Census Bureau. 2000. "Factfinder. Fact Sheet for a Race, Ethic, or Ancestry Group." Accessed at http://factfinder.census.gov.

PART I

THE BACKLASH AND ITS EFFECTS

CHAPTER 2

CITIZENSHIP, DISSENT, EMPIRE: SOUTH ASIAN MUSLIM IMMIGRANT YOUTH

SUNAINA MAIRA

IN THE WAKE of the September 11 attacks, questions of citizenship, racialization, and religious and national identities have taken on new, urgent meanings for Muslims living in the United States. South Asian Muslim youth, in particular, are coming of age at a moment when their religious and national affiliations are politically charged issues. This chapter addresses the impact of 9/11 on South Asian Muslim immigrant youth living in a New England town I call Wellford. It explores the ways in which they make sense of citizenship, particularly cultural citizenship and their everyday understandings of belonging and exclusion, in relation to state policies after 9/11. How do South Asian Muslim youth make sense of the state and its powers as it shapes their daily experiences of family, migration, work, and education? How do they think of the nation and national belonging in relation to the United States as well as to India, Pakistan, or Bangladesh? How do they imagine their relationships with young people from other ethnic and national groups and other histories of belonging, exclusion, and dissent?

Focusing on Muslim immigrant youth allows us to understand some of the paradoxes of national belonging, alienation, and political expression for a generation of immigrants that is coming of age at this particular moment. Youth are generally the targets of nationalizing discourse by the state and civil society, for example, in institutions such as public high schools, where ideas of national identity and civic virtue are inculcated to produce good citizens. Immigrant youth are particularly important because they are often perceived as not American enough, or as desiring to "become American" but being "caught between two worlds," and thus culturally suspect. For South Asian Muslim immigrant youth this perception is even more acute, especially after 9/11; they are viewed in mainstream discourse as not just culturally or religiously alien, but also as potential recruits for religious fundamentalist movements or anti-American ideologies, or at best, having divided loyalties at a time when national unity is seen as critical.

CULTURAL CITIZENSHIP

Citizenship is a fundamental notion underlying relationships among individuals, communities, and the nation-state because these are inflected by issues of ethnic and racial identity, religion, and transnational identification (Young 1990). It has traditionally been thought of in political, economic, and civic terms (Marshall 1950), but the universalizing ideal is, in reality, challenged by practices of inclusion and exclusion. These make it important to consider the cultural dimensions of citizenship.

Research has increasingly focused on the concept of cultural citizenship, or cultural belonging in the nation (in this case, the United States), and highlighted how the trope of national belonging, so powerful in modernity, is not just based on political, social, and economic dimensions of citizenship but is also defined in the social realm of belonging (Shanahan 1999). Cultural citizenship is a critical issue for immigrants and non-white Americans, in that the rights and obligations of legal citizenship are shaped by differences of race, ethnicity, gender, sexuality, and religion (Berlant 1997; Coll 2002; Miller 1993). The post-9/11 scrutiny of Muslim Americans has made it particularly apparent that the formal promise of equality to citizens and dominant understandings of American national identity are mediated by cultural understandings of citizenship, as has been the case throughout United States history (Sassen 2004, 184). Cultural definitions of citizenship and dominant understandings of who is truly American mediate the rights afforded to citizens and immigrants and cultural constructs of terrorists (now jihadists), borders, and security.

My work examines young Muslim Americans' understandings of cultural citizenship, national belonging, and the ways they negotiate relationships of power in different realms of their everyday life (Bhavnani 1991; Buckingham 2000). Focusing on youth is important because they are generally viewed as the next generation of citizens, who symbolize the cultural and political future of the nation and are invested with adult hopes and fears (France 1998, 200). The category of youth is itself socially constructed and in traditional Western perceptions of adolescence, is viewed as a liminal stage when social identities and political commitments are being formed. Much of the public discourse about Muslim American youth after 9/11 is tinged with deeper social and national anxieties about how Muslim, South Asian, and Arab Americans will position themselves in relation to the United States and what course American society will take. Examining the experiences of youth thus brings into sharper relief the cultural and political anxieties about Muslims in post-9/11 America.

It is important to note, however, that the war on terror and the assault on civil liberties unleashed by the USA PATRIOT Act were not immaculately conceived on September 11, 2001. They have a long gestation in the plans for aggressive military expansion and global political and economic domination for what is called a New American Century, developed well before 2001 by the group of neo-conservatives aligned with George W. Bush, and also in the military interventions and anti-immigrant policies of previous administrations that laid the groundwork for this intensified, unilateralist assertion of American power after 9/11 (Bacevich 2002; Burbach and Tarbell 2004).[1] These policies are rooted in a long history of United States imperial power that has used both direct and indirect control (Ho 2004; Kaplan 1993). United States imperialism has been marked by nebulous, nonterritorial forms of domination that do not resemble traditional colonialism (Magdoff 2003; Smith 2005).[2] In the larger work from which this article is drawn, I discuss the theoretical debates about the United States empire and the role of the lone superpower since the fall of the Berlin Wall and the consolidation of neoliberal capitalism (Maira forthcoming). Scholarship on the United States empire has analyzed the "benevolent imperialism" that purports to bring democracy and freedom to the rest of the world through military and political interventions, often covert and secret, and shapes the collective denial or amnesia about empire within the "cultures of U.S. imperialism" (Kaplan and Pease 1993; Harvey 2003; Rogin 1993; Williams 1980).

The national consensus for United States foreign policies is strengthened through historical processes of scapegoating outsiders and conflating internal and external enemies (Stoler 2006, 12). United States foreign policy is linked to the "policing of domestic racial tensions" and disciplining of subordinated populations through gender and class hierarchies at home (Pease 1993, 31). The experiences of South Asian Muslim youth in the United States in relation to national belonging are inevitably intertwined with the role of the United States on the global stage, and are shaped by the United States' policies toward Muslims domestically and overseas. I first provide a brief overview of the state policies and civil society backlash that affected Muslim Americans in 9/11, which will provide a backdrop for the analysis of the ethnographic research.

THE WAR ON TERROR

Excluding or distancing Arab and Muslim Americans from normative cultural belonging is embedded in state policies and social categorizations that pre-date 9/11 but were heightened under the Patriot Act.[3] The construction of Muslims and Arabs as suspect citizens in the war on terror is rooted in

17

Orientalist views of Islam and the Middle East tied to Western and imperial engagements in the region (Said 1978). This suspicion of Muslim terrorists and Islamic fundamentalists intensified after 9/11 in hyper-Orientalized views, and sometimes hostile assaults and harassment of Arab and Muslim Americans (see, for example, Akram 2002). Many South Asian Americans, Arab Americans, and Muslim Americans (or individuals who appeared Muslim) have been victims of physical assaults and profiling as part of the anti-Muslim backlash and demonization of Arabs in the United States.[4] There was a shift in United States race politics after 9/11, where the racialized fault lines were no longer just between white Americans and racial minorities, or even the binary of black and white Americans, but between those categorized as Muslim or non-Muslim, American or foreign, or citizen or noncitizen. This has led to a racialization of Muslim identity that is not, technically, a racial identity but instead a religious category, intertwined with twenty-first century United States racial formation through processes that resemble other practices of racial profiling.

As part of the domestic war on terror, the mass detentions of Muslim immigrant men in the aftermath of 9/11, without any criminal charges, have deeply affected South Asian Muslim—particularly Pakistani—immigrant communities. The Justice Department, as public criticism began to mount, stopped releasing numbers of persons detained in the post-9/11 sweeps in November 2001. So, according to civil rights lawyers, though the official estimate was 1,182, a more conservative figure for detentions until May 2003 was at least 5,000 (Cole 2003, 25). Nearly 40 percent were thought to be Pakistani nationals, though virtually none were identified publicly and the locations they were held remained secret (Schulhofer 2002, 11). After 9/11, Muslim families began experiencing the disappearances of husbands, brothers, and sons, and many families ended up leaving the country after indefinite separations and loss of family support (Chang 2002, 69–87). There have been, for example, mass deportations of Pakistani nationals on chartered planes, some leaving in the middle of the night from New York State (Ryan 2003, 16).

In June 2002, the National Security Entry-Exit Registration System (Special Registration) was established, requiring men from twenty-four Muslim-majority countries—including Pakistan and Bangladesh, as well as North Korea—to be interviewed, photographed, and fingerprinted at federal immigration facilities.[5] Many of these men, however, never came out: 2,870 were detained and 13,799 were put into deportation proceedings (Nguyen 2005, xviii). After the mass arrests of Iranian men complying with Special Registration in southern California in December 2002, some undocumented immigrants and those with pending immigration applications, including several hundred Pakistanis, tried to flee to Canada.[6] The war on terror has also drawn large numbers of immigrants who were not from Arab or Muslim communities into its dragnet (for example, Nguyen 2005, xx, 18), as part of ongoing anti-

immigrant sentiments and immigration raids, but there has been a dispropor-
tionate targeting of Muslim immigrant men, mostly undocumented and working
class, detained for immigration violations without being convicted on terrorism charges.

The detentions and deportations of Muslim and Arab immigrants have
altered the composition and social fabric of immigrant communities and
instilled fear, suspicion, and self-censorship, as I found in the Muslim immigrant
community in Wellford. Around the country, areas with large concentrations
of Muslim populations saw an exodus of immigrants seeking to avoid arrest
or deportation, such as Brooklyn's Little Pakistan on Coney Island Avenue
(Ryan 2003). More than 15,000 undocumented Pakistanis reportedly left the
United States for Canada, Europe, and Pakistan by June 2003, according to
the Pakistani Embassy in Washington (Swarns 2003). Pakistani immigrants
were disproportionately targeted for detention and deportation, even though
there were no Pakistani nationals involved in the 9/11 hijackings. Although
Pakistan has been a key ally to the United States in its war on terror in the region,
the U.S. government claimed it was clamping down on Islamist guerrilla networks linked to both al Qaeda and Taliban in northwest Pakistan, along the
border with Afghanistan, and thus Pakistanis in the United States became suspect.[7] This is one of many examples that illustrates how the war on terror con-
nects American foreign policy concerns with domestic issues of citizenship,
immigration, criminalization, and incarceration, reshaping communities and
altering the social geography of Muslim America.

Although the fear and anxiety about racial profiling diminished over time
for South Asian immigrants—particularly Indian Americans who were Hindu,
Christian, or even Sikh—it persists for Muslim and Arab Americans who
continue to be targets of the war on terror and are subject to surveillance,
FBI interviews, and discrimination in the workplace, which is increasingly
invisible in the mainstream media and thus unknown to the larger public.[8]
There is a heightened sense of vulnerability in Muslim immigrant communities,
particularly among working class immigrants who cannot as easily afford legal
counsel. State policies of profiling directed at Muslim Americans have fostered
and exacerbated religious cleavages between Muslims, Hindus, and Sikhs, and
highlighted existing anti-Muslim sentiments within Indian American communities. In some cases, the backlash has also led to an affirmation or strengthening
of Muslim or pan-Muslim identification and fostered new, cross-ethnic alliances,
as I found in my research.

Post-9/11 racial profiling has led to new, or in some cases growing, affiliations
between Arab Americans and South Asians, particularly South Asian Muslims,
as well as alliances with other immigrant communities in civil and immigrant
rights coalitions. Although Arab Americans and Muslim Americans have experienced racism and Islamophobia for many years, many South Asian Americans
suddenly found themselves the objects of intensified suspicion and surveillance

as part of the domestic war on terror. South Asians in this country have generally had a different relationship than Arab Americans and Muslim African Americans to the national security state, due to varied histories of migration and relationships of the United States with their home states.[9] Arab American communities have long experienced scrutiny and surveillance, due to their criticism of United States policies in the Middle East and support of the Israeli occupation of Palestine.[10] For South Asian Americans, by contrast, the crisis of civil rights after 9/11 is the most virulent example of large-scale scapegoating of South Asians in the United States since the anti-Indian riots on the West Coast at the turn of the twentieth century (Jensen 1988) and, on a smaller scale, the Dotbuster attacks targeting South Asians in Jersey City in 1986 and 1987 (Misir 1996), leading many South Asian Muslims to confront issues of racism and racial identification.

SOUTH ASIAN MUSLIM IMMIGRANT YOUTH IN WELLFORD

Wellford is an interesting site for this research, for while media attention and community discussions of racial profiling were primarily focused on South Asians in the New York–New Jersey area, the impact of the war on terror was felt in places where South Asians have not been as visible or as organized in the public sphere, such as New England. It is interesting to focus on a community, such as Wellford, known to be politically liberal, because it sheds light on the kinds of political expressions such a setting enables, encourages, or fails to safeguard in a climate of repression, particularly for Muslim immigrant youth.

Wellford is a small, predominantly white city transformed in the 1990s by accelerated gentrification and increasing immigration, which expanded the population of workers from different parts of the world.[11] The Wellford public high school has an extremely diverse student body reflecting the city's changing population, with students from Latin America, the Caribbean, Africa, and Asia.[12] In 2002 and 2003, there were about 400 foreign-born students in the high school. Reflecting the immigrant communities in the city, the largest groups were Haitians, Latinos, Portuguese-speaking students from Brazil and Cape Verdes, and South Asians. South Asian students have been coming to the high school since they began arriving in Wellford about fifteen years ago. The majority of Muslim students were from India, Pakistan, Bangladesh, and Afghanistan, followed by those from Ethiopia, Somalia, and Morocco. About sixty students were of South Asian origin, including a few Nepali and Tibetans, about half immigrant and half second-generation.

The South Asian immigrant youth in Wellford I focus on were part of the most recent wave of immigration and were predominantly working- to lower-middle class. Since the 1980s, a second wave of labor migrants from South

Asia has arrived, changing the presumed model minority profile of the South Asian immigrant community. Many have entered on family reunification visas rather than through the professional-technical categories that drew an influx of upwardly mobile, highly educated immigrants after the Immigration Act of 1965. The South Asian immigrant student population had arrived recently (within the previous five to seven years), and had minimal to moderate fluency in English. The majority of the Indian youth were from Muslim families, most from small towns or villages in Gujarat in western India. Several were actually related to one another because their families have sponsored relatives as part of an ongoing chain migration. Entire families have migrated from the same village in Gujarat, recreating their extended family networks in the same apartment building in Wellford. At least half of the South Asian immigrant youth in the school lived in high-rise apartment complexes in north Wellford. The remainder lived in the Prospect Square area, an ethnically and racially diverse neighborhood that is undergoing gentrification.

The parents of these youth generally worked in low-income jobs in the service sector, and the students worked after school, up to thirty hours a week, in fast food restaurants, gas stations, retail stores, and as security guards. The families of the South Asian (Sunni) Muslim youth were not very involved in local Muslim organizations or mosques in the area, which drew from a diverse Arab, North African, Asian, and African American population. They tended to socialize mainly with people from their own ethnic community, and generally did not affiliate with the local Indian or Pakistani community organizations or even Muslim American associations, which tended to involve mainly middle- to upper-middle-class, suburban families.[13] The expressions of cultural citizenship of these youth were rooted in the specificities of their urban, working class experience, which I found was often completely unknown to their more privileged South Asian American counterparts in the area.

RESEARCH METHODS

This ethnographic study is based on field work and interviews in Wellford in 2002 and 2003. I conducted a total of sixty-seven interviews, which included thirty-eight high school students, of whom twenty-five were South Asian Muslim and the remainder non-Muslim South Asian or non-South Asian Muslim. Of the South Asian Muslims, twelve were Indian, eight Pakistani, and five Bangladeshi (roughly in proportion to their representation in the high school). I ended up speaking with twenty-five female students and thirteen male students, conducting interviews in both Hindi and English.[14] I also interviewed second-generation South Asian youth, parents of immigrant and non-immigrant students, teachers, staff, youth program organizers, South Asian and Muslim community and religious leaders, city officials, and activists of diverse backgrounds working on immigrant and civil rights issues.

My field work included participant-observation in various sites where immigrant youth construct and perform understandings of cultural citizenship in their everyday lives: the school, homes, workplaces, and community or cultural events. I visited the high school on an average of twice a week from September through mid-December 2002. While I was doing the field work, I was a volunteer, since the fall of 2001, with the South Asian Mentoring and Tutoring Association (SAMTA), a community-based support program for South Asian immigrant students in the high school's bilingual program. As a member of SAMTA's school committee, I helped organize biweekly workshops in coordination with the International Student Center for South Asian students on social, cultural, and academic issues. SAMTA organized after-school activities for the students, such as trips to see films about South Asian immigrants or cultural performances by local student groups, and I often acted as unofficial chaperone at these events.[15]

It is a complicated issue to be documenting the experiences, immigration histories, and political views of Muslim immigrant youth at a time of heightened state surveillance and public scrutiny of their communities. There have been many cases of detention and deportation of Muslim Americans linked to political speech and statements about United States foreign policy that have also involved youth, such as that of a teenage Bangladeshi girl from New York who was deported after she wrote an essay about suicide bombing and Islam and visited radical Islamic chat rooms on the Internet (Bernstein 2005). To protect the identity of these young immigrants as much as possible—especially because Wellford has only one public high school—I have changed the name of the town where I did the research but still tried to describe the local context, and have used pseudonyms for all the students I interviewed. I am aware that these devices are largely symbolic rather than practical shields of protection, but this attempt, however limited, is probably the minimum responsibility of an ethnographer studying high school youth during a time of war and surveillance. Equally important, I hope these strategies will call attention to the implications of the thirst for knowledge of targeted communities and the ways narratives about Muslim Americans are framed by the state, academy, media, and public culture at large.

CULTURAL CITIZENSHIP

South Asian Muslim youth in Wellford have to grapple daily with the meaning of the state's role in their lives and with the implications of war, violence, and racism for the politics of national belonging. I found that nearly all my conversations with these youth and their parents would inevitably turn to the subject of legal and cultural citizenship, because this was an issue that had profoundly shaped their lives and driven their experiences of migration. Most of these young immigrants desired and had applied for official United States citizenship;

about half already had green cards, and the remainder were a mix of citizens and undocumented immigrants. A few, such as Zeenat, a Gujarati girl, said that they wanted U.S. citizenship so that they could vote, and several said that they wanted to be able to travel freely between the United States and South Asia, to be mobile in work and family life. After 9/11, of course, citizenship seemed to become less a matter of choice for immigrants—particularly Muslims and South Asian or Arab Americans—and more a necessary step they hoped would shield them against the assault on civil rights. The tensions between the legal promise and cultural dimensions of citizenship were implicitly acknowledged by these youth, who realized that formal citizenship was an instrumental strategy for work, mobility, and education but would not necessarily bring cultural inclusion.

Cultural citizenship is the "behaviors, discourses, and practices that give meaning to citizenship as lived experience" in the context of "an uneven and complex field of structural inequalities and webs of power relations" (Siu 2001, 9). The concept of cultural citizenship has been developed by Latino studies scholars who support new social movements for rights based on class, gender, sexuality, ethnicity, and race, connecting issues of cultural recognition to struggles for economic and political rights (Rosaldo 1997; Flores and Benmayor 1997). Other theorists, such as Aihwa Ong, view citizenship as a process the state uses to discipline populations and to enshrine values of "freedom, autonomy, and security" (2003, xvii). This Foucauldian approach is skeptical about transforming the identity of citizen in that it relies on a politics defined by the state's disciplining power, not to mention the force of capital. Being a citizen in a neo-liberal state such as the United States is more akin to being a consumer of state services or social goods (Cohen 2003; Schudson 1998). Cultural citizenship is embedded in the contradictions of liberal multiculturalism and the inequities of global capital, and so is necessarily politically ambiguous in its liberatory possibilities (Kymlicka 1995; Hutnyk et al. 2000).[16]

My research suggests that there are three major ways in which South Asian immigrant youth understand and practice cultural citizenship: *flexible citizenship, multicultural* or *polycultural citizenship,* and *dissenting citizenship.* These terms are drawn from the ways in which the young immigrants in my study expressed and practiced cultural citizenship, through everyday behaviors, expectations, and desires. My analysis builds on existing theories of flexible and multicultural citizenship, extending them but also suggesting new, critical forms (polycultural and dissenting). The forms of citizenship that emerged from this study are not exclusive of one another, nor do they exist in some kind of hierarchy of efficacy. They are also not static categories but dynamic processes that cross social, economic, and political boundaries, and are simultaneously expressed by immigrant youth in response to the conditions of their transnational adolescence. These three categories of cultural citizenship are not disconnected from forms of economic and legal citizenship, as the experiences of these youth demonstrate, and also point to the limitations of rights-based discourses.

FLEXIBLE CITIZENSHIP

The lives of immigrant youth are transformed by the migration choices of their parents, and by the state and economic policies that drive their families to cross national borders. Flexible citizenship is used to describe the emergence of new uses of citizenship by migrants in response to the conditions of transnationalism, specifically, the use of transnational links to provide political or material resources not available within a single nation-state (Basch, Glick Schiller, and Szanton Blanc 1994; Ong 1999). Actors now make claims that express what some call postnational citizenship, which is partly outside the national realm, or denationalized citizenship, based on a transformation of the nation itself, but both forms co-exist as the national state continues to be significant (Sassen 2004, 190–1). Immigrants strategically use formal citizenship for legal and economic purposes while expressing varying, sometimes multiple, national affiliations (Ong 1999). Flexible citizenship exists independently of formal dual citizenship, which entails a legal status as citizen of two nation-states. For the South Asian immigrant youth in my study, identification with the home nation as well as linguistic-regional identities (such as Gujarati for the Indian students, or Pathan for the Pakistanis) were very important. Their desires for formal United States citizenship did not conflict with their affiliations with their home nation-states but were layered in a flexible understanding of national belonging, embedded in mobility and migration. I found that flexible citizenship was linked to three cultural processes of "self-making and being-made" in relation to national belonging (Ong 1996, 737): transnational family, social, and economic ties; popular culture practices; and experiences of labor.

First, flexible citizenship for these youth was part of a transnational, long-term, family-based strategy of migration in response to economic pressures on those living in, or at the edge of, the middle class in South Asia. They understood citizenship and immigration documents as artifacts created by the state that they needed to move across national borders and to be reunited with their families, and transnational marriages and social networks are common in their families. However, these transnational arrangements were also the source of disruption of family ties and emotional bonds. These youth came to the United States sponsored by relatives who were permanent residents or citizens, in some cases fathers who had migrated alone many years earlier. At least two boys had been separated from their fathers for about fifteen years; Faisal said his father had left Pakistan for the United States right after he was born, and in effect missed his son's childhood while he was working in the United States and supporting his family through remittances. By the time Faisal came to the United States as a teenager, however, his older brother was too old to enroll in high school and had to struggle to get a GED diploma and find a job with his limited English skills. It is ironic that South Asian immigrants, and Asian Americans more generally, are held up in the United States as model minority citizens who embody exemplary family values, presumably emphasizing stable, nuclear family units. Yet these immigrants could also be viewed as the model citizens of global capitalism, willing to scatter family members across the globe and separate parents from their children, exemplifying the actual family values that the globalized free market engenders (Cole and Durham 2007).

Some of these youth imagined their lives spanning national borders and spoke of returning to South Asia, at least temporarily, once they had become United States citizens and perhaps when their parents had retired there. For example, Ismail, who worked as an IT assistant after school, wanted to set up a transnational high-tech business so that he could live part-time in Gujarat and part-time in Wellford, while supporting his parents. He saw this as a development strategy for nonresident Indians (or NRIs, a term coined by the Indian government) to fulfill their obligations to the home nation-state, using the benefits of United States citizenship. Official practices of flexible citizenship for the benefit of home nations have been encouraged by the Indian government, which developed policies to encourage NRIs to invest in the Indian economy, especially as foreign currency reserves declined in the early 1990s (Sharma and Gupta 2006, 26). The Indian government offers PIO (persons of Indian origin) cards and dual citizenship to foreign citizens of Indian origin, but both categories exclude Pakistani and Bangladeshi citizens of Indian origin. The challenges to flexible citizenship for South Asian Muslims need to be considered on both sides of the transnational terrain in which citizenship is claimed and contested, in the United States and in South Asia.

Second, for many of these immigrant youth, identification with South Asia is based largely on transnational popular culture, on Bollywood films, South Asian television serials, and Hindi music that they access through video, DVDs, satellite television, and the Internet. Jamila, a Bangladeshi immigrant girl, spoke of visiting Internet chat rooms for diasporic Bangladeshi youth as well as youth in Bangladesh. She alluded to an identification with a transnational youth community; commenting that Bangladeshis "in London, they're like, they're almost the same as me." This kind of transnational identification through cyberculture and new media was common for these youth, many of whom spent their free time between classes surfing the Web or checking email in the International Center, because few had access to the Web at home.

The home is an important site for consuming South Asian popular culture. These youth, for example, rarely went out to the cinema or other public spaces of cultural consumption because of financial and time constraints. In almost all the apartments I visited, large-screen televisions and entertainment centers seemed to be the point of pride in the living room, and some families subscribed to South Asian satellite television services to watch national and regional news programs and shows from South Asia. The students I spoke with regularly watched Hindi movies or television serials at home with their families or with South Asian friends. Popular culture, then, is the avenue through which these youth explore and fashion national and transnational identities. As Nestór García Canclini argues, "for many men and women, especially youth, the questions specific to citizenship . . . are answered more often than not through private consumption of commodities and media offerings than through the abstract rules of democracy or through participation in discredited legal organizations" (2001, 5).

Third, flexible citizenship is also linked to issues of labor and enacted by these youth in the workplace. South Asian Muslim youth and their families have come to the United States, in some sense, as migrant workers seeking economic opportunities. These students work in low-wage, part-time jobs in retail and fast food restaurants and struggle in school to get credentials for class mobility. Flexible citizenship does not only resist or only serve global capitalism but often manages to do both. Under neo-liberal capitalism, cultural citizenship is embedded in and mediated by work practices, because these young workers provide the flexible labor that the globalized United States economy relies on for maximum profit. They work at the same jobs generally occupied by young people of diverse ethnic backgrounds in the U.S. (Newman 1999; Tannock 2001) but find that the opportunities available to them are limited because immigration and citizenship policies discriminate between U.S.- and foreign-born workers. These youth understand work to be tied to the law, and to the regulatory powers of the state as it defined them as immigrants, aliens, or Muslims, but also experience it culturally and socially, in relation to the city and to public culture.

However, both academic and popular discussions of Muslim American youth after 9/11, or even before, have generally neglected the role of labor in shaping experiences of difference or exclusion. Understanding the position of South Asian Muslim immigrant youth in the labor economy is important for critically analyzing the relationship of various groups of South Asian, Muslim, or Arab Americans to the nation-state, before and after 9/11. Practices of inclusion or alienation are based on economic as well as cultural and political processes. What makes the situation of the young South Asians in this study particularly acute is that they were immigrants, youth, *and* also happen to be Muslim, so they experienced multiple levels of marginalization in the labor market and economies of citizenship. South Asian immigrant workers do not have the same access to cultural citizenship as nonimmigrant workers because they are not white and, in the post-9/11 moment, because they are identified as Muslim. Their participation in public culture in the United States, in fact, is largely through work; their relations outside the school and community are mainly with other immigrant or young workers and with employers. Walid, a Pakistani boy, lamented that he could never go out into the city with his friends because they all worked different schedules, and he had to work night shifts for his weekend job as a security guard. Work dictated the contours of his leisure time and his relationship to the city, and that of the other youth in this study.

These young people entered the labor market to support their families but also struggled to keep up in school, improve their English, learn about the American college system, and get financial aid to go to college. Farid, who had come to the United States at an early age and spoke English fluently, was frustrated that he could not even get a part-time job working in the Star Market grocery store like his other friends. A few of these young people had parents or relatives who had been laid off as the city struggled with the impact of economic recession. Compared to more affluent or highly credentialed South Asian immigrants, these working class youth are more ambiguously positioned in relation to what Ong calls the American neoliberal ideology of citizenship that emphasizes "freedom, progress, and individualism" (1996, 739). In the United States and other "consumerized republics" that place mass consumption at the center of nation-building, "self-interested citizens . . . view government policies like other market transactions, judging them by how well served they feel personally," thus assuming the combined role of citizen-consumer (Cohen 2003, 9). South Asian immigrant youth participate in this neoliberal mode of relating to the nation-state through consumption and work, even if their exclusion from its full benefits and their struggle as immigrants means that they do so more through their aspirations for class mobility and their consumption of notions of the American Dream.

Working class South Asian immigrant youth see the limits of the model of the self-reliant consumer-citizen—and of the American Dream—in their own lives, and that of their families. Fatima and Tasmeena, two Gujarati sisters, both worked at a Dunkin Donuts store in Wellford where the other workers were Indian, Brazilian, and Haitian. Tasmeena told me that they were paid only $7 an hour, and Fatima noted that the store manager owned two houses and that his son drove a "very nice" car. The sisters seemed well aware that they were being underpaid, and that there was a hierarchy of employers and workers that seemed unjust. They were learning the meanings of class hierarchies and wage scales in the American labor market at the same time as they were learning cultural codes of belonging in the United States. They confronted ideas of belonging to the U.S. nation-state and of productive neoliberal citizenship in the workplace as well as the school, through vocational education programs, internships, and other avenues offering credentials in their aspirations for upward mobility. However, their participation in internships and other city youth employment programs was minimal, partly because of their limited English skills and their lack of knowledge about these opportunities.

The neoliberal state uses legal-juridical regulations of citizens and workers to regulate the supply of low-wage, undocumented, noncitizen labor for employers who wish to depress wages and keep labor compliant. The work of citizenship as a disciplining technology of the state that keeps labor and immigrants vulnerable to exploitation and suppresses dissent is very evident after 9/11 with the ongoing arrests and deportations of immigrant workers for visa violations (Vimalassery 2002). There is a greater fear among noncitizens who have transnational ties, political or familial, that are increasingly suspect when the threat to national security is attributed to foreign nations and global networks. "The privilege of transnational identification," Sally Howell and Andrew Shryock argue, "has been, for Arabs in Detroit, the first casualty of the war on terror" (2003, 445). Travel across national borders, money transfers, including donations to Islamic charities, and transnational businesses and organizations have all been monitored and used to detain Arab and Muslim immigrants as the state has broadened its definitions of involvement with terrorism in the Patriot Act.[17] Small businesses owned by South Asian and Arab immigrants were raided on the suspicion that they were somehow funding militant groups, with nationwide raids of Pakistani-owned jewelry stores and sweeps of Indian-owned convenience stores in California in 2002.[18]

Muslim and Arab entrepreneurs and workers have suffered economically for taking advantage of their transnational networks, and families have lost the support of economic remittances from overseas. Even if all these South Asian immigrant youth were not engaged in official transnational practices involving business or organizational networks, they all did feel the power of the state to limit their mobility across national borders and undermine their strategies for flexible citizenship. The youth I spoke with expressed the general anxiety among Muslim Americans about state regulations of immigration status and work, and how this might affect their education. For example, a Pakistani girl, Mariyam, who had graduated from high school was unable to go to college or fulfill her goal to study medicine because she was undocumented. Her story was poignant because she was an extremely bright young woman who radiated purposefulness. Flexibility is always in tension with control, and is a strategy that is in practice constrained by the state and by ideologies of who can and cannot move or waver.

Yet, in the face of such regulations of citizenship and its cultural boundaries, it became apparent to me that these young Muslim immigrants thought about citizenship in ways that were themselves flexible, shifting, and contextual. This may perhaps reflect a consumerist approach of selectively drawing on various models of citizenship as appropriate, but it also reflects a deeper, strategic sensibility about belonging in relation to the nation-state. In some cases, it seems that religious identity actually prompted youth to think of themselves as belonging to the United States or at least identifying with its concerns, if not identifying as American. Ismail said to me in the fall of 2001, "Islam teaches [us that] what country you live in, you should support them . . . See, if I live in America, I have to support America, I cannot go to India." Ismail was the same boy who said that he ultimately wanted to return to India and support its development. But this simultaneous evocation of transnational and national loyalties is not as contradictory as it first appears. Ismail was able to frame his relationship to Islam in a way that would help him think through questions of national allegiance at a moment when Muslims were being framed as non-citizens because of a particular construction of Muslims as anti-American. Ismail instead used Islam to claim affiliation with the United States and to support a flexible definition of citizenship. His comments are one strand in a complex debate among Muslim Americans about the compatibility, even the centrality, of a new "American Islam" and of participation in American public and political life to the "evolving international umma," or worldwide Muslim community (Leonard 2003, 101). Although Ismail did not speak directly to these larger debates about the "relationship between state, society, and religion" among American Muslims (see Mattson 2003, 199), he seemed to voice a pragmatic strategy that reflects a rather sophisticated understanding of citizenship as necessarily mobile, drawing on different ideological resources to respond to the exigencies of diverse moments and places.

A similar expression of Muslim cultural citizenship emphasizing loyalty to the United States was increasingly adopted by moderate Muslim American clerics and commentators after 9/11 as part of a plea for inclusion in the nation and distance from Islamist extremism. At a Boston rally in November 2001 protesting the imminent war in Iraq, Imam Talal Eid of the Islamic Center of New England said that he spoke for peace as a United States citizen who believed that Muslim Americans could contribute to the "civilizing" of America. This is an interesting turn on Samuel Huntington's (1996) anti-Islamic argument about the clash of civilizations, pitting Islam versus the West; however, the imam's statement still upheld the idea that what is at stake is the relationship between cultural civilizations. Even if he privately disagreed with the premise of cultural inclusion in the United States, public statements such as this implicitly reinforce the notion of peace-loving, "good" Muslims who are willing to be made into loyal citizens of the United States, as opposed to "bad" Muslims who critique the expansionist policies and imperial strategies of the United States under the guise of promoting democracy (Mamdani 2004, 15). Although flexible citizenship is sometimes based on claims to so-called good Muslim citizenship, these positions are highly contested and debated within South Asian, Muslim, and Arab American communities. Flexible citizenship is clearly an economic and family strategy for South Asian immigrant youth but also part of a cultural strategy that allows them to manage diverse national affiliations and ideological constructions of Muslim political subjectivity in the war on terror.

MULTICULTURAL-POLYCULTURAL CITIZENSHIP

South Asian immigrant youth understand belonging in the U.S. nation-state and in Wellford through the prism of cultural, racial, and religious difference. Will Kymlicka (1995) conceives of multicultural citizenship in relation to minority cultural rights—the rights of minority groups within multiethnic nations to express their cultural identity—an idea that increasingly shapes national belonging in the United States through notions of cultural difference. The discourse of American multiculturalism is quickly absorbed by immigrants, students, and youth because the state uses education, the law, bureaucratic processes, media images, and official rhetoric to propagate and celebrate the doctrine of inclusion, especially since the 1960s and 1970s. Many immigrant youth talked about national belonging and relationships with others in terms of multicultural citizenship, even if only implicitly, given that multiculturalism is such a pervasive discourse of cultural belonging in the arena of education. The high school, implicitly and explicitly, promoted the notion through visual symbols and support for ethnic-based student activities that mixed a political and cultural recognition of difference.

These vernacular understandings of multicultural citizenship emerge from the pluralism embedded in the social fabric of relationships. Most of these youth had friendships that crossed ethnic and racial boundaries and would spend leisure time with Latino, Caribbean, African American, and Asian students, and especially with Muslim African youth from Somalia, Ethiopia, or Egypt, potentially forming an incipient pan-Islamic identity. Yet it was also apparent that students, like those in most American high schools and colleges, tended to cluster by ethnic group after school or in the cafeteria. Ismail commented that his friendships with non-South Asian students were sometimes questioned by other desi (South Asian) youth, but he argued for a more expansive conception of community: "They don't like it, but I say if you want to live in a different world, you have to exist with them. . . . if you're gonna live in the desi community, you're only going to know desi people, not the other people." Interestingly, Ismail also traced the value he placed on multiculturalist co-existence to a view of India as a multiethnic nation: "India is a really good place to live in . . . because they've got a lot of religions, different languages, different people." However, this was before the horrific February 2002 massacre of Muslim Indians in the Gujarat riots that shattered many Indians, especially Muslims. Perhaps Ismail, too, would have been less sanguine or more open about his critique of Indian pluralism, though this is obviously a sensitive issue for Indian Muslims, whose national loyalties are sometimes suspect (see Varadarajan 2002; Panikkar and Muralidharan 2002).

Multicultural citizenship is enacted at the level of nation-state as well as the local level. Engin Isin argues that the "work of modern nationalism" is done in the city, the sphere in which people engage most immediately with ideas of rights and belonging through forms of urban citizenship (2000, 15). The city provides not a "singular, abstract public sphere" but "intensely concrete" and "plural public spaces"; in fact, it is generally the primary context for constructing, engaging in, or being rejected from public spheres for these South Asian immigrant youth. For them, belonging in the United States meant belonging in the city, which provided a specific, local context for their ideas of what being in America meant. Although a small city, Wellford is nonetheless an urban context in which different social groups shape collective identities, enact claims of belonging, struggle for rights, and make demands on the state. The diverse social groups that encounter one another in the space of the city forge collective identities as a basis for expressing rights and obligations but are also divided by the emphasis of multicultural citizenship on cultural, racial, ethnic, and gendered difference (Isin 2000, 15).

Multicultural citizenship is appealing in neo-liberal states such as the United States, because it encourages citizens to turn to a politics of representation rather than one of systemic change by fostering a cultural, rather than structural, analysis of social inequity (Fraser 1997, 186). After 9/11, the categories of Muslim, Arab, and South Asian American were constructed as another kind of cultural difference, but one that did not always fit easily with the American narrative of assimilation for ethnic and racial minorities. "Muslim" is of course not a racial category, and thus Moustafa Bayoumi refers to the tragic irony of racial profiling after 9/11 (Bayoumi 2001, 73). Muslim American youth have been forced to play the role of spokespersons for Islam, giving speeches at their schools and in community forums about their religion and culture as part an expanded discourse of multicultural diversity. A coordinator of a Muslim youth group at the Wellford mosque noted that it is a role that also brings pressure or fatigue. The role of native informant not only makes members of marginalized or targeted communities responsible for compensating for the failures of the American educational system or the racism and ignorance of the media and civil society, but also draws them into the multiculturalist presumption that injustice can be resolved simply by awareness of difference. The framework of liberal multiculturalism evades broader analyses that connect domestic race politics and economic inequity to United States foreign policy and international politics.

American multiculturalism has attempted to subsume the assault on the civil liberties of Muslim and Arab Americans into a racialized framework of minority victimhood. Muslim Americans—or the trio of Arab, Muslim, and South Asian Americans (the new shorthand of AMSAs)—are constructed as belonging to just another, culturally distinct, ethnicized, or quasi-racial category whose problems can be contained within a discourse of domestic racism and addressed by inclusion. However, some Muslim Americans have realized the inherent limitations of multicultural citizenship. When I spoke to Syed Khan, an Indian immigrant on the board of one of the local mosques and founder of Muslim Community Support Services, in the fall of 2002, he expressed his frustration with the discrepancy between the White House's public rhetoric of multicultural inclusion and government policies of surveillance, detention, and deportation: "Initially leaders including Bush had spoken up [against racial profiling], but afterwards, when it wasn't as critical, outreach to Muslim

31

Americans has stopped completely. Now, it's bashing time."[19] Other South Asian Muslims active in the community were quick to point out to me the outpouring of support from neighbors and friends after 9/11. It is true that individual acts of solidarity have coexisted with acts of discrimination, private and state-sponsored, on a mass scale (Hing 2002; Prashad 2003; Robin 2003). Racial profiling operates on multiple levels and through these contradictions of rhetoric and policy.

I argue that the targeting of Muslim, Arab, and South Asian Americans in the war on terror is based on political, not simply racial, profiling. evident in earlier circumstances, such as the Iran hostage crisis and the first Gulf War, and tied to United States interventions in the Middle East. The construction of Muslim, Arab, and South Asian Americans as the enemy is more akin to a form of Green McCarthyism than (just) to the common domestic form of racial profiling (Prashad 2003), however ambiguously defined the notion of race is in the United States. The image of the Muslim terrorist has replaced the threat of the communist that was used to fan the Red Scare. The exclusion of Muslim Americans from cultural citizenship is part of a political discourse that defines American interests and national identity in opposition to a foreign enemy and an enemy within. Regimes of tolerance and intolerance legitimizing American foreign policies are linked to supposedly apolitical understandings of cultural difference and essentialized notions of "civilizational conflict" (Brown 2006). This was evident in the vocabulary of intolerance used to target Muslim and Arab Americans after 9/11, including the South Asian Muslim high school youth in this study. Accusations such as "you're a terrorist" or "bin Laden's your uncle" entered into what might otherwise have been just an outbreak of youthful aggression among boys. These epithets are part of a deeply gendered Orientalist discourse about Islam and the Arab world as essentially antidemocratic and antimodern, portraying Muslim males as militant and misogynist and Muslim females as submissive and oppressed.

The responses of South Asian Muslim youth to the anti-Muslim backlash revealed interesting issues of interethnic racism and cross-ethnic affiliations that have not received adequate attention in discussions of Muslim Americans. One of the anti-Muslim incidents in Wellford occurred in the school, when an African American girl accused two Pakistani boys, Adil and Walid, of "killing people" and reportedly called them "Muslim niggers"— another new racial epithet after 9/11 that suggests that Muslim is one of the more degraded identities. The girl was eventually suspended and Adil, who was a friend of the girl's brother, tried to intervene and soften her punishment. Both the Pakistani boys emphatically refused to portray the incident as a black-South Asian or black-Muslim conflict; they insisted that this was the case of a lone individual who Walid half-jokingly said must have been drunk or high. Adil thought that black Americans were more critical of nationalist responses to 9/11 than white Americans, even though he was hesitant to extend this generalization to their responses to the United States' war in Afghanistan.

For Walid and Adil, the aftermath of 9/11 prompted a heightened self-consciousness about racialization that seemed, if anything, to reinforce the black-white racial polarization. Walid thought that African Americans were not as shattered by the attacks because, in his view, their legacy of slavery leads them to feel alienated from the nation-state. Although this racialized difference after 9/11 is more complex than Walid suggests, what is significant is that he believed that blacks shared his experience of marginalization. Walid did not, however, completely dismiss the resurgent nationalism of many Americans after 9/11, saying, "The first thing is they're born here in the USA, so that's their country. . . . We are immigrants. . . . If something happens back home, like, and someone else did [something], we're gonna be angry too, right?" For Walid and other immigrant youth, the response of African Americans seemed more significant than that of Latinos or even Arab Americans because, on the one hand, they were the largest group of minority students in the school, and, on the other, African American identity symbolizes a contested United States citizenship. Post-9/11 politics seem to have drawn some of these Muslim youth into an understanding of citizenship based on racialized fissures in claims to national identity and on cross-ethnic affiliations with other minority youth.

These responses suggest a potentially polycultural citizenship, based not on the reification of cultural boundaries that underlies liberal multiculturalism, but on a complex set of political affiliations and social boundary crossings situated in the realm of power relations (Prashad 2001). The historian Robin Kelley's (1999) notion of polyculturalism suggests that cultures are inevitably already hybridized, and that there are no discrete, pure cultures. Building on this notion, polycultural citizenship suggests a more complex notion of difference that allows for political as well as cultural identifications between groups and is situated in the realm of power relations (see Maira 2002). Polycultural citizenship emerges from the relationships of different groups with the state and in cross-border affiliations based on particular historical and material conjectures.

This is not an idealization, however, of the complexities of race politics. Polyculturalism does not exist in the absence of antiblack racism in the South Asian immigrant community, given that racialized antagonisms and suspicion in the school are indeed absorbed by some immigrant youth, and that interracial tensions and prejudices exist, as they do in all communities. There is room in the notion of polycultural citizenship to acknowledge the resentment and competition among groups, particularly marginalized groups, rooted in daily struggles for turf or resources. These young immigrants simultaneously invoke a multiculturalist discourse of pluralist coexistence and polyculturalist

affiliations embedded in their everyday social and political experiences of affiliation and exclusion.

DISSENTING CITIZENSHIP

The polycultural affiliations of South Asian Muslim immigrant youth were, in
some cases, based on shared sentiments of dissent with other minority youth.
These immigrant youth voiced dissenting views about the war on terror that
most South Asian middle class community leaders in Wellford did not express
publicly after 9/11, due to the state's sweeping powers of surveillance and targeting of political speech deemed anti-American. In the face of such repression,
I found some South Asian Muslim immigrant youth practicing dissenting
citizenship: an engagement with the state based on a critique of its politics and
policies. Dissenting citizenship is still a form of cultural citizenship, however,
because it engages with the role and responsibility of the nation-state even as
it challenges nation-based discourses of rights.

These youth emphasized the importance of political justice and respect
for international human rights, denouncing both the terrorist attacks and
militarized state aggression as a means of retribution. As Adil said to me in
December 2001:

> You have to look at it in two ways. It's not right that ordinary people over there
> [in Afghanistan], like you and me, just doing their work, get killed. They don't
> have anything to do with . . . the attacks in New York, but they're getting killed.
> And also the people in New York who got killed, that's not right either.

Jamila, a Bangladeshi girl, said, "I felt bad for those people [in Afghanistan] . . .
because they don't have no proof that they actually did it, but they were all
killing all these innocent people who had nothing to do with it." Ayesha, a
Gujarati Indian girl who could very easily pass for Latina and evade obvious
identification as Muslim or Arab, chose to write the words "INDIA + MUSLIM"
on her bag after 9/11. For her, this was a gesture of defiance responding to the
casting of Muslims as potentially disloyal citizens. She observed, "Just because
one Muslim did it in New York, you can't involve everybody in there, you know
what I'm sayin'." Not all the students were as bold as Ayesha in challenging
the profiling of Muslims and publicly claiming a Muslim identity—which she
did without wearing a hijab, contrary to expectations of what religious identification looks like for Muslim females—but they all they implicitly criticized
both the war on terror and assault on their civil rights.

The school was perhaps the only public space where these Muslim immigrant
students felt comfortable expressing their political views, because of the liberal
political climate and the support of progressive teachers and staff; high schools

in other towns in the area, or around the nation, were not as openly supportive of dissenting views or critical of the profiling of Muslim Americans. Polycultural identifications with other minority youth, particularly African Americans, also led some youth to imbibe a discourse of racial identity and civil rights that shaped their dissenting stance after 9/11. After the anti-Muslim incident in the high school, the International Student Center organized a student assembly about the war on terrorism and the attack on civil liberties. Adil, Walid, and a Gujarati Muslim girl, Shireen, delivered eloquent speeches condemning racism to an auditorium filled with their peers. Adil said that when he was threatened by some young men in Boston after 9/11, "I could have done the same thing, but I don't think it's the right thing to do." Adil's call for a nonviolent response was a powerful one at a moment when the United States was at war with Afghanistan as retribution for the attacks on the Twin Towers. Shireen said, "We have to respect each other if we want to change society. You have to stand up for your rights." South Asian Muslim immigrant youth were being drawn into race politics and civil rights debates in the local community, although it was not clear what the impact of this politicization would be over time. But, a year later, on the anniversary of September 11, when the International Student Center organized another student assembly, Shireen's younger sister and another Gujarati Muslim girl voluntarily made similar speeches that were reported in the local press. Even though these working class youth do not have the support of, or time to participate in, community or political organizations, they were willing to voice a dissenting view in the public sphere. However, such dissent, whether by South Asian Muslim immigrant youth or by South Asian or Muslim Americans more generally, is not necessarily overt, consistent, or public, let alone guaranteed. As the state acquired sweeping powers of surveillance with the Patriot Act, there were numerous incidents of FBI and police investigations of "unpatriotic" activity that stifled public dissent, particularly among vulnerable immigrant and Muslim American communities (see Rothschild 2007).

An overt, though on some levels also subtle, moment of political discussion with a group of South Asian Muslim youth occurred in May 2003, when the students watched a documentary film, *Bridge to Baghdad*, as part of a SAMTA workshop. The documentary was filmed just before the invasion of Iraq and focused on an exchange, by satellite television, of a group of college-age youth in New York and Baghdad. The South Asian students were mesmerized by the film and a couple of the boys were particularly excited by an interview with a young Iraqi man who had a heavy metal rock band. In a poignant scene, a young Iraqi woman showed viewers the supplies stocked in her basement and freezer in preparation for the invasion. The girls giggled when a young Iraqi woman in hijab swore in response to a question from the American youth that she had never dated anyone before. When the debate about the imminent war turned into a heated exchange among some of the youth in the film, the young Iraqi woman asked the American students how they would feel if an army, "say,

35

an Iraqi army," came to invade their country and remove their leader. A young white woman responded that many Americans were actually opposed to the war and a young antiwar activist of color jokingly responded that she would actually be happy if an army came to get rid of Bush. The students in the workshop burst out laughing. Later, in a discussion between the SAMTA volunteers and the students about the film, Zeenat remarked, "It's not right that the war will affect innocent people."

The gendered response to the film was apparent in the identification of the girls with the issues of dating and the boys with the young metal rocker. On the face of it, this response fits neatly with the dominant way in which issues of gender for Muslim American youth have been discussed in the mainstream American media, pinning the question of hijab and social control onto young Muslim women, and the image of rebelliousness—implicitly tied with a presumably Western mode of modernity—onto young Muslim men. But the film also evoked more complex responses that challenged gendered stereotypes of submissive Muslim girls and angry Muslim boys, for the girls were drawn to the young Iraqi woman in the documentary who voiced the strongest dissent against the United States' occupation. At the same time, the boys were both fascinated by the young Iraqi musician's rock star hairstyle and moved by his anxiety about the impending war, identifying both via fashion and fear.

Gender inflected understandings of cultural citizenship for these youth in ways not immediately obvious, given that boys and girls showed very little difference in their expressions of cultural citizenship. Yet these youth are forced to respond to dominant constructions of cultural citizenship for Muslim males and females that are deeply gendered. There is a general preoccupation in American mainstream discourse and mass media with women in hijab and with presumably oppressed Muslim women who need to be liberated from their traditions to be brought into the fold of the nation. At the same time, there is a deep anxiety about young Muslim men as potential terrorists and religious fanatics disloyal to the nation and, unlike women perhaps, ultimately unassimilable. A particular space has been constructed for Muslim and Arab women in the post-9/11 debate about the war on terror that is very revealing of the ways in which Muslimness, and also Arabness, is gendered in the public sphere.

In the high school, for example, more South Asian Muslim girls than boys spoke at public events, at least during the research, even though the boys were the most visible targets of profiling. This may or may not have been intentional, but what is striking is the gendered representations of Muslim and Arab females and males and underlying discourses of Orientalism and liberal feminism. Muslim and Arab women have played a particular role in the American mass media and public discussions that both challenges and supports Orientalist perspectives on Muslim and Arab culture and, in particular, the status of women. These gendered representations of Muslim identity perform a classically Orientalist role (Said 1978; Shaheen 1999), drawing on stereotypes of inherently oppressive cultures to justify military interventions, domestic profiling, and the exclusion or inclusion of different categories of Muslimness. This gendering is linked to Orientalist images of submissive Muslim women and fanatical Muslim men that are defied, if not overtly by public statements, then by the actions and self-presentations of Muslim immigrant youth in this study.

The responses of these youth were obviously rooted in their identities as Muslims. Their critiques were more rooted in regional and religious identity than the universalizing ideal of cosmopolitanism suggests and yet, at the same time, was far more critical of American nationalism and state powers than liberal theorists of cosmopolitanism allow (for example, see Nussbaum 2002). Their dissenting views critiqued United States policies by associating assaults on civil rights within the United States to overseas military interventions and assaults on human rights in Afghanistan and Iraq. Dissenting citizenship captures some of the ambivalence these youth experience, in that the United States is simultaneously a place invested with their parents' desire for economic advancement and security and their own hopes to belong in a new home, and also the site of alienation, discrimination, fear, frustration, and anxiety about belonging. A few young immigrants, such as Shireen and Samira, had expectations that the United States would live up to its ideals of freedom and equal rights, but most seemed to emphasize simply that the actions of the United States should be held to an international standard of human rights that should apply within America as well as to other nation-states, including India and Pakistan.

It is this link between the domestic and global faces of the war on terror that makes these perspectives an important mode of dissent. The link is generally obscured, preventing populations from understanding how their subjugation or marginalization within the nation is connected to dominance overseas (Pease 1993). For example, the war on terror is in effect an extension of the war on immigrants waged since the late 1980s, in that it has stripped civil rights from noncitizens and extended the assault on immigrant rights heightened with the anti-immigrant Proposition 187 in California in 1994, the heightened policing of international borders, and the 1996 immigration acts (Hing 2000; Moore 1999, 87). The targeting of a population demonized as Other, and the absorption of previously targeted communities into a unifying nationalism and climate of fear, shifts attention away from the ways in which the war at home and the war abroad actually work in tandem.

Muslim immigrant youth are subjects of both wars. Their dissenting citizenship is, as mentioned, very much rooted in their identities as Muslims, for they are targeted as Muslims by the state, and sheds light on the links between United States policies at home and abroad. It goes against the grain

37

of what I call the imperial feeling of post-9/11 America, the complex of psychological and political belonging to empire that is an often unspoken, but always present, structures of feeling (Williams 1980, ix), infusing the relationship of the individual to the state. These feelings constitute the affective response of those living within the United States to its imperial power—often a mix of anxiety, ambivalence, fear, guilt, hope, assurance, desire, or denial—that shape the habitus and everyday dispositions of life in post-9/11 America (Bourdieu 1977).[20]

At the same time, it seems that these young immigrants implicitly understood the limits of a dissenting citizenship and state-based rights for they have had to grapple with the failures of both home and host states to guarantee protection and equal rights to Muslim subjects. For example, the massacres in Gujarat and the military standoff between India and Pakistan that preceded it, reinforced the ambiguous religious and national identifications of Indian Muslims. With the heightened nationalism in India during the Kargil conflict with Pakistan in 1999 and the rising tide of Hindu fundamentalism, Indian Muslims were viewed with intensified suspicion as potential traitors and not authentically Indian.[21] This was understandably a difficult subject even for their parents to speak about to me, but in more private spaces some expressed the vulnerability that Muslim immigrants have felt both in the United States and at home. Their cultural citizenship and loyalties are in question in both nation-states, which have used very similar public rhetoric associating Muslims with the war on terrorism and undermining their civil rights.

Some wonder if this intensified politicization of Muslim identity will lead to the emergence of a new political generation of Muslim, South Asian, or Arab American youth, as it did in Britain (Jacobson 1998; Modood 2002). I think there is still not enough evidence to make a generalized statement about this, partly because the post-9/11 surveillance, detentions, and deportations have crushed political dissent in the affected communities and made it difficult for young people, especially immigrants, to say anything that would depart too radically from what is considered acceptable political critique at a given moment. As Corey Robin points out, repression historically works on two levels to silence dissent: on a state level, but also as important, on the level of civil society, where individuals internalize repression and censor themselves (2003). Dissenting critiques of domestic racial profiling and United States foreign policy in the Middle East were most strongly expressed by South Asian youth who had grown up in the United States and perhaps felt less vulnerable than those who did not have citizenship, such as Ayesha and Farid. Yet the sometimes subtle and coded expressions of dissenting citizenship by these immigrant students, expressed through humor and visual rather than verbal statements, tell us something about the nature of dissent at a time of political repression. There are a variety of ways in which Muslim American youth have chosen to respond to the post-9/11 targeting. The experiences of this generation will shape their future relationship to the nation-state, in the United States and beyond, and to multiple communities of affiliation.

CONCLUSION

The post-9/11 moment underscores that notions of citizenship expressed by Muslim immigrant youth, some of which I have explored here, are constructed in a dynamic relationship with various institutions and policies of the state, and manifestations of the state are themselves mutable and multifaceted. I want to note that the term *post-9/11* has come to signify a range of ideologies and processes. For many, it has become a shorthand to variously signify the war on terror; the relation between the U.S. state and Muslim, Arab, and South Asian Americans; anti-terrorist policies; and linkages among Islam, fundamentalism, and national security. It is important to remember that there are also important continuities before and after 9/11 that are often not acknowledged enough. My use of *post-9/11* is not meant to signify a radical historical or political rupture, but rather a moment of renewed contestation over ongoing issues of citizenship and transnationalism, religion and nationalism, civil rights and immigrant rights.

Focusing on cultural citizenship sheds light on how immigrant youth understand their relationship to the state in their everyday lives. Through ethnographic research, it is possible to examine cultural practices that express ideas of national belonging and political subjectivity that may not always be expressed through an explicitly ideological or political vocabulary. Clearly, these youth understand the experience of being Muslim after 9/11 in relation to a range of contexts that extend beyond religious practices and identifications: family, work, education, popular culture, and social relationships. This research, and the larger project from which it is drawn, focus on everyday notions of cultural citizenship to show that constructions of the Muslim-ness are embedded in the micro-politics of daily life and also in state policies and discourses that immigrant youth are forced to respond to as Muslim actors. A nuanced understanding of the impact of 9/11 on Muslim immigrant youth requires an analysis of the interaction between national ideology, state policy, social practice, and individual and collective identities. The study aims to provoke further work in the burgeoning field of post-9/11 area studies that will provide a deep and honest analysis of questions of affiliation and exclusion, fear and dissent, empire and belonging, that face young Muslim immigrants in the United States today.

This study was funded by the Russell Sage Foundation and supported by my able research assistants, Palav Babaria and Sarah Khan. Thanks to Louise Cainkar for her editorial feedback on an earlier version.

NOTES

1. For example, the goal of "maintaining U.S. global military supremacy in perpetuity" and a proactive military "omnipotence," was crystallized, if not fully realized, during the Democratic regime of Clinton, supported by the Pentagon's post-cold war plan for restructuring the armed forces, Joint Vision 2010 (Bacevich 2002, 131).

2. There are different strategies of dominance used by the United States imperial power: "control over international bodies (the United Nations, World Bank, International Monetary Fund, World Trade Organization), covert actions, global surveillance methods, direct military interventions, political machinations, and deadly economic sanctions of the sort used against Iraq" (Boggs 2003, 6).

3. It is also important to note that state practices and legal regimes have long been used to target aliens and political radicals in the United States—from the Alien and Sedition Act of 1798 that criminalized dissent, to the Palmer Raids of 1919 and 1920 that led to mass roundups and deportations of anarchists and union members, and the anti-Communist witch hunts of the McCarthy era (Hing 2004).

4. There were 700 reported hate crimes against South Asian Americans, Arab Americans, and Muslim Americans, including four homicides (two involving South Asian American victims), in the three weeks following September 11, 2001 (Jeff Coen, "Hate Crimes Reports Reach Record Level," *Chicago Tribune,* October 9, 2001). At least 200 were reported in this period against Sikh Americans alone (Jane Lampan, "Under Attack, Sikhs Defend their Religious Liberties," *Christian Science Monitor,* October 31, 2001). The Council on American-Islamic Relations reported that it had documented 960 incidents of racial profiling in the five weeks after 9/11, with hate crimes declining and incidents of airport profiling and workplace discrimination on the increase (Associated Press, San Jose, Calif., "Hate Crime Reports Down, Civil Rights Complaints Up," October 25, 2001).

5. The re-registration component of the program was officially ended by the Department of Homeland Security in December 2003, after protests by immigrant, civil rights, and grassroots community organizations, while other aspects of the program remained in place, and the detentions and deportations continue.

6. By March 12, 2003, the Canadian immigration service reported 2,111 refugee claims by Pakistanis since January 1 (Ryan 2003, 16).

7. Ironically, from the same area that provided the mujahideen whom the CIA armed and trained to fight its proxy war in Afghanistan in the 1980s (for more, see Rashid 2000).

8. The Council on American Islamic Relations (CAIR) reported that since 2001, hate crimes began declining and incidents of airport profiling and workplace discrimination increased; despite underreporting, the U.S. Equal Employment Opportunity Commission (EEOC) received so many complaints of discrimination that it had to create a special category, Code Z (Mary Beth Sheridan, "Backlash Changes Form, Not Function," *Washington Post,* March 4, 2002). By 2003 the

EEOC had received over 800 complaints by individuals who had been dismissed from their jobs or harassed at work for being identified as "Muslim, Arab, Afghani, Middle Eastern, South Asian, or Sikh" (Nguyen 2005, xx).

9. While South Asian immigrants to the United States in the early twentieth century were involved in transnational movements to liberate India from British rule that were surveilled in the United States, post-colonial South Asian immigrants have generally come to the United States seeking economic advancement and have, for the most part, not engaged in political challenges to U.S. state policies (Jensen 1988).

10. Those who have protested United States policy in the Middle East have been targeted by the government at various moments since the 1967 Israeli-Arab war, from the FBI's monitoring of the General Union of Palestinian Students in the 1980s, to the attempted deportation of the pro-Palestinian activists known as the LA 8, to the nationwide monitoring and interviews of Arab American individuals and organizations before and during the first Gulf War (Cole and Dempsey 2002, 35–48; see also Cainkar 2002; Green 2003).

11. Wellford's population is 68.1 percent white American, 11.9 percent African American, 11.9 percent Asian American, and 7.4 percent Latino (U.S. Census Bureau 2000). This, of course, does not include undocumented immigrants. The native population is 74.1 percent and foreign-born is 25.9 percent; 17.7 percent are not citizens and 31.2 percent speak a language other than English. The median household income in 1999 was $47,979, which is above the national median, but 12.9 percent lived below poverty level, slightly above the national level, which some explain due to the significant presence of students.

12. The high school has approximately 2,000 students, of which about 40 percent are white and the remaining 60 percent are minorities. African Americans are the largest of these (about 25 percent), followed by Latinos (15 percent), and Asian Americans (about 7 percent). In 2000 and 2002, 33 percent of students had a first language other than English and 14 percent were in the bilingual program, which suggests that the immigrant student population in the school is somewhere between these figures.

13. The 2000 census reported 2,720 Indian immigrants (2.7 percent of the population), 125 Pakistanis, and 120 Bangladeshis in Wellford (U.S. Census Bureau 2000).

14. Although I had ideally hoped for a gender balance among interviewees, I discovered that the boys were simply not as comfortable talking to girls and women. This is a factor that might generally be true of adolescent boys and was particularly true of these youth, who were recently arrived immigrants and tended to socialize in gender-segregated circles.

15. I was very aware that I was sometimes helping to shape the context in which questions of cultural citizenship were being discussed, and the larger project takes a self-reflexive approach to ethnographic writing as do many critical ethnographers who acknowledge that research is co-produced and wish to lay bare the scaffolding of the ethnographic process, rather than erase their presence.

41

16. One of the chief contradictions is that movements for cultural citizenship critique the state while still remaining within the framework of engagement with the state or inclusion within it, even if they challenge or reject the notion of rights and identities as defined solely by the nation-state.

17. Neil MacFarquhar, "Fears of Inquiry Dampen Giving by U.S. Muslims," *New York Times,* October 30, 2006.

18. Irina Slutsky, "Indian Couple Seeks Release: Jewelry Store Investigation," *The Bradenton Herald,* July 17, 2002.

19. Khan's comment was echoed by Muslim American leaders who noted George W. Bush's meeting with Muslim activists at the White House had not been accompanied by a shift in policies concerning Muslim Americans (Rachel Zoll, "U.S. Muslims Say Bush Ignores Them," Associated Press, August 17, 2002).

20. Cultural historians have also demonstrated the ways in which identification with and support of imperial policies is made possible by popular culture representations and media spectacles that justify United States militarism and dominance (for example, Kaplan 1993; Pease 1993).

21. See Ahmad 2000, 301–23.

REFERENCES

Ahmad, Aijaz. 2000. "Of Dictators and Democrats: Indo-Pakistan Politics in the Year 2000." In *Lineages of the Present: Ideology and Politics in Contemporary South Asia.* London and New York: Verso.

Akram, Susan. 2002. "Orientalism Revisited in Asylum and Refugee Claims." In *Moral Imperialism: A Critical Anthology,* edited by Berta Esperanza Hernandez-Truyol. New York: New York University Press.

Bacevich, Andrew. 2002. *American Empire: The Realities and Consequences of U.S. Diplomacy.* Cambridge, Mass.: Harvard University Press.

Basch, Linda, Nina Glick Schiller, and Cristina Szanton Blanc, editors. 1994. *Nations Unbound: Transnational Projects, Postcolonial Predicaments, and Deterritorialized Nation-States.* Amsterdam: Gordon and Breach.

Bayoumi, Moustafa. 2001. "How Does It Feel To Be a Problem?" *Amerasia Journal* 27(3): 69–77.

Berlant, Lauren. 1997. *The Queen of America Goes to Washington City: Essays on Sex and Citizenship.* Durham, N.C.: Duke University Press.

Bernstein, Nina. 2005. "Questions, Bitterness and Exile for Queens Girl in Terror Case." *New York Times,* June 17, 2005. Accessed at http://www.nytimes.com/2005/06/17.

Bhavnani, Kum-Kum. 1991. *Talking Politics: A Psychological Framing for Views from Youth in Britain.* Cambridge: Cambridge University Press.

Boggs, Carl. 2003. "Introduction: Empire and Globalization." In *Masters of War: Militarism and Blowback in the Era of American Empire,* edited by Carl Boggs. New York and London: Routledge.

Bourdieu, Pierre. 1977. *Outline of a Theory of Practice.* Cambridge: Cambridge University Press.

Brown, Wendy. 2006. *Regulating Aversion: Tolerance in the Age of Identity and Empire.* Princeton, N.J.: Princeton University Press.

Buckingham, David. 2000. *The Making of Citizens: Young People, News, and Politics.* London: Routledge.

Burbach, Roger, and Jim Tarbell. 2004. *Imperial Overstretch: George W. Bush and the Hubris of Empire.* London: Zed Books.

Cainkar, Louise. 2002. "No Longer Invisible: Arab and Muslim Exclusion After September 11." *MERIP Middle East Report* 32(224): 22–29. Accessed at http://www.merip.org/mer/mer224/224_cainkar.html.

Canclini, Nestór García. 2001. *Consumers and Citizens: Globalization and Multicultural Conflicts* Minneapolis, Minn.: University of Minnesota Press.

Chang, Nancy. 2002. *Silencing Political Dissent: How Post-September 11 Anti-Terrorism Measures Threaten Our Civil Liberties.* New York: Seven Stories/Open Media.

Cohen, Lizabeth. 2003. *A Consumer's Republic: The Politics of Mass Consumption in Postwar America.* New York: Alfred A. Knopf.

Cole, David. 2003. *Enemy Aliens: Double Standards and Constitutional Freedoms in the War on Terrorism.* New York: New Press.

Cole, David, and James Dempsey. 2002. *Terrorism and the Constitution: Sacrificing Civil Liberties in the Name of National Security.* New York: The New Press.

Cole, Jennifer, and Deborah Durham. 2007. "Introduction: Age, Regeneration, and the Intimate Politics of Globalization." In *Generations and Globalization: Youth, Age, and Family in the New World Economy,* edited by Jennifer Cole and Deborah Durham. Indianapolis, Ind.: Indiana University Press.

Coll, Kathleen. 2002. "Problemas y necesidades: Latina Vernaculars of Citizenship and Coalition-Building in Chinatown, San Francisco." Paper presented at Racial (Trans)Formations: Latinos and Asians Remaking the United States, Center for the Study of Ethnicity and Race. Columbia University, March 2002.

Flores, William V., and Rina Benmayor, editors. 1997. *Latino Cultural Citizenship: Claiming Identity, Space, and Rights.* Boston, Mass.: Beacon Press.

France, Alan. 1998. " 'Why Should We Care?': Young People, Citizenship and Questions of Social Responsibility." *Journal of Youth Studies* 1(1): 97–111.

Fraser, Nancy. 1997. *Justice Interruptus: Critical Reflections on the Postsocialist Condition.* New York: Routledge.

Green, Jordan. 2003. "Silencing Dissent." *ColorLines* 6(2): 17–20.

Harvey, David. 2003. *The New Imperialism.* Oxford: Oxford University Press.

Hing, Bill O. 2000. "No Place for Angels: In Reaction to Kevin Johnson." *University of Illinois Law Review* 2000(2): 559–601.

———. 2002. "Vigilante Racism: The De-Americanization of Immigrant America." *Michigan Journal of Race and Law* 7(2): 441–56.

———. 2004. *Defining America Through Immigration Policy.* Philadelphia, Pa.: Temple University Press.

Ho, Enseng. 2004. "Empire Through Diasporic Eyes: A View from the Other Boat." *Comparative Studies of Society and History* 46(2): 210–46.

Howell, Sally, and Andrew Shryock. 2003. "Cracking Down on Diaspora: Arab Detroit and America's War on Terror." *Anthropological Quarterly* 76(3): 443–62.

Huntington, Samuel. 1996. *The Clash of Civilizations and the Remaking of World Order.* New York: Simon & Schuster.

Hutnyk, John, Stephen Corry, Iris Jean-Klein, and Richard Wilson. 2000. "The Right to Difference is a Fundamental Human Right." In *The Right to Difference Is a Fundamental Human Right,* edited by Peter Wade. GDAT debate no. 10. Manchester: Group for Debates in Anthropological Theory, University of Manchester.

Isin, Engin. 2000. "Introduction: Democracy, Citizenship and the City." In *Democracy, Citizenship and the Global City,* edited by Engin Isin. London: Routledge.

Jacobson, Jessica. 1998. *Islam in Transition: Religion and Identity Among British Pakistani Youth.* London: Routledge.

Jensen, Joan. 1988. *Passage from India: Asian Indian Immigrants in North America.* New Haven, Conn.: Yale University Press.

Kaplan, Amy. 1993. "Left Alone with America: The Absence of Empire in the Study of American Culture." In *Cultures of United States Imperialism,* edited by Amy Kaplan and Donald Pease. Durham, N.C.: Duke University Press.

Kaplan, Amy, and Donald Pease, editors. 1993. *Cultures of United States Imperialism.* Durham, N.C.: Duke University Press.

Kelley, Robin D. 1999. "People in Me." *ColorLines* 1(3): 5–7.

Kymlicka, Will. 1995. *Multicultural Citizenship: A Liberal Theory of Minority Rights.* Oxford: Oxford University Press.

Leonard, Karen I. 2003. *Muslims in the United States: The State of Research.* New York: Russell Sage Foundation.

Magdoff, Harry. 2003. *Imperialism Without Colonies.* New York: Monthly Review Press.

Maira, Sunaina. 2002. "Temporary Tattoos: Indo-Chic Fantasies and Late Capitalist Orientalism." *Meridians: feminism, race, transnationalism* 3(1): 134–60.

———. Forthcoming. *Missing: Youth, Citizenship, and Empire After 9/11.* Durham, N.C.: Duke University Press.

Mamdani, Mahmood. 2004. *Good Muslim, Bad Muslim: America, the Cold War, and the Roots of Terror.* New York: Pantheon.

Marshall, T. H. 1950. *Citizenship and Social Class.* Cambridge: Cambridge University Press.

Mattson, Ingrid. 2003. "How Muslims Use Islamic Paradigms to Define America." In *Religion and Immigration: Christian, Jewish, and Muslim Experiences in the United States,* edited by Yvonne Haddad, Jane Smith, and John Esposito. Walnut Creek, Calif.: AltaMira.

Miller, Toby. 1993. *The Well-Tempered Subject: Citizenship, Culture, and the Postmodern Subject.* Baltimore, Md.: Johns Hopkins University Press.

Misir, Deborah. 1996. "The Murder of Navroze Mody: Race, Violence, and the Search for Order." *Amerasia* 22(2): 55–75.

Modood, Tariq. 2002. "The Place of Muslims in British Secular Multiculturalism." In *Muslim Europe or Euro-Islam: Politics, Culture, and Citizenship in the Age of*

Globalization, edited by Nezar AlSayyad and Manuel Castells. Lanham, Md.: Lexington Books.

Moore, Kathleen. 1999. "A Closer Look at Anti-Terrorism Law: American Arab Anti-Discrimination Committee v. Reno and the Construction of Aliens' Rights." In *Arabs in America: Building a New Future,* edited by Michael Suleiman. Philadelphia, Pa.: Temple University Press.

Newman, Katherine S. 1999. *No Shame in My Game: The Working Poor in the Inner City.* New York: Alfred A. Knopf and the Russell Sage Foundation.

Nguyen, Tram. 2005. *We Are All Suspects Now: Untold Stories from Immigrant Communities After 9/11.* Boston, Mass.: Beacon Press.

Nussbaum, Martha C. 2002. "Patriotism and Cosmopolitanism." In *For Love of Country,* edited by Martha Nussbaum and Joshua Cohen. Boston, Mass.: Beacon Press.

Ong, Aihwa. 1996. "Cultural Citizenship as Subject-Making: Immigrants Negotiate Racial and Cultural Boundaries in the United States." *Current Anthropology* 37(5): 737–62.

———. 1999. *Flexible Citizenship: The Cultural Logics of Transnationality.* Durham, N.C.: Duke University Press.

———. 2003. *Buddha is Hiding: Refugees, Citizenship, the New America.* Berkeley, Calif.: University of California Press.

Panikkar, K. N., and Sukumar Muralidharan, editors. 2002. *Communalism, Civil Society and the State: Reflections on a Decade of Turbulence.* New Delhi: SAHMAT.

Pease, Donald. 1993. "New Perspectives on U.S. Culture and Imperialism." In *Cultures of United States Imperialism,* edited by Amy Kaplan and Donald Pease. Durham, N.C.: Duke University Press.

Prashad, Vijay. 2001. *Everybody Was Kung Fu Fighting: Afro-Asian Connections and the Myth of Cultural Purity.* Boston, Mass.: Beacon Press.

———. 2003. "The Green Menace: McCarthyism After 9/11." *The Subcontinental: A Journal of South Asian American Political Identity* 1(1): 65–75.

Rashid, Ahmed. 2000. *Taliban: Militant Islam, Oil and Fundamentalism in Central Asia.* New Haven, Conn.: Yale University Press.

Robin, Corey. 2003. "Fear, American Style: Civil Liberty After 9/11." In *Implicating Empire: Globalization and Resistance in the 21st Century World* Order, edited by Stanley Aronowitz and Heather Gautney. New York: Basic Books.

Rogin, Michael. 1993. " 'Make My Day!' Spectacle as Amnesia in Imperial Politics [and the Sequel]." In *Cultures of United States Imperialism,* edited by Amy Kaplan and Donald Pease. Durham, N.C.: Duke University Press.

Rosaldo, Renato. 1997. "Cultural Citizenship, Inequality, and Multiculturalism." In *Latino Cultural Citizenship: Claiming Identity, Space, and Rights,* edited by William F. Flores and Rina Benmayor. Boston, Mass.: Beacon Press.

Rothschild, Matthew. 2007. *You Have No Rights; Stories of America in an Age of Repression.* New York: New Press.

Ryan, Oliver. 2003. "Empty Shops, Empty Promises for Coney Island Pakistanis." *ColorLines* 6(2): 14–16.

Said, Edward W. 1978. *Orientalism.* New York: Vintage.

Sassen, Saskia. 2004. "The Repositioning of Citizenship: Emergent Subjects and Spaces for Politics." In *Empire's New Clothes: Reading Hardt and Negri,* edited by Paul A. Passavant and Jodi Dean. London: Routledge.

Schudson, Michael. 1998. *The Good Citizen: A History of American Civic Life.* Cambridge, Mass., and London: Harvard University Press.

Schulhofer, Stephen J. 2002. *The Enemy Within: Intelligence Gathering, Law Enforcement, and Civil Liberties in the Wake of September 11.* New York: Century Foundation Press.

Shaheen, Jack G. 1999. "Hollywood's Reel Arabs and Muslims." In *Muslims and Islamization in North America: Problems and Prospects,* edited by Ambreen Haque. Beltsville, Md.: Amana Publications.

Shanahan, Suzanne. 1999. "Scripted Debates: Twentieth-Century Immigration and Citizenship Policy in Great Britain, Ireland, and the United States." In *Extending Citizenship, Reconfiguring States,* edited by Michael Hanagan and Charles Tilly. Lanham, Md.: Rowman & Littlefield.

Sharma, Aradhana and Akhil Gupta. 2006. "Rethinking Theories of the State in an Age of Globalization." In *The Anthropology of the State: A Reader,* edited by Aradhana Sharma and Akhil Gupta. Malden, Mass.: Blackwell.

Siu, Lok. 2001. "Diasporic Cultural Citizenship: Chineseness and Belonging in Central America and Panama." *Social Text* 19(4 69): 7–28.

Smith, Neil. 2005. *The Endgame of Globalization.* London: Routledge.

Stoler, Ann L. 2006. "Intimidations of Empire: Predicaments of the Tactile and Unseen." In *Haunted by Empire: Geographies of Intimacy in North American History,* edited by Ann L. Stoler. Durham, N.C., and London: Duke University Press.

Swarns, Rachel L. 2003. "More Than 13,000 May Face Deportation." *The New York Times,* June 7, 2003, A1.

Tannock, Stuart. 2001. *Youth at Work: The Unionized Fast-Food and Grocery Workplace.* Philadelphia, Pa.: Temple University Press.

U.S. Census Bureau. 2000. American Fact Finder—Census 2000 Summary File. Accessed at http://factfinder.census.gov/.

Varadarajan, Siddharth, editor. 2002. *Gujarat: The Making of a Tragedy.* New Delhi: Penguin Books.

Vimalassery, Manu. 2002. "Passports and Pink Slips." *SAMAR (South Asian Magazine for Action and Reflection)* 15: 7–8, 20.

Williams, William A. 1980. *Empire as a Way of Life. New York: An Essay on the Causes and Character of America's Present Predicament.* New York: Oxford University Press.

Young, Iris M. 1990. *Justice and the Politics of Difference.* Princeton, N.J.: Princeton University Press.

CHAPTER 3

Detroit Exceptionalism and the Limits of Political Incorporation

Sally Howell and Amaney Jamal

NATIONAL AND international media often turn their attention to Detroit when exploring connections between the United States and the Middle East. So too do federal authorities. In the immediate aftermath of the 9/11 attacks, the special relationship between Arab Detroit, the media, and law enforcement agencies intensified significantly. America was in crisis, and prevailing anxieties were felt by and projected onto Arab and Muslim Americans in unique ways. The Detroit suburb of Dearborn, with its heavy concentration of newly arrived Lebanese, Iraqi, Yemeni, and Palestinian immigrants, was an early target of investigation and concern. Here, journalists and Arab community leaders were already on a first-name basis, fear of a backlash was palpable, and an alleged sleeper cell was identified and raided within days of the attacks. Working class mosques, colorful Arabic storefronts, women and girls wearing headscarves, and Arabic speakers gathering to watch Al Jazeera broadcasts in their homes and businesses made Dearborn an alluring backdrop for initial coverage of the "war on terror." The images these stories purveyed, whatever the intentions of the reporters and their agencies, encoded two contradictory assumptions. One was that Detroit's Arab communities and their experiences after 9/11 were somehow representative of the experiences of Arab Americans nationwide. The other was that Detroit's Arab communities, by virtue of their visibility, accessibility, and concentrated Otherness, were in fact exceptional to national patterns. In this chapter we examine the post 9/11 backlash in Detroit in light of both assumptions.

The tension between Detroit as representative of Arab America and Detroit as exceptional to Arab America has a long history among Arab American activists and Arab Americanist scholars (Shryock and Abraham 2000). Like so much else concerning Arabs in America, this tension acquired a political urgency after 9/11 that has not waned. When President George W. Bush uttered his famous challenge on September 20, 2001, "Either you are with us, or you are with the terrorists," many in Michigan felt the statement targeted their community quite specifically. Were local Arabs with us, or with the terrorists? County, state, and municipal officials, business leaders, and clergy rushed in to assure Arab Americans that their loyalty was not in doubt and that discrimination against local Arabs and Muslims would not be tolerated. Arab Detroiters donned protective American flags, held large, televised memorial services for the victims of the attacks, and issued strongly worded condemnations of the attacks and the motivations behind them. Although thousands of suddenly vulnerable Arabs suffered insults or abuse at the hands of their fellow citizens, thousands more received gestures of goodwill and support from non-Arab neighbors. These local experiences of protection and solidarity contrasted sharply with events transpiring on the national stage, where the president's challenge appeared to elicit a different response, where the USA PATRIOT Act (Patriot Act) was swiftly passed by Congress, and where Arab and Muslim Americans (as well as those who resembled them) suddenly found themselves humiliated on airplanes, detained and deported (if lacking citizenship) without legal counsel, and subjected to unprecedented surveillance and governmental scrutiny. It appeared that the federal government had a less certain, and certainly less affirmative, answer to the president's challenge than leaders in Detroit did.

To frame Arab Detroit as exceptional, we must go beyond portraying it as a demographic anomaly and ask instead whether the local experience of the 9/11 backlash was qualitatively different from the experience elsewhere. If the answer is yes, it is also imperative that we consider how and why Detroit achieved this exceptional status. Borrowing loosely from recent scholarship that challenges the concept of American exceptionalism, we argue that Detroit's exceptionalism is a double-edged sword.[1] It does not imply a simple binary wherein Arab Americans are either proof of the American dream, of egalitarianism, the rule of law, and tolerance, or proof of the American nightmare, of discrimination, violence, and bigotry. Rather, it suggests a complex amalgam of both realities, in which ignorance and fear live side by side with solidarity and progress. Arab Detroit is exceptional, we will argue, due to the power of a local community—with its own local history and political culture—to insulate itself from a national public culture that sees Arabs (and Muslims) as a problem and has difficulty separating "good" Arabs from "bad." Michigan's Arabs, through the work of many individuals and the efforts of many successful ethnic institutions, have been incorporated to a remarkable degree into local structures of economic, social, and political capital. At the national level, by contrast, Arabs have found their efforts to organize and influence governmental policies, especially foreign policies, blocked (Samhan 2006; Suleiman 2006). This power differential between local and national arenas, which has become more critical in the post-9/11 period, gives special significance to the question of Detroit's role as an Arab American community versus its role as exemplar of the Arab American community. Drawing on data from the Detroit Arab American Study (see appendix), from national surveys, from conversations with Arab American community leaders,[2] and from our observations of recent events, we will examine the social, political, and economic repercussions of the "war on terror" in Arab Detroit. Insofar as Detroit's experience in the aftermath of the 9/11 attacks was a departure from the norm, what are the factors that account for this difference and, more critically, what are the consequences of this difference? Given the size, longevity, and genuine incorporation of this diverse community, the question of its representational status has profound implications for the future of Arab and Muslim communities nationwide.

SETTING THE DEMOGRAPHIC STAGE: "MICHIGAN IS OUR NEW YORK"

Among scholars and Arab American community leaders, Detroit's exceptional nature has been highlighted for multiple, often conflicting purposes.[3] On the one hand, Detroit, and more specifically Dearborn, is cast as the golden city of assimilationist desires, where, in the late 1990s, Arab Americans included in their ranks the CEO of Ford Motor Company, a United States senator, and the head of the United Auto Workers. At the same time, however, Detroit is home to a large number of recently arrived Arabs. Many have found success as professionals, or as gas station and liquor store owners. Many languish in low-income jobs, cleaning the homes of others, working as busboys in Detroit's casinos, providing nonunionized labor to Detroit's shrinking industrial sector, or driving ice cream trucks. Dearborn is often viewed as little more than an Arab ghetto, where pressure to Americanize is minimal and almost all one's social and consumer needs can be met in the Arabic language. Alternatively, Dearborn's thriving Lebanese business district has become a tourist destination for non-Arabs eager to sample the enclave's wares. Affluent suburban Arabs flock to Dearborn on weekends to shop for bargain vegetables, freshly butchered halal meat, and the delicacies of a half dozen bakeries. The Dearborn enclave has also produced (among many others) two of the oldest, most influential mosques in America and the country's most celebrated Arab American community organization: ACCESS (the Arab Community Center for Economic and Social Services). These organizations have gained for Dearborn Arabs a measure of political clout and influence at the state level that is unrivaled elsewhere.

For all these reasons, Arab Detroit is not representative of Arab America as a whole. Yet anomalous demographics are not enough to explain Detroit's exceptional status. For Arab American leaders and the scholars who work with and among them, Detroit's exceptional nature is based equally on the complex mix of imagery found in collective representations of local Arab communities.

It is at once a marginalized ghetto, a site of mobilization and political incorporation, a prospering marketplace, a model of effective police-community relations, a classroom for Americanization, a refuge from oppressive Arab regimes, a sanctuary for retrograde conservatives, an exploitable labor pool, a conduit for trade with the Arab world, and a zone of federal scrutiny and harassment. We first highlight several demographic features that distinguish Detroit from other Arab American communities and analyze how these demographics have intersected with community history to produce an exceptionally well-enfranchised ethnic American enclave.

Distinguishing feature #1. Arab Detroit is as old as the oldest Arab American communities. But its population, by comparison, is also far more recently arrived and far more fluent in Arabic and other third languages.

Arab immigrants began arriving in Detroit in the 1880s, and by 1897 a small colony of Syrians, as they were known at the time, had established itself on Detroit's East Side, working mostly as peddlers. This early settlement attracted fellow sojourners from the mountainous regions of today's Lebanon. Like many who arrived in Detroit during this period, the Syrians were drawn by the high wages Henry Ford and other automobile manufacturers were offering, especially after 1914. By 1921, two Arab churches had been established in Detroit, and the nation's first mosque had opened its doors in Highland Park (Howell 2007). Arab immigrants and their descendents continued to settle in Michigan throughout the twentieth century. They built dozens of economic, cultural, and sectarian institutions, and produced politicians, union activists, captains of industry, celebrity entertainers, and even a presidential candidate (Ralph Nader's family is originally from Detroit). Despite this long and pedigreed local history, Arab Detroit is today, as it was in 1914, a majority immigrant community. This fact more than any other accounts for Detroit's anomalous relationship to Arab America as whole.

The Detroit Arab American Study (DAAS) in 2002 and 2003 found that, in a sample of 1,016 adults of Arab and Chaldean ancestry, 75 percent were born outside the United States. Were children factored into the equation, this number would drop sharply, but would still be much higher than the national average for Arab Americans of 41 percent (Arab American Institute Foundation 2006). More than three quarters (79 percent) of local Arabs and Chaldeans are U.S. citizens, a high percentage relative other immigrant populations.[4] In a region of the country not receiving large numbers of immigrants,[5] Arabs in Detroit stand out as foreign. Eighty-five percent of our sample speaks Arabic, and in some cases a third language, at home, in comparison to 53 percent of Arabs nationwide (Arab American Institute Foundation 2006). Arab Detroiters are nonetheless fluent in English, on a par with Arab Americans nationwide. Although the high percentage of immigrants and Arabic speakers in the DAAS tends to distract attention from the tens of thousands of Arab Americans whose families have lived in Michigan for generations, it is not the presence of one community or the other that makes Detroit unusual. Rather, it is the degree to which both populations effectively interact as a composite, overarching Arab American community that is rare.

Distinguishing feature #2. Arab Detroit has far more Muslims than Arab America as a whole, and a larger percentage of Shi'a Muslims in particular.

About 58 percent of Arabs and Chaldeans in Detroit identify as Christian, and 42 percent as Muslim. Among Arab Christians, Catholics are the largest group (73 percent), followed by Orthodox (24 percent), and Protestants (3 percent). Arab Muslims have a Shi'a majority (56 percent), and a Sunni minority (35 percent), though Sunnis make up the majority of Muslims in the Arab countries and worldwide. Arab Christians outnumber Arab Muslims in Detroit, as they do nationally, but the margin locally is not large. Muslim Arabs represent less than a third of Arabs nationwide (23 to 33 percent).[6] These differences play a significant role in framing the Detroit community as an exception to Arab America as a whole.

Distinguishing feature #3. Arab Detroit contains America's best-known Arab immigrant enclave, Dearborn, where a large number of mostly Muslim Arabs live in very high concentration. No other American city includes such a highly visible and large Arab enclave.

Arab Detroit is not famous simply for the size and diversity of its Arab communities. It is known primarily for the high concentration of Arabs who live in and around Dearborn, home of the Ford Motor Company, Michigan's oldest mosque, the nation's most influential Arab American organization, ACCESS, and an Arab population that accounts for a solid thirty-five percent of the city's 98,000 residents (American Community Survey 2005). Dearborn Heights, an adjacent township, and several Detroit neighborhoods abutting Dearborn, also have high concentrations of Arabs. The presence of this immigrant enclave, with its thriving business districts, residential neighborhoods that are often more than 90 percent Arab, and multitude of community activists and organizations, has put Dearborn at the center, nationally and locally, of all things Arab American. This singular enclave, however, is by no means the totality of Arab Detroit. In fact, only 29 percent of the DAAS sample lives in Dearborn and Dearborn Heights. Nine percent lives in Detroit and Hamtramck, but the majority of local Arabs (62 percent) are scattered throughout Detroit's suburbs, typically in much smaller concentrations. In general, Muslims and Christians tend not to live in the same neighborhoods. About two-thirds of Arab Muslims (64 percent) live in the Dearborn area, whereas very few Christian Arabs (only 5 percent) do.

Distinguishing feature #4. Arabs in Detroit are both richer and poorer than the general population. Compared to other Arab Americans nationally, those living in Detroit are less well educated.

Socioeconomic factors also distinguish Arab Detroit from Arab Americans at large. Although nationally Arabs have achieved high levels of educational and economic success, the heavily immigrant population in Detroit, often arriving

51

from rural and war-torn regions of the Middle East, makes the economic and educational profile of Detroit distinctive. Only 72 percent of Arab Detroiters have high school degrees, compared to 88 percent of Arabs nationwide, and where more than 43 percent of Arab Americans nationally have a bachelor's degree or higher, only 23 percent in the Detroit area do (Arab American Institute Foundation 2006). The relatively high number of Arabs and Chaldeans without a high school degree is reflected in income figures. Income levels also show a gap between those educated in America and those who came here as adults. Twenty-four percent claim an annual family income of less than $20,000, compared to 18 percent of the general Detroit population.[7] On the other hand, 25 percent report annual family incomes of $100,000 or more per year, compared to only 16 percent in the larger population. Arabs and Chaldeans born in the United States are more affluent still: 36 percent report an annual family income of $100,000 or more, and only 7 percent report less than $20,000. Finally, Arabs and Chaldeans own their own businesses in greater numbers than others (19 percent and 14 percent respectively) and are more likely to be self-employed (31 percent and 16 percent). When compared to Arab Americans nationally, however, 37 percent of whom own their own businesses, Arab Detroiters look more like others in Detroit and less like Arab Americans in general (Arab American Institute Foundation 2002).

Again, the socioeconomic gaps that divide those educated in the Middle East from those educated in the United States are stark and have led to a higher poverty rate among Arabs in Detroit than elsewhere. The presence of an Arab working class in Detroit has had positive consequences for the population as whole. Low-income Arabs have two effective, increasingly prominent organizations that lobby for their concerns. ACCESS and the Arab American and Chaldean Council (ACC) opened their doors in the early 1970s in reaction to new immigration from distressed Arab countries and a series of economic downturns in the auto industry that left immigrant workers vulnerable. Both ACCESS and ACC built successful alliances between Arab immigrants in need, Arab immigrant professionals and human service providers, and American-born Arabs committed to community-based activism. Although many Arab and Chaldean service organizations have developed since the 1970s, ACCESS and ACC have the strongest track records. Each has an annual operating budget of more than $12 million and each is well connected to state and local governments. These organizations bring together rich and poor, immigrant and American-born, enclave dwellers and suburbanites, Christians and Muslims. More significant, they collaborate extensively with non-Arab organizations throughout the Detroit area and have brought Arab Americans into the mainstream of local public culture (Howell 2000).

Distinguishing feature #5. Arab Detroit has an unprecedented number of elected officials, law enforcement officers, appointed government officials, and other public servants.

Arab Detroiters are uniquely situated in positions of local power and influence. The City of Detroit, for example, is a border town, home to the Ambassador Bridge and the Detroit-Windsor Tunnel, which carry between them nearly a third of all traffic crossing the U.S.-Canada border (Border Transportation Partnership 2004). The Ambassador Bridge is rare among American border crossings in that it is privately owned and operated. It is rarer still for being owned by an immigrant from Lebanon, Manuel Maroun. Likewise, when international travelers arrive at the Detroit Metropolitan Airport, they pass through a terminal bearing the name of another Lebanese American, former Wayne County Road Commissioner Michael Berry. Flight schedules and ground traffic at the airport are managed by Hassan Makled, director of Air-field Operations, who, like Berry, is an active member of the Islamic Center of America.[8] All this coming and going is carefully monitored by Detroit and Wayne County Homeland Security Task Forces, both of which are led, in part, by Lebanese American law enforcement officers who are also Shi'a Muslims. These men are among more than sixty deputized Arab Americans in Wayne County alone, where Azzam Elder, a Palestinian American, was recently named deputy Wayne County executive and his wife, Charlene Makled Elder, a Lebanese American Muslim, now serves as a circuit court judge. The Elders are two of at least thirty-six Arab Americans in Michigan to hold political appointments, and the state is home to at least twenty-three Arab American judges and elected officials.[9] This list, with its perhaps surprising inclusion of Arab Americans who work for Homeland Security task forces, is perfectly mundane in Detroit. It does not include the much larger number of Arab Americans who sit on the boards of local hospitals and the United Way, serve as regents of state universities, or are active participants in the local ACLU, UAW, Civil Rights Board, or many of the state's important nonprofit organizations. Although no other state can rival Michigan's high number of Arab public servants, similar patterns of community service by Arab Americans can be found across the United States.

Clearly, Detroit is quite unlike Arab America as a whole. It is more recently arrived, more bilingual, more Muslim, less well educated, has a higher percentage of economically marginal households, is home to the largest and most visible Arab American enclave, and its members have a higher level of representation in municipal, county, and state government. In the words of Ismael Ahmed, former director of ACCESS, "Michigan can and should be a model of political participation" (2006, 50), making it, in the words of another well known Arab American activist, James Zogby "our New York" (Ahmed 2006). But do these differences make Detroit exceptional to Arab America in other ways as well? Is daily life, or community life, in Detroit somehow different from daily or community life elsewhere in Arab America? Given, for instance, that many of the demographic features that distinguish Detroit are associated nationally with increased vulnerability to hate crimes and discrimination, it should follow that

Arab Detroiters were more vulnerable to the 9/11 backlash than other Arab Americans. We show, in the section that follows, that this was not the case. Likewise, we might assume that the federal crackdown on Arab and Muslim transnational networks, fueled in part by the Patriot Act (Howell and Shryock 2003), would have had a greater impact on Detroit's large immigrant and Muslim population. Our findings do not contradict this assumption, but suggest that the impacts are ambiguous and difficult to assess.

BACKLASH, PART 1: ARAB AMERICAN SECURITY

9/11 occurred on a Tuesday. By Wednesday, we started receiving phone calls in our mosque, at our parochial school on Ford Road, threatening to come bomb our buildings, kill the school kids in retaliation for 9/11. I have to admit that I got a little scared myself. . . . I suggested that the school be shut down. . . . That was Wednesday. We shut the school down in the middle of the day. . . . By Thursday morning, then Sheriff Robert Ficano became aware of the threats that were being made to the most visible place probably in the country—Arab American Dearborn. . . . ACCESS started getting phone calls making threats, the mosques did, several of the mosques, some of the other organizations. You know the temperament of the country was—you had to take them seriously. . . . So Ficano and myself and a few other Arab officers got together and we called a meeting of the imams of all of the mosques in Dearborn and some of the surrounding mosques that border Dearborn in Detroit. . . Ficano offered to set up protection for the mosques for the prayer that was coming up on Friday, the next day, and it was agreed. What we did is we went out and sought volunteers from the sheriff's department who would work a few hours every Friday, beside their regular shift, at the various mosques. We did that and we were able to put at least 2 police officers at every mosque in Dearborn for the Friday prayer and every mosque that requested it. (Ronald Amen, former Wayne County deputy sheriff, interview, January 8, 2005)

When we examine the backlash data from the DAAS and national studies, we find stark contrasts between Detroit and Arab America as a whole, contrasts that suggest the efforts of Ron Amen, Robert Ficano, and thousands of concerned and well-placed citizens like them did indeed make a tremendous difference throughout the Detroit area. The percentage of DAAS respondents who reported having a bad experience after the attacks because of their race or ethnicity was 15 percent, significantly less than the 25 percent reported in a national Zogby poll (Arab American Institute Foundation 2002).[10] The majority of these discriminatory acts involved verbal insults or threats (61 percent). Some 43 percent of DAAS respondents reported worrying more about the future facing their families in the United States after the attacks, but this number is also significantly lower than the 66 percent nationwide. The gap between Arab Detroit and the rest of Arab America also extends to questions regarding willingness to exchange civil liberties for more security. By and large, the national Arab American community was much more likely (at 49 percent) to agree to give up some of their liberties than Arabs in Detroit were. Only 20 percent of DAAS respondents were willing to selectively forgo their civil liberties.

These numbers suggest that Detroit fared better in the post-9/11 period than the rest of Arab America, a finding that alternately surprised, disturbed, and reassured the Arab Detroiters we shared it with, especially those who work in frontline occupations directly affected by the backlash and the war on terror. Rena Abbas-Chami, deputy director of the Michigan arm of the American Arab Anti-Discrimination Committee (ADC), said in a February 2005 interview that the number of discrimination reports her office received skyrocketed from four to five a week to several hundred in September and October of 2001. ADC's staff was so overwhelmed they began referring their clients directly to their national office and to a hate crimes hotline they established with Wayne County immediately after the attacks. "Dearborn seemed to be the epicenter of the threats to avenge 9/11," Ron Amen said. Dearborn, and Arab Detroit more generally, were indeed vulnerable. The public visibility the community gained in the 1990s, when multicultural inclusion was the order of the day, now made Arab Americans feel exposed. Rumors flew about young men being dragged from their cars and beaten up on the outskirts of Dearborn. People stayed at home as much as they could. One story, which circulated nationally, claimed that Dearborn was placed under martial law (Niraj Warikoo, "Rumor Mill Spins Fast and Furious," *Detroit Free Press*, September 13, 2001, 12A). Law enforcement agencies in Michigan were also concerned about the vulnerability of Arab Americans and responded, especially in Dearborn and Wayne County, with unprecedented patrols of Arab American neighborhoods, business districts, and houses of worship to provide a sense of security and calm (Thacher 2005).

Likewise, the number of DAAS respondents who reported receiving a gesture of kindness from a non-Arab after the attacks was twice as high (33 percent) as those who reported an act of discrimination (15 percent). This informal support was matched by local officials, corporate leaders, educators, and other opinion makers. Imad Hamad, director of ADC Michigan, found himself meeting with Dearborn's mayor, Mike Guido, and chief of police, Greg Guibord, just before noon on September 11 to discuss the possibility of a backlash and how best to thwart troublemakers while reassuring the community at large (Interview, July 20, 2005). These local policing efforts were highly successful, with only two hate crimes reported in Dearborn (Arab population roughly 30,000) in 2001 and 2002. Human Rights Watch called these local campaigns exemplary and has since encouraged other cities to follow

Table 3.1   Metro Detroit: Place of Birth and Backlash

	Bad Experience	Worry	Give Up Civil Liberties
U.S.-Born	19%	46%	22%
Foreign-Born	14	55	19
	Pearson chi2(1) = 2.4788 Pr = 0.105	Pearson chi2(1) = 9.6802 Pr = 0.002	Pearson chi2(1) = 3.3876 Pr = 0.066

Source: Detroit Arab American Study (DAAS) (2003).
Note: N = 1,016

Dearborn's lead (Singh 2002). It seemed as though every elected official in the state issued a statement about tolerance.[11] The breadth and depth of public support shown to Arab Detroit went a long way toward making Dearborn residents feel, in the words of Maysoun Khatib, a Michigan Civil Rights Commission program officer, that the city wore an "invisibility cloak" protecting it from hostility and attack (Interview, January 23, 2005). "People know us," attorney Bill Swor explained. "My intuition, my experience tells me that because the Arab community in Detroit has been here 100 years, 120 years, has been a greater part of the fabric [of the city] for a longer period of time and is integrated in the [local] infrastructure . . . then I guess you buy the good as well as the bad and it is harder, even if you don't like the guy, it is harder to be overtly hostile" (Interview, November 9, 2004).

By examining which parts of Detroit's Arab community were most vulnerable after the attacks, and which witnessed the greatest solidarity from non-Arabs, we can illustrate how the public outpouring of support for Arab Detroiters in the post-9/11 period helped ensure the security of this population. Nationally, it was immigrants (29 percent) and Muslims (42 percent) who reported the largest percentages of bad experiences after the attacks, or those with a poor command of English (Zogby International 2002). In Detroit, however, despite its unusually large percentage of foreign-born and Muslim Arabs, the numbers look very different. Not only was the overall backlash in Detroit less severe, but when the data is disaggregated at the local level, it is also clear that Michigan's most vulnerable populations, in particular, fared better than their counterparts in other states (on vulnerable Arab populations in California and Illinois, see especially Naber 2006; Cainkar 2006). Foreign-born Arabs in Detroit reported fewer bad experiences than their U.S.-born counterparts, 14 percent to 19 percent (see tables 3.1 and 3.2). Likewise, the percentage of negative experiences reported by Muslims, 20 percent, though higher than those reported by Arab Christians, 13 percent, is less than those

Table 3.2   National Patterns: Place of Birth and Backlash

	Bad Experience	Worry	Give Up Civil Liberties
U.S.-Born	19%	60%	57%
Foreign-Born	29	70	44
	Pearson chi2(1) = 7.1967 Pr = 0.007	Pearson chi2(1) = 6.5727 Pr = 0.010	Pearson chi2(1) = 7.3857 Pr = 0.007

Source: Zogby International (2002).
Note: N = 505

reported nationwide, 42 percent and 16 percent (see tables 3.3 and 3.4). And, in an unusual turn of events, the more fluent in English DAAS respondents were, the more likely they were after the attacks to report having had a bad experience related to their race or ethnicity.

Similarly, although Muslims in Detroit (71 percent) and elsewhere (82 percent) report greater worries about their future in the United States than Christian Arabs (39 percent in Detroit and 57 percent nationally), Michigan Arab populations overall report significantly less than the national average (43 percent of the DAAS to 66 percent of the Zogby data). In fact, though Christians nationally (58 percent) and in Detroit (30 percent) were more willing to trade civil liberties for security than Muslims were (presumably because they did not feel as implicated in the 9/11 attacks), Detroit Muslims were significantly less likely to accept this compromise than Muslims nationwide (6 percent to 35 percent). Finally, although the percentage of foreign-born Arab Detroiters who worry about their future is greater than that of the American-born (55 percent to 46 percent), this percentage is still significantly lower than national

Table 3.3   Metro Detroit: Religion and Backlash

	Bad Experience	Worry	Give Up Civil Liberties
Muslim	20%	71%	6%
Christian	12.7	39	30
	Pearson chi2(1) = 7.5987 Pr = 0.006	Pearson chi2(1) = 89.9708 Pr = 0.000	Pearson chi2(1) = 70.8574 Pr = 0.000

Source: Detroit Arab American Study (DAAS) (2003).
Note: N = 1,016

Table 3.4   National Patterns: Religion and Backlash

	Bad Experience	Worry	Give Up Civil Liberties
Muslim	42%	82%	35%
Christian	16	57	58
	Pearson chi2(1)	Pearson chi2(1)	Pearson chi2(1)
	= 38.9386	= 30.9507	= 24.1392
	Pr = 0.000	Pr = 0.000	Pr = 0.000

Source: Zogby International (2002).
Note: N = 505.

figures. Only 19 percent of Detroit's foreign-born Arab population is willing to trade civil liberties for security, which is less than half the national average of 51 percent. Overall, our data suggest that Arab Detroit weathered the post 9/11 backlash with fewer scars than the Arab American community nationwide and that Arab Detroiters, relative their counterparts elsewhere, are more confident about their future in the United States and more assertive of their rights as citizens. These findings are most pronounced among those Arab populations that are most vulnerable nationwide—namely, immigrants and Muslims.

THE IMPACT OF PARTICIPATION IN ARAB AMERICAN ETHNIC INSTITUTIONS

What accounts for these differences? The answer lies in Arab Detroit's unparalleled amalgam of successful institutions, politically incorporated individuals, economic clout, and concentrated populations. They are what make Detroit exceptional, and they are most effectively expressed in a profusion of ethnic associations. DAAS findings suggest that participation in ethnic associations correlates directly to greater empowerment among Arab Detroiters. Of DAAS respondents, 39 percent report being involved in an Arab ethnic association, "including advocacy groups like ADC, the Yemeni Benevolent Association, or the Chaldean Federation." These organizations act as gateways to a larger political world, linking local residents to mainstream institutions at the local, regional, and national levels. Police departments, elected officials, service providers, churches, universities, marketers, and many others go through Detroit's community organizations when hoping to reach local Arab Americans. Sometimes ethnic associations act as surrogates for the communities they represent, monopolizing contacts and resources, but they also act as conduits through which incorporation is pursued (Howell 2000; Jamal 2005; Shryock 2004).

Table 3.5   Participation in Ethnic Associations and Solidarity

Participation	Solidarity		Total
	No	Yes	
No	73%	27%	100%
Yes	57	43	100

Pearson chi2(1) = 15.2591
Pr = 0.000

Source: Detroit Arab American Study (DAAS) (2003).
Note: N = 996; N (participation in ethnic associations = no) = 612; N (participation in ethnic associations = yes) = 384.

Among DAAS respondents, participation in ethnic associations is linked to both positive and negative post 9/11 outcomes. The 39 percent of DAAS respondents who reported participating in ethnic associations had different experiences than those who reported active membership (or regular attendance) in churches, mosques, or village clubs. For example, when compared to nonmembers, members of ethnic associations were 15 percent more likely to have reported experiencing an act of solidarity by a non-Arab after the 9/11 attacks (43 percent to 27 percent; see table 3.5). On the other hand, members of ethnic associations were less likely to express confidence in the federal government (43 percent of members reported high levels of confidence compared to 59 percent of nonmembers). Members were also less likely to think Arabs and Muslims accused of supporting terrorism could receive a fair trial, (44 percent to 55 percent) suggesting that members are more skeptical of American political institutions (see tables 3.6, 3.7). Nonetheless, as presented in table 3.8, members are also far more likely to contact a government official to express an opinion on a political issue (16 percent) than are Arabs who do not belong to such groups (6 percent). Membership in an Arab ethnic association brings with it greater skepticism about the American political system. It also brings increased opportunity to engage, sometimes productively, with mainstream political institutions.

BACKLASH, PART 2: THE FEDERAL LAW ENFORCEMENT AGENDA

Everybody saw George Bush go to the mosque in Washington, D.C., take his shoes off and enter the prayer room, the masjid area, as a show of solidarity with the Muslims in this country, and certainly, initially, we all thought that was a really good thing for him to have done and we appreciated that and really looked

Table 3.6   Participation in Ethnic Associations
             and Confidence in U.S. Government

| | Confidence | | |
Participation	Low	High	Total
No	41%	59%	100%
Yes	57	43	100

Pearson chi2(1) = 15.1053
Pr = 0.002

Source: Detroit Arab American Study (DAAS) (2003).
Note: N = 950; N (participation in ethnic associations = no) = 578; N (participation in ethnic association = yes) = 372.

to him to defend our civil rights. And then it all appeared to be a dog and pony show. As the situation evolved a few weeks later we started to see Muslims and Arabs just disappearing from the country. Actually they were being arrested, incarcerated, held without charge, without contact, without an attorney, just kind of disappearing. Sometimes their families didn't even know where they were for several weeks before the government finally deported them . . . And then, the infamous Patriot Act came into existence and we could actually see in black and white that all those things that George Bush said to us when he was running for office prior to 9/11, about how he was going to do away with profiling, about how he was going to do away with secret evidence, turned out to be a lie. Not only did he not do away with those things, he actually put his attack dog, John Ashcroft, in a position to strengthen those violations of our civil rights as Arab Americans, as Muslim Americans. (Interview, Ron Amen, 2005)

When Arab Detroiters talk now about the impact of the 9/11 attacks, their greatest concern, echoing Ron Amen, is the erosion of their civil liberties and the profiling of their communities by law enforcement and the media. They speak of the silencing effect on those who want to criticize United States and Israeli policies in the Middle East.[12] They worry about the constriction of economic and cultural flows that connect the United States and the Arab world, and the simultaneous expansion of American military campaigns in the Muslim world. It is not always easy to see, but in Washington and the national media, Arab Americans are portrayed as potential threats to American security and as potential assets in the Bush administration's campaign to reshape the Middle East and fight the "war on terror" (Hagopian 2003). This situation

Table 3.7   Participation in Ethnic Associations and Government Contact

Participation	Written Letter to Government		Total
	No	Yes	
No	94%	6%	100%
Yes	84	16	100

Pearson chi2(1) = 30.3196

Pr = 0.000

Source: Detroit Arab American Study (DAAS) (2003).
Note: N = 1,003; N (participation in ethnic associations = no) = 618; N (participation in ethnic associations = yes) = 385.

has yielded a heady mix of opportunity and constraint for Arab Americans, just as it has delivered an especially violent mix of opportunity and destruction to the Arab world. Nowhere in America has the two-edged nature of increased federal attention been more apparent than in Detroit's Arab communities. If Arab Detroit's exceptional nature sheltered it from angry, intolerant individuals bent on revenge, did it also protect Arab Americans from ill-informed federal agents who saw culprits and conspirators around every corner? Did it situate Detroit's Arab organizations to capitalize on new economic and cultural possibilities that followed (and were a part of) the backlash or did it force them to redirect their energies toward defensive educational and legal campaigns? Did it empower Arab Americans to influence policy on the national level now that many Arab ethnic associations were working closely with federal agencies? We will next explore how Detroit has responded to what Hussein Ibish, former spokesperson for ADC, has described as the Bush administration's "message" to Arab Americans: "private citizens should not and cannot discriminate against Arabs and Muslims, but we [the federal government] can and will" (Ibish 2003).

THE HUNT FOR TERRORISTS IN DETROIT COURTROOMS

In the days immediately following the 9/11 attacks, the FBI, INS, and local law enforcement agencies rounded up and detained without charge more than 1,100 Arab, South Asian, and Muslim men as part of Investigation PENTTBOM, which sought out individuals who were suspected, on the most speculative of evidence, of having known beforehand about the 9/11 attacks or

Table 3.8   Participation in Ethnic Associations
and Ability to Obtain a Fair Trial

Participation	Ability		Total
	No	Yes	
No	45%	55%	100%
Yes	56	44	100

Pearson chi2(1) = 12.3494
Pr = 0.000

Source: Detroit Arab American Study (DAAS) (2003).
Note: N = 950; N (participation in ethnic associations = no) = 574; N (participation in ethnic associations = yes) = 372.

of planning additional terror attacks (U.S. Department of Justice 2003). For the most part, these men were held without charges and in complete secrecy, often in solitary confinement. More than half were eventually deported, though none have been linked, directly or indirectly, to the 9/11 conspiracy. As the investigations widened over several months, the numbers grew to more than 5,000 detained, 155 in Detroit (Cole 2003). Detroit may not have been the epicenter of the public backlash against Arabs and Muslims in the United States, but it was in many ways the epicenter of the Justice Department's campaign to apprehend terror suspects and reassure the public that it was doing all it could to hunt down and prosecute those with terrorist ties. On the anniversary of the 9/11 attacks, for example, Mark Corallo, a Justice Department spokesman in Washington, announced that the FBI office in Detroit had more than doubled in size in 2002, that their agents were receiving full cooperation from "wary community leaders acting as cultural guides into the local Arab world," and that the Detroit office was at the forefront of "the largest investigation in the history of the United States" (Tamara Audi, "Terror War Hits Home—Secret Sweep: Detroiters Caught in Widening Investigation," *Detroit Free Press,* November 12, 2002, 1A). This vast deployment of man hours and new powers of surveillance yielded not the terrorists Bush was hoping for, but a tripling of the arrest rate of local Arab and Muslim petty criminals and visa over-stayers (Greg Krupa and John Bebow, "Immigration Crackdown Snares Arabs," *Detroit News,* November 3, 2003, 1A). As Bill Swor, a Detroit attorney who has worked on several prominent terrorism-related cases, pointed out to us, these investigations had a chilling effect on the community. "When every federal investigation involving an Arab, whether a citizen or a resident alien, is vetted through the terrorism unit . . . and every illegal act treated as a federal offense . . . and each case is charged at grotesque levels, finding the most serious charges we can bring, the community remains traumatized because the community knows that it is being not only watched, but targeted" (Interview, 2004).

On September 17, 2001, five days after the attacks, the FBI raided a house in Detroit. They were looking for Nabil Almarabh, a noncitizen whose name had appeared on a pre-9/11 terrorism watch list. Almarabh was not in Detroit, but his four noncitizen housemates were each detained after a cache of false identity papers and other "suspicious" Arabic documents were found in their apartment. They were quickly dubbed an "operational combat sleeper cell" of al Qaeda terrorists by John Ashcroft, a label referenced frequently in news stories about Detroit for the next several years. Farouk Ali-Haimoud, Ahmed Hannan, Karim Koubriti, and Abdel-Ilah Elmardoudi were eventually indicted on terrorism charges when a former housemate testified, in exchange for a plea bargain, that they had attempted to recruit him for a terrorist cell. Ali-Haimoud and Hannan were acquitted of terror-related charges in 2003, but a year later, to much public fanfare, Elmardoudi and Koubriti were convicted of conspiring to provide material support and resources to terrorists. The case was not yet closed, however. The convictions were overturned a few months later—and the charges against both men were thrown out—when the U.S. Attorney's office in Detroit was forced to admit that their former lead prosecutor, Richard Convertino, had withheld "impeachment and exculpatory material" from the defense (U.S. Attorney Stephen J. Murphy, personal communication, May 20, 2005). Convertino quickly resigned, but after three years of unprecedented investigative work and relentless international publicity, the government had failed to prove that anything remotely resembling a "sleeper cell of al Qaeda terrorists" had lived in Detroit.[13] Instead, Convertino has been indicted on charges of conspiracy, obstruction of justice, and making false declarations during the "Detroit sleeper cell trial" (Department of Justice press release, March 29, 2006). His case went to trial in October 2007.

A former special-agent-in-charge of the FBI in Michigan admitted that in 2001 and 2002, the Detroit FBI office strongly encouraged the public to volunteer terror related tips, many of which proved to be misleading and to have been motivated by personal vendettas. "Terrorism is the hot button right now," said John Bell. "If you want to get law enforcement on someone, you accuse him of being a terrorist" (Fang 2003). Bill Swor described the resulting legal cases as both "frivolous and insidious, a waste of resources . . . a witch hunt." In its defense, the U.S. Attorney's office in Detroit claims to "have had a number of other successful prosecutions that are aimed at disrupting terrorism that have not specifically charged crimes of terrorism, per se, but nonetheless, helped prevent terrorist attacks. These prosecutions generally fall into two categories, cases based on intelligence information, and cases that protect vulnerabilities in our homeland security" (Stephen J. Murphy, personal communication, 2005). When pressed for information on the number of such cases tried in Detroit, or anywhere else, for that matter, local officials have been unwilling to provide further answers. The White House has been less cautious about reporting such numbers. In 2005 President Bush claimed that more than half of the 400 suspects against whom terrorism-related charges had been filed since 9/11 had been successfully convicted. His use of these numbers drew heavy criticism. On June 12, 2005, the *Washington Post* asserted that only thirty-nine people, not 200, had been convicted of crimes related to terrorism or national security, and only a few of the cases involved plots against the United States. The overwhelming majority involved convictions on minor crimes, such as making false statements or violating immigration law. The median sentence meted out regardless of the charges brought to trial was eleven months, a sentence that seemed unlikely to deter people genuinely involved in campaigns against the United States or its allies (Dan Eggan and Julie Tate, "In Terror Cases, Few Convictions," A01). To date, six Arab Americans with ties to Detroit have been found guilty on charges related to providing material support for terrorism. All had connections to Hezbollah, not al Qaeda.[14]

Although Arab Detroiters were relieved to see the sleeper cell convictions overturned, they are nonetheless alarmed by the prejudicial manner in which these cases (and many others like them) have been handled and by the inflammatory news coverage that accompanied each arrest and trial (Jamal 2004). The FBI's local antiterrorism unit, renamed the national security unit in 2006, continues to surface when Arab or Muslim Americans are under investigation for offenses unrelated to terrorism. In August of 2006, for example, five young men who were buying large quantities of discounted cell phones for resale in other markets were also accused of providing material support to terrorists. That all five were Arab Muslims did not go unnoticed by attorneys or the media. In one case, the men were in possession of photographs of the Mackinac Bridge. News headlines accused them of plotting to blow up the famous Michigan landmark. The other young men were found with a manual from Royal Jordanian Airlines in their car and, on the basis of this alleged evidence, they were accused of plotting to infiltrate the airline also for terror-related purposes. The manual, like the car, belonged to an employee of the airline, the mother of one of the accused. All charges against each of the five men were eventually dropped, but not before damning headlines, such as "2 Dearborn Men Linked to Terrorism" (*Detroit Free Press*, August 10, 2006, 1B) or "3 Arraigned on Terror Charges" (*Detroit Free Press*, August 13, 2006, 1B) had done their work. Local Arab and Muslim community leaders in Detroit were furious with federal authorities for how the cases were handled and very publicly bungled, accusing law enforcement agents and those who reported on the young men as equally guilty of racial profiling.[15]

These cases, based on the flimsiest of circumstantial evidence, have done little to strengthen public trust in federal agencies that now regularly justify their investigations, prosecutions, and deportations of Arab and Muslim defendants with intelligence reports that are not made public. The U.S. Attorney for eastern Michigan, Stephen J. Murphy, admitted that "it would not be surprising to learn that the arrest rate of Arab Americans has increased since 9/11 in light of our investigative priorities" (Personal communication, May 20, 2005). And, rather than tapering off over the years as investigations in Detroit have yielded scant return on the money and man hours invested, or as Congress and the Supreme Court have finally begun to challenge the Bush administration's interpretations of First Amendment protections, homeland security and antiterrorism are considered among the few growth sectors in Michigan's rapidly shrinking economy. In 2006, shortly after the White House revealed its program of domestic surveillance and wiretapping operations[16] the FBI, announced another doubling—the third since 9/11—of the number of their Michigan agents who are pursuing terror related investigations. They also broke ground on a new facility in Detroit in 2007, planning to triple the square footage of their local office space and increase their security (Joe Swickard, "FBI to Have New Offices in Detroit," *Detroit Free Press*, August 29, 2006, 1A). The U.S. Attorney's office in Detroit, likewise, added two attorneys to their terror unit in 2006 (Paul Egan, "Terror Unit Boosts Staffing: U.S. Attorney's Office in Detroit Will Add Two Assistants to Force, One of Largest in U.S.," *Detroit News*, March 21, 2006, 1B), and Governor Granholm has made attracting new homeland security jobs to the state a key anchor of the state's 21st Century Jobs Fund (Granholm 2006). The growth of this particular economic niche has Arab leaders in Detroit worried that federal agents are interested in their communities only insofar as they are useful for "propaganda purposes," military recruitment, and "spying" (Drees 2006).

A DAMPER AGAINST DISCRIMINATION?

A tally of abuses meted out by government agencies against Arabs and Muslims and legal briefs filed in response[17] would say little, however, about the larger transformations Arab institutions have undergone in reaction to the "war on terror" and the new political realities it has generated. It is often difficult to determine whether these changes are driven by rewards or punishments, by a sense of belonging or exclusion. Amid the profiling and attempts to marginalize Arab Americans as a political constituency that prevails at the national level, changes that have taken place on the ground in Michigan have often had positive effects, strengthening an Arab community that was already confident and well connected before September 2001.

Churches and mosques in Michigan, like those elsewhere in the country, have made a concerted effort to welcome outsiders, hosting film crews, open houses, and ecumenical events. They have also strengthened their support for one another. Human service organizations like ACCESS and ACC have provided hundreds of cultural sensitivity workshops for law enforcement agencies, corporations, school districts, lawyers, and reporters. The list is long and impressive and includes training for State Department officials and the United States military. ADC Michigan, the Council on American-Islamic Relations (CAIR), and the Michigan Civil Rights Commission now provide regular workshops on civil rights issues of relevance to Arabs and other citizens. Although many of these educational outreach programs are over a decade old, the funds available to support them have grown exponentially since the 9/11 attacks (for a careful analysis of culture work in the pre- and post-9/11 period, see Shryock 2004). Millions of dollars have been spent on these efforts in recent years, with support coming from a variety of corporate, government, and foundation sponsors. This largess enabled the Arab American National Museum, the first of its kind in the United States, to open its doors in Dearborn in 2005. Likewise, ADC Michigan broke ground on a new, multimillion dollar Arab American Center for Civil and Human Rights (ACCHR) in 2007. New funding has also been made available to scholars, resulting in the Detroit Arab American Study and a plethora of edited volumes, including this one, published by presses and funded by foundations that had little interest in niche communities like Arab and Muslim Americans before September 11, 2001. Mosques, too, continue to invest in public outreach; their construction projects and educational programs have yielded impressive results. Since the 2001 attacks, over a dozen mosque building projects have been completed, more than doubling the square footage of prayer space available in Dearborn and Detroit.[18] This climate of growth and success is welcomed by Arab Detroiters. They recognize that each of these developments improves their ability to assert and defend their claims to full American citizenship. Community leaders are equally aware, however, that these developments bring with them significant costs.

National and local foundations are not the only parties with a newfound interest in sponsoring research on Arab Americans or supporting events and publications that reach Arab American audiences. A motley array of individuals and organizations are lining up to benefit from these opportunities. The number of weekly and monthly newspapers and magazines published by Arabs in Detroit has doubled in recent years, for example, and most are financed, in no small part, by the full-cost, full-page recruitment ads placed in them by the U.S. Army, the FBI, the CIA, and businesses operating in and out of occupied Iraq. Likewise, the CIA has become a prominent, if unlikely, sponsor of the East Dearborn Arab International Festival since 2004, their information booth conspicuous among the falafel stands and carnival rides. Such sights have become commonplace at Arab events in the Detroit area, especially those organized by the American Arab Chamber of Commerce and ACCESS, both of which have developed close ties to the U.S. Departments of State, Homeland Security, and Commerce in recent years.

Together with the League of Arab States and the Gulf Cooperation Council, these otherwise local organizations hosted an event in 2003 called the U.S.-Arab Economic Forum. Intended to increase trade between the Arab Gulf states and Detroit, the event drew heavy criticism from local activists. "The feeling in the region that the United States is on a crusade against Arabs and against Islam is as bad as I have ever seen it," said Osama Siblani, publisher of the *Arab-American News*. "This is not the time to be having this summit. . . . Who in his right mind is going to come and invest from the Arab world when he knows if he comes here he's going to be stripped, searched and humiliated at the airport." Forum organizer Ahmed Chebanni adamantly defended the project, arguing that "peace and prosperity go hand in hand. By using Arab-Americans as a business vehicle, we will establish a real, meaningful dialogue and create a basis for long-term dialogue" (Jennifer Brooks, "Divisions Cloud Promise Surrounding Arab Forum," *Detroit News,* September 26, 2003, 1A). In a political climate where actual economic ties between everyday American citizens and their relatives and communities in the Middle East were being seriously curtailed and support for Islamic charities was dwindling due to seizures and political posturing by the federal government (Howell and Shryock 2003), this optimism proved difficult to sustain. Even Wayne County Executive Robert Ficano could mention only another round of seven digit contributions to the Arab American National Museum (a division of ACCESS) as a tangible, realized benefit of this partnership (Haimour 2005). "We do not wish to judge others. We do not wish to preach to others. We certainly do not wish to coerce others. We wish to help others, and by so doing, help ourselves," said Colin Powell in his address to the forum (2003). Yet his speech also cautioned Arabs, both American and foreign, to check their criticisms of Israel and opposition to the American invasion of Iraq at the door. If coercion does not account for this partnership, then the opportunism of community leaders offers little solace to those who are left of the margins on the post-9/11 boom in all things Arab American.

Just as Arab organizations have been met halfway in their educational and civil liberties campaigns by concerned foundations, corporations, public institutions, and government agencies, Arab Americans have also met federal law enforcement agencies half way, some would say more than half way, in their many investigations in the Arab American community. Within a week of September 11, more than 4,000 Arabs from Detroit called to volunteer their services to the FBI and CIA as translators of stockpiled communications intercepts (Niraj Warikoo, "Arabic Speakers Answer U.S. Need," *Detroit Free Press,* September 19, 2001, 7A).[19] Arab Americans were no less eager to catch genuine terror suspects than other Americans were. They had a special interest and often specialized skills that could be of help in this regard. It was in this spirit that ADC Michigan pulled together a coalition of fifteen Arab

American organizations for monthly meetings with the regional leadership of the FBI, the U.S. Attorney's office, and an additional dozen federal agencies after the 9/11 attacks. Imad Hamad, director of ADC Michigan, and John Bell, then special agent in charge of Detroit's FBI office, had already worked together through the National Conference for Community and Justice. It was through this relationship that Building Respect in Diverse Groups to Enhance Sensitivity (BRIDGES) was established as a forum for dialogue where "both sides" could communicate freely (Personal communications, 2005).

The first major accomplishment of this task force was the creation of a series of best practice guidelines that the FBI in Michigan followed in November 2001 when it began questioning more than 500 of the state's Arab and Muslim noncitizens as part of a national effort that included 7,600 noncitizens nationwide. ADC was able to monitor these investigations locally, both in 2001 and on the three subsequent occasions when the FBI repeated this process, making pro bono attorneys available on request, providing a helpline for those with questions, insisting that interviewees receive advance letters to explain the program's voluntary nature, providing translators, and insisting that federal agents not confront respondents at school or in the work place. Stephen J. Murphy asserts that the process also enabled law enforcement to conduct these investigations without "alienating" the Arab American community, and to be more efficient and effective by pairing federal agents with local law enforcement officers (Personal communication 2005; see also Thacher 2005). Although the process was inherently discriminatory—profiling informants along religious and national lines—and the best practice guidelines were reached only after extensive and heated debate, the execution of these interviews in Michigan was significantly less disruptive of individual lives and community-law enforcement relations than elsewhere. In particular, Eastern Michigan was one of only four districts where letters were uniformly mailed in advance to interviewees and one of only two districts where the U.S. Department of Immigration and Naturalization was kept out of the interview process (Ramirez, O'Connell, and Zafar 2004, 24).

In 2005, several of the people we interviewed for this project were cautiously, if also strategically, optimistic about the benefits that flowed from the BRIDGES alliance, pointing to a sustained dialogue between the state and the community that enabled all parties to clarify legal, linguistic, and cultural matters in ways that improved the application of federal laws on the ground. Arab leaders argued that the process made the law enforcement community more accountable to Arab concerns, and law enforcement agreed, adding that it also brought greater trust and public support. Both sides recognized that the familiarity encouraged by an ongoing airing of principles, concerns, and grievances was able to produce better law enforcement and greater cooperation among those involved. Both groups were also able to monitor and safeguard one another in ways not yet operative in other parts of the country. Hamad mentioned that he had seen improvements in how each federal agency cooperated with ADC Michigan, with the exception of Immigration, and both Hamad and Murphy provided a list of Arab Americans who sought and received assistance from law enforcement agencies. Several individuals, for example, had their names removed from federal no-fly lists, several hate crimes against Arab Americans were prosecuted with speed and efficiency, and a few federal detainees who posed no threat or flight risk were freed while their cases were pending trial (Personal communication, 2005).

Some are encouraged to see Arab American complaints handled in this face-to-face terrain where justice can occasionally be facilitated, but BRIDGES has not yet been able to challenge the status quo in which the presumption of innocence seems to have been reversed and due process is lacking for Arab and Muslim defendants. As time passes, the volatility of the BRIDGES alliance has made it less effective and less easy to sustain. Kenwah Dabaja, when Michigan field director of the Arab American Institute, described BRIDGES as too inconsistent in its efforts, meeting less and less frequently, often in reaction to the latest crisis (Personal communication, 2007). Even when the group meets according to schedule, outside events can easily sidetrack their discussion. In September 2006, the head of the Department of Justice's Civil Rights Division, Assistant U.S. Attorney Wan Kim, was scheduled to address BRIDGES members in a public forum. Although he did manage to introduce himself and outline the progress his department has made prosecuting hate crimes and other forms of discrimination against Arabs and Muslims since 9/11, the meeting itself was completely overrun by comments about the cell phone cases mentioned earlier and angry complaints about a raid on Life for Relief and Development (LIFE), an Islamic charity headquartered in the Detroit area that took place the day before the BRIDGES meeting and just before the onset of Ramadan. Daniel Roberts, special agent in charge of Detroit's FBI office, argued that the raid was timed to take place before rather than during this month of fasting (and charitable giving) to be "sensitive to community concerns." LIFE was not closed down, nor were its assets frozen, but it took the FBI most of the month of Ramadan to issue a public statement to this effect, reassuring Muslims that LIFE could continue to collect their donations. Kenwah Dabaja summed up the FBI's participation in the BRIDGES alliance this way: "I don't get the feeling they are listening."[20]

Despite these tensions, BRIDGES is now considered an ideal model of community-law enforcement relations by observers outside Michigan and it is being replicated in other parts of the country (Ramirez, O'Connell, and Zafar 2004), a process that is supported by Arab American activists and by the Department of Justice alike. In a study of such community-law enforcement initiatives nationwide, the Soros Foundation attributes the success of BRIDGES to the remarkable degree of institutional incorporation the Arab community in Michigan has achieved. The BRIDGES story is the latest chapter in a long history of local activism in which Arab Americans have made political gains by working with city hall, as it were, while actively fighting against it. Imad Hamad laments the fact that BRIDGES, though replicated in other locations, has met with only local success in eastern Michigan and has been able to intervene positively only on a case-by-case basis. "Of course, the dialog needs to be with policy makers and not just those who implement policies," he argues. "For BRIDGES to make a difference outside Michigan, we need to communicate with those in D.C. and not only those who are in Detroit" (Interview, 2005).

CONCLUSION

Imad Hamad's appeal was echoed by each of the Arab Americans we interviewed, who suggested that the federal government, especially the law enforcement agencies managing the state of exception created of our ongoing crisis, would benefit tremendously from the insight of Arab and Muslim professionals, not simply as translators, role-playing actors,[21] field agents, or civil rights watchdogs, but as intelligence officers, presidential advisors, and policy makers. Arabs in Michigan have achieved genuine political incorporation. At the state level, they shape the way social services are delivered, health data is collected, automobiles are designed and manufactured, world music is packaged, homeland security measures are implemented, and gasoline, milk, and other goods are distributed and sold. As in other ethnic communities, most of this work is accomplished without reference to collective identities, while ethnic institutions stand by to carefully catalog and augment these efforts, ensuring that Arabs are a political constituency local governments must acknowledge and support. This process has been decades in the making, but the events that transpired on and after 9/11 compelled officials to recognize that the fate of Michigan and of Dearborn, in particular, are intertwined now with the fate of their Arab citizens. This is why the public backlash in Michigan was significantly less severe than in other communities.

At the national level, Arabs have not achieved this sort of inclusion, and until they do, the exceptional privileges they have gained in Detroit will remain fragile. Arab leaders in Detroit are acutely aware of the limitations of this status, as is Imad Hamad, whose sensitivity to the difference between the local and the national is rooted in personal experience. In September 2003, the FBI in Washington sought to recognize Hamad's singular contribution to the BRIDGES effort by awarding him their highest civilian honor, the Exceptional Public Service award. Hamad soon found himself slandered by a national media campaign that described him as "a man who supports terrorism and was himself a suspected terrorist" (Schlussel 2003). He was further humiliated when the FBI declined to award him the honor they had already announced to the media. As the public controversy around the award escalated, Arab

American members of the BRIDGES alliance threatened to withdraw. Hamad was forced to defend his past, reassure the public that he is not a terrorist, and plead with BRIDGES partners to continue their collaboration with a government agency that was clearly ambivalent about Hamad and insensitive to the community he represents.[22]

Awareness of the difference between local and national politics is keen among Detroit's major Arab American institutions, each of which has found itself performing the defensive maneuvers described earlier; defending their pasts and promoting their institutional histories, investing vast resources in reassuring the public that they are not and do not support terrorists, and urging their constituents to not lose faith as they collaborate in increasingly complex ways with the FBI, CIA, Department of State, and other federal agencies that are interested in Arab Americans only as potential threats to American security or potential allies in the United States' "war on terror." In Arab Detroit today, local social service providers, arts presenters, civil liberties advocates, and Muslim charities find themselves working closely with, and often accepting the patronage of, federal agencies that specialize in security issues, foreign and domestic espionage, criminal investigations, and other forms of governmental discipline and control. Occasionally, Arab American groups are enlisted, mostly as window dressing, in American campaigns to transform the Middle East, economically, politically, and militarily.[23] This work stands at a remove from the bread and butter efforts of Detroit's Arab ethnic associations to provide services and address community needs, activities that have garnered them strong grassroots support. When Arab organizations are included in what are called public diplomacy and community policing efforts but are not treated as full partners with a voice in setting agendas and negotiating strategies, they risk weakening their grassroots strength and eroding Arab confidence in American public institutions and government. The new status quo suggests that, at the national level, Arab Detroit is being reconfigured as a constituency defined not by its genuine integration with a city and its society, but by its imputed associations with foreignness and danger. If this odd feature of Arab Detroit's political incorporation continues to receive institutional support, it may produce tragic (and unintended) consequences for a community that has withstood the 9/11 backlash and now looks forward, longingly, to a more stable era of acceptance.

APPENDIX

DAAS Data

1. Birth [U.S.-born or foreign-born]
2. Religion [Muslim or Christian]

3. Bad experience

   Question: Since 9/11, have you personally had a bad experience due to your Arab or Chaldean ethnicity? [yes or no]

4. Worry

   Question: Since 9/11, as an Arab (Chaldean) I worry more about the future facing me and my family here in the United States. Do you strongly agree, agree, neither agree nor disagree, disagree or strongly disagree? [strongly agree, agree, neither agree nor disagree, disagree, strongly disagree]

5. Willingness to give up civil liberties [index variable]

   a. Do you support increasing surveillance of Arab Americans by the government? [yes or no]

   b. Do you support giving the police powers to stop and search anyone who appears to be Arab or Muslim, at random? [yes or no]

   c. Do you support detaining some suspicious Arabs and/or Muslims even if there is not sufficient evidence to prosecute them in the courts? [yes or no]

6. Fair trial

   Question: Do you think Arabs or Muslims who are accused of supporting or engaging in terrorism can receive fair trials in the U.S.? [yes or no]

7. Confidence in the U.S. government:

   Question: How much confidence do you have in the government in Washington, D.C.? [a great deal, a lot, not very much, none]

8. Solidarity

   Question: In the weeks after 9/11, did anyone who was not of Middle Eastern background show you support or solidarity? [yes or no]

9. Contact government

   Question: In the past twelve months, have you called or written a government official to express your opinion on a political issue? [yes or no]

10. Participation in ethnic organizations

    Question: [Are you] an active member, inactive member, or neither [in an] ethnic association, including advocacy groups like ADC, the Yemeni Benevolent Association or the Chaldean Federation? [active, inactive, or neither]

ZOGBY DATA

1. Willingness to give up civil liberties

    Question: Is it justified or not justified for law enforcement officials to engage in extra questioning and inspections of people with Middle Eastern accents or features? [justified or not justified]

2. Bad experience

    Question: Since the terrorist attacks on the U.S. on September 11, have you personally experienced discrimination because of your ethnicity? [yes or no]

3. Worry

    How worried are you about the long-term effects of discrimination against Arab Americans? [very worried, somewhat worried, not worried at all]

NOTES

1. See, for example, Seymour Lipset's 1996 cautionary analysis of the exceptionalism myth. He argues that the proverbial city on the hill was never a beacon of freedom to all but instead that the rights and privileges of American citizenship have always been distributed unequally, based on racial and class formations held in place by dominant ideologies and violence. Our work relocates the promise and pain of Lipset's observations to a contemporary immigrant community where both blades of the double-edged sword are being sharpened to great effect.
2. Bill Swor, Rena Abbas-Chami, Maysoun Khatib, Ron Amen, and Imad Hamad participated in lengthy interviews with Sally Howell. Most of these conversations were recorded on tape. Several others, who prefer to remain anonymous, provided details and helped formulate the ideas in this paper. Barbara McQuade, from the U.S. Attorney's office in Detroit, responded helpfully to an earlier draft of this paper, and Stephen J. Murphy, U.S. Attorney, eastern Michigan region, and John Bell, former FBI special agent in charge for Detroit, both replied in writing to questions we submitted to the U.S. Attorney's office in Detroit. We thank each of the individuals, named and unnamed, who contributed to this research and analysis.
3. Ismael Ahmed attributes this quote to James Zogby, adding that Arab Detroiters "can and should be a model of political participation" for Arab Americans nationwide (2006, 50).
4. Census 2000 provides the following figures for percentage of immigrants who are naturalized citizens, by region: Europe, 56 percent; Latin America, 30 percent; Africa, 36 percent; Asia, 51 percent; North America, 46 percent; and Oceania, 34 percent (see U.S. Bureau of the Census 2000, table FPB-1).

5. More than 90 percent of Detroit area residents are American-born (Detroit Area Study 2003). The census does not collect information on religion. The national breakdown cited here is drawn from a survey of Arab Americans conducted in 2000 by Zogby International and reported by the Arab American Institute (Arab American Institute Foundation 2001). A 2002 survey by Zogby International found that Muslim Arabs constituted 33 percent of the sample.

6. The U.S. Census does not collect information on religion. The national breakdown cited here is drawn from surveys of Arab Americans conducted in 2000 and 2002 by Zogby International (see http://www.aaiusa.org/demographics and Zogby [2002]).

7. Respondents were asked about the total family income for the respondent and all family members residing in the household.

8. Hassan Makled retired from his position at the Detroit Metropolitan Airport in 2006.

9. These numbers are the authors' calculation based initially on the Arab American Institute's 2007 *Roster of Arab Americans in Public Life* and updated as new appointments have been announced and approved (Arab American Institute Foundation 2007). Ronald Amen provided the number of deputy sheriffs for Wayne County.

10. The DAAS was conducted in 2003, and the Zogby International polls in 2002. It may appear that the Zogby poll numbers are higher than the DAAS numbers because of the timing of these studies; however, hate crimes across the nation have been on the rise each year since 9/11, as reported by both ADC (2002, 2003a, 2003b) and CAIR (2001, 2002, 2003, 2004, 2005, 2006). Furthermore, the DAAS question we cite here asked respondents specifically whether they had had a bad experience since 9/11. We ask a separate question about discriminatory acts "in the past year" that is not analyzed here but does confirm the national pattern of escalating numbers.

11. When Governor John Engler visited Arab American leaders in Dearborn on September 27, 2001, and assured them that "there is never any excuse for discrimination against anyone" (Niraj Warikoo, "Engler, Arab Americans Talk: Governor Condemns Discriminatory Acts," *Detroit Free Press,* September 28, 2001, 3B), the timing of his visit received local criticism, following, as it did, rather than preceding President Bush's visit with Arab American leaders in Washington.

12. This silencing effect predates the 9/11 attacks, but has become more pronounced since. It was especially apparent in the Detroit area during the 2006 Israeli-Hezbollah War when Arab American leaders were routinely described as Hezbollah supporters in the media and then dismissed. This smear campaign reached its peak on September 12, 2006, when gubernatorial candidate Dick DeVos canceled his planned appearance at an Arab American Political Action Committee (AAPAC) dinner in Dearborn following the lead of a local writer in the *Detroit Jewish News* who argued that "no legitimate candidate for public office should go before the Dearborn-based [PAC] . . . because its leadership has defended Hezbollah" (Robert Sklar, Editorial, September 6, 2006, 7). The president of AAPAC was likewise

introduced at a public forum by the head of Michigan's FBI field office as a supporter of Hezbollah (Osama Siblani, personal communication, 2006).

13. Hannan and Koubriti were recently re-indicted, this time on a charge of insurance fraud. This new case is pending.

14. The guilty pleas include *U.S. v. Makki* and *U.S. v. Kourani.* A third man, Nemr Ali Rahal, was arrested in May 2005 for raising $600 to support the families of suicide bombers connected to Hezbollah (David Shepardson, "Dearborn Man to Be Tried in Terror Case: Authorities Claim He Stole More than $400,000, Collected Money for Hezbollah," *Detroit News,* May 4, 2005, 3B). Finally, four men pleaded guilty in Detroit in 2006 to a variety of racketeering and counterfeiting charges related to a money making scheme to benefit Hezbollah in part, Youssef Bakri, Imad Hamadeh, Theodore Schenk, and Karim Nasser. For many Lebanese and other Arabs, Hezbollah's status on the U.S. State Department's list of Foreign Terrorist Organizations (FTO) is problematic. Hezbollah has had a violent past, but the organization's political party today plays a significant role in the Lebanese parliament and its social service arm has long aided the disenfranchised Shi'a of the South. It is credited with forcing Israel, after a grueling twenty-year occupation, to end their occupation of South Lebanon and again in 2006, with defending this same region of the country against the full force of an Israeli air, sea, and land assault (Deeb 2006). At a 2005 public forum in Dearborn, "Charitable Giving and Terrorism Sanctions," Chip Poncy of the U.S. Treasury Department warned Arab and Muslim Americans that they must regulate themselves to ensure that their charitable donations are not being rerouted to support terror. Members of the audience objected to Hezbollah's inclusion on the FTO list, arguing that it was placed on the list because it opposes Israel, not because it is a threat to the United States or to American citizens.

15. See *Detroit Free Press* articles from August 10 to August 16, 2006.

16. This program was challenged in court by the ACLU of Michigan, with support from several of the Arab and Muslim organizations mentioned elsewhere in this paper. It was found unconstitutional in a Detroit courtroom (David Ashenfelter and Joe Swickard, "Ruling on Wiretaps Faces Fierce Challenge—Detroit Judge: Program Illegal," *Detroit Free Press,* August 18, 2006, 1A).

17. ADC Michigan and ACCESS, for example, joined the ACLU of Michigan in filing the first challenge to the USA PATRIOT Act in July of 2003 and have continued to advocate on behalf of local Arab and Muslim defendants (ACLU 2003).

18. This exponential growth in mosque construction corresponds to a precipitous drop in the funds given to international Islamic charities. Six of the largest and best known Islamic charities operating between the United States and the Muslim world have been closed and their assets frozen since September 2001 (Nail MacFarquhar, "Muslim Charity Sues Treasury Dept. and Seeks Dismissal of Charges of Terrorism," *New York Times,* December 12, 2006, 24).

19. The FBI does not use volunteer labor. Between 2001 and 2005, the Detroit office of the FBI hired fifteen Arabic translators. Hundreds applied, but the hurdles to

75

employment are many. The agency has no tests for competency in Arabic beyond their classical Arabic, written exam (Personal communication, Laura Waters, Detroit FBI recruitment officer, 2005). The Department of Homeland Security has also had a difficult time hiring and retaining Arab Americans in its Michigan offices, according to an anonymous former officer, although details have been impossible to track down. Independent security contractors have also sprung up in Michigan to handle work outsourced by federal agencies. They seem to have a better track record at hiring Arabic speakers.

20. By Ramadan 2007, six major Muslim charities in the United States, three from Michigan, had been closed and had their assets frozen. Several others are under investigations. Very few charges have been levied against any of these agencies or their employees and the evidence against them has not been shared with those under investigation. Muslim community leaders now assert that the Treasury Department is among the least forthcoming federal agencies, indicating the significance of this financial warfare to the operationalization of the "war on terror" (see Muslim Public Affairs Council 2007).

21. Iraqi Americans in the Detroit area are now regularly flown to American military bases in several states to act the part of Iraqi insurgents, innocent civilians, and government ministers for military training exercises (see John Milburn, "Afghan, Iraqi Immigrants Play Their Countrymen in Military Training Exercises in Kansas," *Associated Press,* October 15, 2007, or Robert F. Worth, "National Guard at War at Home To Prepare for Real Thing in Iraq," *New York Times,* December 27, 2003, 1).

22. Hamad's alleged crime was to support Palestinian nationalist aspirations—through legal channels—when he was not yet a citizen. Like the thousands of Arab and Muslim men who have been detained and deported since 9/11, Hamad's deportation proceedings and citizenship appeal dragged on for years, and the evidence used against him was kept secret for security reasons.

23. This trend has been especially pronounced in relation to the United States' invasion and occupation of Iraq. See, for example, "Bush Shares Hopes for Iraqi Homeland," *Detroit Free Press,* April 29, 2003, 1A.

REFERENCES

Ahmed, Ismael. 2006. "Michigan Arab Americans: A Case Study of Electoral and Non-Electoral Empowerment." In *American Arabs and Political Participation.* Washington: Woodrow Wilson International Center.

American Civil Liberties Union (ACLU). 2003. "ACLU Applauds Introduction of Senate Bill to Fix Now Infamous "Section 215" of the USA PATRIOT Act." Press release. July 31, 2003. New York: American Civil Liberties Union.

American Community Survey. 2005. "Data Profile Highlight, Dearborn, Michigan." Washington: U.S. Census Bureau.

Arab American Anti-Discrimination Committee (ADC). 2002. "The Arab American Experience After September 11: Healing the Nation." Washington: Arab American Anti-Discrimination Committee.

———. 2003a. "Impact of September 11 on Traditional Openness to Immigrants and Non-Immigrants: An Arab-American Community Perspective." Washington: Arab American Anti-Discrimination Committee.

———. 2003b. "Muslim/Arab Employment Discrimination Charges since September 11." Washington: Arab American Anti-Discrimination Committee.

Arab American Institute Foundation (AAIF). 2001. "Arab American Demographics." Washington: Arab American Institute. Accessed at http://www.aaiusa.org/arab-americans/22/demographics.

———. 2002. "Profiling and Pride: Arab American Attitudes and Behavior Since September 11." Washington: Arab American Institute.

———. 2006. "Select Social and Demographic Characteristics for Arab Americans." Washington: Arab American Institute.

———. 2007. *2007 Roster of Arab Americans in Public Service.* Washington: Arab American Institute. Accessed at http://www.aaiusa.org/page/-/Roster/2007Roster_web_.pdf.

Cainkar, Louise. 2006. "The Social Construction of Difference and the Arab American Experience." *Journal of American Ethnic History* 25(2–3): 243–78.

Canada-U.S.-Ontario-Michigan Border Transportation Partnership (Border Transportation Partnership). 2004. *Planning/Need and Feasibility Study Report.* Detroit, Mich.: Detroit River International Crossing Study.

Council on American-Islamic Relations (CAIR). 2001. *Accommodating Diversity.* Washington: Council on American-Islamic Relations.

———. 2002. *Stereotypes and Civil Liberties.* Washington: Council on American-Islamic Relations.

———. 2003. *Guilt by Association.* Washington: Council on American-Islamic Relations.

———. 2004. *Unpatriotic Acts.* Washington: Council on American-Islamic Relations.

———. 2005. *Unequal Protection.* Washington: Council on American-Islamic Relations.

———. 2006. *The Struggle for Equality.* Washington: Council on American-Islamic Relations.

Cole, David. 2003. *Enemy Aliens: Double Standards and Constitutional Freedoms in the War on Terrorism.* New York: The New Press.

Deeb, Lara. 2006. "Hizballah: A Primer." *Middle East Report Online.* Accessed at http://www.merip.org/mero/mero073106.html.

Detroit Arab American Study (DAAS). 2003. Unpublished dataset. Ann Arbor, Mich.: Institute for Social Research.

Drees, Caroline. 2006. "In Terror War, American 'Outreach' Has US Muslims Wary." May 8, 2006. *Reuters.*

Fang, Bay. 2003. "Under Scrutiny, Always: An Arab American Community and Its Legion of FBI Watchers." *U.S. News and World Report,* January 6, 2003: 26.

Granholm, Jennifer M. 2006. *Jobs Today, Jobs Tomorrow: Governor Granholm's Plan to Revitalize Michigan's Economy.* Lansing, Mich.: State of Michigan. Accessed at http://www.michigan.gov/documents/GFuturePlan_160459_7.pdf.

Hagopian, Elaine. 2003. "The Interlocking of Right-Wing Politics and U.S. Middle East Policy: Solidifying Arab/Muslim Demonization." In *Civil Rights in Peril,* edited by Elaine Hagopian. Chicago, Ill.: Haymarket Press.

Haimour, Muhannad. 2005. "Michigan Leaders Pave Way for Business in the Middle East." *Forum and Link* 1(16): 14–16.

Howell, Sally. 2000. "Cultural Interventions: Arab American Aesthetics between the Transnational and the Ethnic." *Diaspora* 9(1): 59–82.

———. 2007. "America's First Mosques." In *Encyclopedia of Islam in the United States,* edited by Jocelyne Cesari. Westport, Conn.: Greenwood Press.

Howell, Sally, and Andrew Shryock. 2003. "Cracking Down on Diaspora: Arab Detroit and America's 'War on Terror'." *Anthropological Quarterly* 76(3): 443–62.

Ibish, Hussein. 2003. "The Civil Liberties of Arab Americans Post 9/11." Civil Liberties Forum, Center for Middle East and North African Studies, University of Michigan, October 17, 2003.

Jamal, Amaney. 2004. "Religious Identity, Discrimination and 9-11: The Determinants of Arab American Levels of Political Confidence in Mainstream and Ethnic Institutions," Presented at meeting of the American Political Science Association, September 2004.

———. 2005. "The Political Participation and Engagement of Muslim Americans: Mosque Involvement and Group Consciousness." *American Politics Research* 33(4): 521–44.

Lipset, Seymour Martin. 1996. *American Exceptionalism: A Double-Edged Sword.* New York: W. W. Norton.

Muslim Public Affairs Council. 2007. "Ramadan and Anxiety over Charity." *DC News & Views.* Accessed at http://www.mpac.org/article.php?id=528.

Naber, Nadine. 2006. "The Rules of Forced Engagement: Race, Gender, and the Culture of Fear Among Arab Immigrants in San Francisco Post-9/11." *Cultural Dynamics* 18(3): 235–67.

Powell, Colin. 2003. "Remarks at U.S.-Arab Economic Forum." Detroit, Michigan, September 29, 2003. Accessed at http://www.state.gov/secretary/former/powell/remarks/2003/24684.htm.

Ramirez, Deborah, Sasha Cohen O'Connell, and Rabia Zafar. 2004. *A Promising Practices Guide: Developing Partnerships Between Law Enforcement and American Muslim, Arab, and Sikh Communities.* New York: Open Society Institute.

Samhan, Helen. 2006. "Losing the Battle: How Political Activism Guarantees Ethnic Integration (in Spite of Defeats Along the Way)." In *American Arabs and Political*

Participation, edited by Philippa Strum. Washington: Woodrow Wilson International Center.

Schlussel, Debbie. 2003. "The FBI's Outrageous Award." Accessed at http://www.debbieschlussel.com/columns/column091303.shtml.

Shryock, Andrew. 2004. "In the Double Remoteness of Arab Detroit: Reflections on Ethnography, Culture Work, and the Intimate Disciplines of Americanization." In *Off Stage/On Display: Intimacy and Ethnography in the Age of Public Culture,* edited by Andrew Shryock. Palo Alto, Calif.: Stanford University Press.

Shryock, Andrew, and Nabeel Abraham. 2000. "On Margins and Mainstreams." In *Arab Detroit: From Margin to Mainstream,* edited by Nabeel Abraham and Andrew Shryock. Detroit, Mich.: Wayne State University Press.

Singh, Amardeep. 2002. *We Are Not the Enemy: Hate Crimes Against Arabs, Muslims and Those Perceived to be Arabs or Muslims after September 11.* HRW Index No. G1406. New York: Human Rights Watch.

Suleiman, Michael. 2006. "A History of Arab-American Political Participation." In *American Arabs and Political Participation,* edited by Philippa Strum. Washington: Woodrow Wilson International Center.

Thacher, David. 2005. "The Local Role in Homeland Security," *Law & Society Review* 39(3): 635–76.

U.S. Census Bureau. 2000. *Profile of Selected Demographics and Social Characteristics. 2000.* Washington: Government Printing Office. Accessed at http://www.census.gov/population/www/socdemo/foreign/STP-159-2000tl.html.

U.S. Department of Justice. 2003. *The September 11 Detainees, A Review of the Treatment of Aliens Held on Immigration Charges in Connection with the Investigations of the September 11 Attacks.* Washington: Government Printing Office.

Zogby International. 2002. "What U.S. Arabs Think." Unpublished dataset. Washington: Zogby International.

CHAPTER 4

BEING MUSLIM AND AMERICAN: SOUTH ASIAN MUSLIM YOUTH AND THE WAR ON TERROR

KATHERINE PRATT EWING AND MARGUERITE HOYLER

IN THIS CHAPTER, we consider some of the responses of Muslim youth growing up in the United States amidst the atmosphere of suspicion associated with the war on terror. We focus on youth from middle class families of South Asian background living in the Raleigh-Durham area of North Carolina, an area that has drawn many professional immigrants and their families to the high-technology companies associated with the Research Triangle Park. At the time of this research, these youth were in their late teens and early twenties. At the time of the September 11 attacks, they were in their early and mid-teens, and in the midst of navigating the social, familial, and identity-related challenges that are a central aspect of growing up in the United States. Given the class of these youth as the children of professionals in middle America, we are concerned with how they have perceived and experienced the changing discourse surrounding Islam and Muslims since 9/11 and how they see it affecting their identities.

Erik Erikson, who played an early role in framing the concept of identity, recognized the power of even a single event to affect the formation, recognition and realization of identity: We are "most aware of our identity when we are about to gain it or when we . . . make its acquaintance" (1959, 127). Such moments of awareness often coincide with a large-scale event capable of triggering the rapid and involuntary repositioning of a group or individual within mainstream consciousness and esteem. For many of the South Asian Muslims involved in our research, September 11 represented just such an event. The attacks of 9/11 placed these young people into a context in which their personal maturation was closely intertwined with the broader political context. The tensions and stigmatizations generated by the aftermath of 9/11 became one of the idioms through which they took up socially articulated identities and expressed some of the anxieties and social stresses associated with navigating high school and college. Identity and its associated labels and practices have thus become a central idiom, in terms of which people inhabit and negotiate social relationships and spaces. The significance and salience of ethnicity, religion, and membership in a majority or minority group, all of which come to be categorized as identities and are often cross-cutting or even mutually inconsistent, are components that add complexity to the process of identity negotiation.[1] We examine how the post-9/11 discursive environment has affected the significance and enactment of a religious identity as Muslim. In our research, we addressed two basic questions: According to South Asian Muslim American youth, has the social and political treatment of Muslims following 9/11 changed their community? How do these youth draw on 9/11 as a discourse for articulating their experiences and identities?

The significance of a religious identity has been shaped by the changing place of religion in American politics. The principle of the separation of church and state articulated in the United States Constitution rests on the notion of the citizen who engages in the public sphere as a rational, autonomous, and equal subject whose religion is legally not relevant. All religions are thus defined in equivalent terms (see Asad 1993), and religious orientation is in principle private and free from government interference. But even before the events of 9/11, religion had become more salient in the public sphere as the Christian right became a powerful political force, especially during the Bush administration. This has been true not only in election rhetoric and the halls of Washington, but also in public schools, where students form religious interest groups that meet on school grounds. Religion becomes a politicized identity and a marker of difference. The events and aftermath of 9/11 have pushed the issue of being Muslim further into the public arena.

One theme that emerged in conversations and interviews was a tension that has been generated between an American identity and a Muslim identity in the wake of 9/11, to the extent that many Muslims and non-Muslims questioned the possibility of inhabiting both identities.[2] The young people with whom we spoke articulated a range of responses to the tension, including ambivalence, a questioning of the desirability of being American, a desire to meld cultures, and efforts to resolve the tension by transcending national and particularistic cultural or ethnic identities. Many expressed increasing awareness of their marginalization and felt that their identities had become more politicized. Although these issues had been present before 9/11, these young people saw this as a significant historical juncture. They believed that two key changes stemming from this juncture have important implications for local communities and for their own relationships to their families, their pasts, and their places in American society. The first was that they, as Muslim American youth, felt impelled to enact and inhabit their Muslim identities in a more deliberate manner than may otherwise have been the case. The second was that the significance of being a Muslim was dramatically redefined. Islam, which before 9/11 had been for many simply a part of their cultural heritage associated with their family's country of origin, came to be sharply distinguished from the concept of culture and detached from an association with any particular place.[3] Many young Muslims resist the equivalence of religion and culture, also downplaying the significance of race and ethnicity, as they renegotiate what it means to be an American citizen and a Muslim. Though this rearticulation is a manifestation of a global discursive process that has been developing for decades and can be seen, for example, in the teachings of the Muslim Students Association, many young Muslims link the emergence of their own intentional identity as a Muslim to the aftermath of 9/11 and the war on terror.

Given this separation from local culture, many draw on Islam as a more encompassing form of belonging, in which Islam has become a means to transcend national and cultural and ethnic identities. The rejection of local cultural practices in favor of what they have learned to consider a more universal Islam, as articulated by their teachers in the mosque and in Islamic study groups, has also affected relationships with parents and attitudes toward their parents' homeland. Paradoxically, this has led some youth to a greater sense of distance from Pakistan or India, in that they see the Islam practiced by their relatives in South Asia as corrupted by a local culture they do not share. Some stressed transnational ties to other Muslims and prioritized religion over ethnicity, an orientation that affected relationships with other, non-Muslim South Asians (for a discussion of this process among Arab youth in the United States, see Naber 2005). Many felt that their friendship groups and social relationships had become more sharply delimited to include only fellow Muslims. The sense of threat to the Muslim community also affected gender relations, stimulating young men to fulfill what they viewed as their Islamic role as protector of young women. The changes associated with 9/11 thus shaped the lives of these youth in numerous ways, contributing to a process in which religious identity moved more fully into the public arena, affecting virtually all social relationships.

SOUTH ASIAN MUSLIMS AND THE ISLAMIC ASSOCIATION OF RALEIGH

The South Asian population in the United States has been growing steadily for nearly half a century. Many South Asians first came to the United States in the 1970s and 1980s to pursue undergraduate and graduate studies, as permitted under the U.S. Immigration Act of 1965. Since then, the South Asian subpopulation has been characterized by upward mobility, a cultural emphasis on education, and notable professional success. Many South Asians were drawn to the Raleigh-Durham area precisely because of their advanced education and scientific expertise: the region is home to the high technology companies of Research Triangle Park, which since it was established in 1959 has become one of the largest science research centers in the country.

Although our research focused on Muslims of South Asian background, this population is not isolated from the larger Muslim community in the area. Mosques in nearby Durham are overwhelmingly African American, and a predominantly South Asian mosque has recently been established in nearby Cary. But the Islamic Association of Raleigh (IAR), the mosque attended by the majority of our research participants, draws Muslims of diverse nationalities and ethnicities. In addition to embodying the diversity of American Muslims, the association also reflects the growth of the Muslim population in the United States. The mosque is currently undertaking a $3 million construction project—one that will double prayer space and create conference rooms and a media center.[4] The IAR is home to an elementary school, which has experienced similar growth. Since its inception in 1992, the Al-Iman School has grown from twelve students to more than 200, and now has twenty instructors.

Much of our fieldwork took place at the IAR, but we also engaged with and heard from South Asian Muslims in a variety of other social contexts. We conducted interviews with nineteen South Asian Muslim youth, ten women and nine men, and with adult members of the community as well. We attended social events hosted by women in the community, including a ladies' party and an all-female high school graduation party. Many of the women in attendance at these events were not associated with a particular mosque, but rather with a local cultural organization, the Pakistani Anjuman of the Triangle area. We also interviewed Muslim students at local universities and met with people in their homes.

Nearly all interviewees were American citizens, whether born in the United States or naturalized. Most young women with whom we spoke wore head scarves. Often, however, they were either the only ones in their extended family to cover, or had been the first to do so. For some, neither relatives in Pakistan, India, or Bangladesh covered, nor did cousins, mothers, or even sisters in the United States.

One of the primary sites where we observed the development and negotiation of a Muslim identity was among young women who attended weekly meetings of a halaqa (study circle) at the Islamic Association of Raleigh. This group is described on the association's Web site as "a social/educational program geared towards team-building, strengthening Islamic identity, and overall Muslim improvement. Sisters get together at the Islamic Center of Raleigh and discuss issues Muslim teenagers face, such as happiness, peer-pressure, Islamic identity, gender-relations, etc."[5] In this space, twelve to eighteen young women gathered and often discussed some of the conflicts they experienced in negotiating the social demands of their American high school experience and the expectations associated with a Muslim identity.[6] The effects of 9/11 were at times apparent in this process of negotiation, manifest in shifts in gender relationships within the Muslim community and greater intentional consciousness associated with wearing hijab.

After 9/11, Muslim organizations began to focus outward toward non-Muslims more than they had in the past. In Raleigh-Durham and elsewhere, Muslim Students Associations (MSAs) shifted into what one student described as an intense mode, in which they spoke not only to peers, but also to teachers and other non-Muslim adults about the meaning of Islam. According to one local university student, his MSA began holding regular "comedy shows, information sessions, [and] banquet dinners" immediately following 9/11, to "show [non-Muslims] that Muslims [were] normal people." This social proactivity has not diminished in the years since the attacks; in the 2004 and 2005 academic year, the club held five such shows.[7]

Mosques, too, underwent significant changes in organization and activity. One young man described the IAR mosque as "evolv[ing] . . . almost to a company of sorts." Its functions as a religious center expanded to incorporate an official committee of outreach and an official committee for media relations. In addition, the mosque designed media shows and Web sites, printed newspapers, and formed a chapter of the Muslim American Society. In the war on terror, it became important to teach non-Muslims about Islam, and to convince them that Islam was a religion of peace and moderation, and not one that sanctioned violence and revenge. The result has been a strengthening of activities and networks within both the local and national Muslim American communities and a sustained effort to increase public awareness of the beliefs, goals, and strengths of that community, making the local practice of Islam more publicly visible.

AMERICAN VERSUS MUSLIM: CHALLENGES TO CULTURAL CITIZENSHIP

As in other parts of the United States, several incidents of hostility against Muslims occurred in the Triangle area immediately following 9/11, and reports of these events reverberated throughout local Muslim communities. Bomb threats were delivered to mosques. Pig's blood was smeared on mosque doors. At local universities, there were a few incidents of students spitting on and throwing rocks at Muslim women. Verbal violence was also reported. One teenage interviewee described separate incidents in which two brothers were called sand niggers, and one was brutally beaten. There were also acts of kindness, inclusion, and support, however, such as a chalk message indicating student support of Muslims that was visible for several days on a sidewalk at one local university. Muslim students noted and appreciated this message.

The message of the anti-Muslim violence seemed clear: Muslims are not "real" Americans. Indeed, Muslims and non-Muslims alike have described the war on terror as a war against Islam. To many young Muslims, anti-Muslim violence conveyed the message that they could not be both Muslim and American and that they would never be considered as such. Our research suggests that this message has been actively contested by Muslim American youth, who have felt the need to argue that there is nothing about Islam per se that makes it incompatible with the principles of American citizenship and belonging.

The aftermath of 9/11, as well as the rhetoric and policies associated with the war on terror, deprived most of the youth we met of a sense of full cultural citizenship[8] as Muslims came to be positioned more explicitly as outsiders and as their religious identity came to be more salient than ethnicity. Before 9/11, many interviewees' families had participated more readily in the status of the so-called South Asian or Indian model minority, in a process analogous to the racial positioning of many Arabs in the United States, who were a kind of invisible minority often racialized as white, as long as religious identity as Muslim was not salient (Naber 2000). The aftermath of 9/11 posed challenges to adolescent Muslims' nascent political identities, even leading some to question the virtues and values of being American and others to anticipate the possibility of having to leave the United States someday (for a discussion of similar concerns in Dearborn, Michigan, see Abraham 2005).

Though the young people we met had not directly experienced local violence, which was actually quite rare even though highly visible when it did occur, government policies—especially the treatment of Muslims traveling on airplanes—produced a more direct, immediate, and pervasive experience of violence and discrimination. This experience has had an effect not only on political orientations, but on the possibility of feeling American. Farah, a twenty-year-old aspiring school teacher, expressed conflict surrounding her American identity that was particularly intense.[9] She considered herself "very American," but her perspective on being a Muslim American was dramatically colored by her father's experience following 9/11:

> It really just breaks my heart that so many people are either—like I know people whose phones have been tapped—my dad, my dad, *my own dad*—if you ever meet my dad, he's the sweetest man. He's soft-spoken, he's such a cute man, pinchable cheeks, everything. He was coming back from a wedding in Canada—and he was just *randomly* selected to be searched. He was strip-searched, interrogated, and videotaped. They went through my dad's wallet. Any phone numbers my dad had, they kept them. They completely violated him. He was *strip-searched* and *videotaped*. Now any time he goes to the airport, he has trouble. Why? Why? My dad has never broken the law. He's lived here longer than he lived in Pakistan. He's been here since 1972. He's a taxpayer. He's never done anything wrong.

He's been a citizen for years and years and years. And that honestly made me upset. It made me so angry. I mean, ugh, that was ridiculous.

Violations of Farah's father's rights as a citizen carried over to the meaning of Farah's own citizenship, and to the relationships she perceived between herself and her government and countrymen. It was evident, too, that Farah perceived her father's violation not only as an abstract offense, an infringement of theoretical rights, but as a very physical invasion. The emotional intensity in her voice, the rigidity of her body as she recounted these events, made it seem as if she were describing a violation of her own person, a violation emphasized in her repetition of the fact that her father was strip-searched. It seemed that Farah superimposed the image of her father's physical exposure onto an imagined occurrence of her own public nudity. Given Farah's careful covering of her own body, this image was particularly threatening. When even the partial exposure of skin and hair is associated with impiety, forced nudity seems not only shameful but sinful. For this reason, too, the officials' treatment of Farah's father is particularly damaging: in addition to violating political delineations of propriety, they represent a breach of the central Islamic value of modesty.

Farah also spoke of her father in terms which might not generally be applied to an authority figure. In her loving description, she maximized the contrast between her experience of her father and the implicit alternative represented by the strip-search: the violent Islamic terrorist who must be broken and humiliated. Her father's powerlessness in the face of a strip search seemed to challenge her sense of the father as a protective figure and her experience of him as the head of the family. It also transformed politics from the realm of the formation of a political identity based on abstract principles to a more immediate, visceral experience that was shared by many Muslims in her community. This memory of her father's experience did not simply color Farah's attitudes toward government and politics, but challenged her identity as American. From her perspective, being very American made the challenges generated by the war on terror even more difficult to manage, because that war positioned her as a threatening outsider.

Paradoxically, then, the South Asian Muslim American adolescents who most emphatically asserted being American were precisely those most tortured by questions about the meanings and manifestations of Americanism, and by popular doubts regarding a Muslim's ability to be truly American. In other words, the youth who feel most integrated culturally are also the ones most painfully aware of their own social exclusion, a common phenomenon among second-generation immigrants. Farah seemed to struggle less with the reconciliation of identities than with what she felt to be her compulsory categorization at the hands of non-Muslims. Indeed, there was little to suggest that she felt a conflict between religious and national allegiances, or any discontinuity between the Muslim and American aspects of her self. Farah felt very much American; in her mind, her parents were the ones who were of another country.

Shahin, a twenty-year-old biology major at a local university, also evinced a degree of national-personal identity conflict that was tied closely to the September 11 attacks:

I think that 9/11 had a lot of negative effects. I had uncles who were in the building, and so feeling the issues from the American perspective of what occurred and the horrendous actions that occurred, so there're definitely those connotations. But at the same time, 9/11 was a wake-up call for both Muslims and non-Muslims. It was a statement—not that I agree whatsoever with what occurred—but it was a statement from Muslims overseas saying, you can't keep treating us like this. And it was a statement to Muslims over here saying, wake up and take what you have and use it.

Shahin indicated that she could relate to Americans—that she was familiar with what she called the American perspective—because several of her family members had been in the twin towers when the attacks occurred. She had thus experienced anxiety and loss even more directly, immediately, and personally than most people in the Raleigh-Durham area had. Shahin drew on her familial connections to solidify a sense of national belonging in relationship to the interviewer. She also drew on her uncles' victimhood to explain her American emotions to us and to herself, validating her American views of September 11. Yet in saying "from the American perspective," she suggests that it is a perspective that she (and others like her) can step into and out of, thus recognizing that her interlocutors might not take for granted or trust her American perspective had she been unable to reference a direct familial connection to September 11.[10]

However, Shahin's identification with the victims of September 11 attacks extended well beyond those persons killed on American soil. Indeed, she expressed a strong connection to the Muslims overseas (whom, she implies, the Western world has long mistreated). She articulated their message in her words: "You can't keep treating us like this." In doing so, she spoke for these overseas Muslims even as she distanced herself from their acts of violence. She also indicated that these Muslims were speaking to her and other Muslims in the United States through the events of September 11. For Shahin, the fundamental messages of the attacks pertained not only to the failings of the Western world in its relations to Muslims overseas, but also very much to her as a member of the Muslim community in the West, and to their—and her—unfulfilled obligations to Muslim brethren. Nonetheless, Shahin balanced these sentiments with clear, pro-American statements, emphasizing that September 11 "had a lot of negative effects."

Shahin's reaction is similar to that of other Muslims in the West. September 11 produced change in the local Muslim community's global religious consciousness. In the words of one young male interviewee, the anti-Muslim backlash seen and felt across the Western world, "brought the Muslims around the world together" and eliminated "quarrelling over smaller issues in Muslim communities." Some felt that sectarian differences within Islam were minimized in the wake of September 11.[11] As another young woman said, "I think every Muslim's goal is to be *just Muslim.* There are so many sects of Islam, but I don't want to identify myself as Sunni or Shiite. I'm just Muslim, and that's how we should treat every other Muslim." She, too, saw the war on terror as a unifying force across Muslim communities, nationally and internationally. Clearly, 9/11 and the resultant backlash did not reduce sectarian divisions among Muslims, even within the Raleigh-Durham area, so what were these people describing? Their statements emphasize being "just Muslim" as a kind of essence. In an environment in which Muslims suddenly became threateningly Other, this otherness is itself experienced as an essence, the common bond of being Muslim.

The challenges to cultural citizenship that most of the youth we talked with experienced seemed to push some toward an orientation that could be characterized as a kind of flexible citizenship. Taking off from Aihwa Ong's work on flexible citizenship, Sunaina Maira (2004) has argued for the existence of flexible citizenship among South Asian Muslim youth in the Boston area: an orientation in which individuals shape for themselves through their degree of participation in popular culture, their selective consumption of goods and services, and the envisioning of futures that might involve pragmatically-motivated migrations. Among the youth we interviewed, an analogous flexible orientation toward citizenship was less an outcome of retaining extensive ties with the country of origins of one's parents and more a result of the fear of being pushed out of a viable American identity and a need to become fully cosmopolitan, unmoored to a specific place that might become unlivable at some point.

Doubts about the value of being American were particularly salient in the commentary of Imran, an architecture student in his early twenties:

I was born and raised here, so I love it here, and I'm an American. I wish I could say that there's hope for [America] and I'm going to be excited to raise my kids here, but I'm not. I hope that things will change but I'm not sure they will. In our situation, it feels like we're going down hill. Our morality is crumbling, our society is crumbling, our respect for the world is going down, our ego is going up and up and up. It's just like the Romans.

In this passage, Imran's use of the pronouns *we* and *our* was striking. He maintained firmly his positioning as American, even as he questioned the desirability of raising his children in the United States, and thereby hints at the possibility of not staying in the United States forever. He explicitly asserted an American identity—a universal assertion among our interviewees born in the United States[12]—and he maintained this identity even when listing negative aspects of an American collective self, expressed in his use of the term *our*. A moment later, however, Imran's pronoun usage shifted, and he separated himself from American society with an allusion to the government:

> I love living here, I *love* American society and the way I was raised. I was born here. But I must say this government is shameless. This society is shameless. The way they've treated the world, and not just the Muslims. Obviously there's a little bit of bias there because they're my Muslim brothers and sisters who are dying and suffering. I think if something of this magnitude had happened to any other group of people, and I saw it with my own eyes and felt the way I feel today about what's going on Iraq, I think I would draw the same conclusions. It's shameless. There's no shame, there's no respect.

Although he also thinks that being Muslim increases his sympathy for the Muslims dying in the wars in Afghanistan and Iraq, Imran suggests that the injustice is so great that he—and by implication all Americans—should feel outraged, as he would also be for any group of people forced to suffer like this.

Imran's emphatic repetitions of "I was born here" suggested that he was highly conscious of his American citizenship: because anyone born in the United States is an American citizen, he is one. But another repetition might be considered differently: Imran's thrice-mentioned love for America and the American way of life seems also to be an attempt to convince his audience—and himself—that he not only is American, but that he wants to be American. In this way, Imran's adamancy regarding his love for America suggested a degree of doubt and insecurity on that point.

> As much as I love it here, I may not be here in twenty or thirty years. It may not be the place to be. We live in a global world today, and America is not the best place, it's not as comfortable or as wonderful as we think it is. There are a lot of places that are wonderful, too, where I could be just as happy or just as comfortable. One day I may have to go somewhere else. I've prepared myself for the worst, but I'm hoping for the best. My dad taught me that: hope for the best, plan for the worst.

Here, Imran was clearly less than optimistic about the nation's future, and about where he will be in the future. His statement can be read as a manifesto of his flexible citizenship and the stirring of a transnational-global sense of belonging, a possibility that many other Americans also experience (see Ong 1998).

He projected a kind of transnational identity reminiscent of the experiences of South Asians in other parts of the world, such as Kenya, who were forced to migrate from their adopted home, an experience that was popularized for an American audience in the film *Mississippi Masala* (Nair 1991). Yet Imran seemed to greet this identity with ambivalence: he was not sure he wanted to be or stay an American, yet rescinding his Americanness was the worst he could foresee for himself. By accepting the possibility of leaving the United States permanently, Imran was preparing for the worst.

It is notable, too, that Imran again used the pronoun *we* towards the end of this excerpt. "America is not [the place] we think it is." In a sense, the usage reinforced his earlier implied dichotomy between the state and American citizens like himself. Just as Imran previously separated himself from American society through references to the government, he has suggested that that separation is so great that he—and other Americans—cannot even understand their government or society. They are unable to see America as flawed, and are incapable of recognizing the ways in which it compares unfavorably to other nations.

The majority of our interviewees were children of first-generation American citizens—whether born or naturalized—who considered themselves culturally and not just nominally or legally American. One young man interviewed during our research was actively involved in the ACLU, and described overturning the Patriot Act in defense of his civil liberties as a "personal [and] ongoing project." Defending the privileges afforded to him by his Americanness was an element of his individual agenda, and a daily focus of his energies and efforts. This young man was actively and politically practicing citizenship by affirming and defending the personal freedoms he located at the core of his national identity as an American.

Many first-generation Muslim Americans have taken it upon themselves to demonstrate publically the compatibility and possible synthesis of Islamic and American identities. This tendency seems to have strengthened considerably in the wake of September 11, 2001. Although, in many settings, individuals' identities are often highly discontinuous and inconsistent (Ewing 1990), the war on terror has rendered it increasingly important among young Muslims to disprove assumptions of discontinuities in their identities in public discourse.

ISLAM IS NOT A CULTURE

Some people with whom we spoke appeared to speak of American and Muslim identities as if they were distinct cultures that must be somehow combined. According to one young woman of Pakistani background, for example, it has become important to "merge the two into something"—and to do so within every Muslim American. Although people did not use the word *hybridity,* statements like this appear to be framed in terms of a hybridity-like model, recognizing and selectively embracing a blend of Islamic and non-Islamic traditions.[13]

Along with many other Muslim youth, this young woman emphasized the importance of blending Muslim and American identities and the necessity of compromising neither one in the process. In a similar discussion, the use of the word *Islamican* was particularly striking. According to a twenty-something woman leading the young women's halaqa at the IAR, "education is becoming Islamican. It's kind of weird."

But for these Muslims, bringing Islam and American culture together emphatically did not mean combining two cultures, as a model of hybridity would suggest. On the contrary, most young people, especially those active in the IAR or the Muslim Students Association, emphasized that Islam is not a culture. Over and over, youth expressed frustration at the all-too-common conflation of cultural and Islamic values. These young Muslims see the necessity of sifting through and removing cultural impurities imbedded within disparate forms of Islam, to isolate and act on the religious convictions that bind all Muslims into one transnational religious community.

The negative formulation that Islam is not a culture is a complex rhetorical positioning that draws on the anthropological concept of culture. This concept of culture, though now a basic part of the world's conceptual apparatus, has a specific history associated with the discipline of anthropology and its colonial past. It was a way that anthropologists could characterize and understand social difference without immediately imposing an explicit hierarchy of value, a perspective that came to be associated with cultural relativism in the works of cultural anthropologists such as Clifford Geertz.[14] In the words of one Muslim teen, "any culture can fit to Islam"—American culture included. In this statement, all cultures are functionally equivalent and in some sense interchangeable. This teen is a cultural relativist, though not when it comes to Islam.

The notion of culture has become a fundamental way of conceptualizing Islam and its relationship to daily life for many diasporic Muslims. In this model, Islam is something fundamentally distinct from any human culture. It has become a priority for young Muslims to separate cultural baggage from the Islam they practice, whatever the source of that baggage. At the same time, national and cultural identities can complement and reinforce Islamic aspects of the self; they are not mutually exclusive. The concept of culture has become a tool for being selective about which cultural elements of their environment are to be embraced and which are to be rejected. Thus, those elements of American culture that are inconsistent with Islam—the consumption of alcohol and pork and American patterns of dating being among the most obvious—are to be avoided and rejected.

The distinction of Islam from culture involved in the self-conscious synthesis of American and Muslim identities is also linked to a shifting relationship to the South Asian cultural practices of their parents and other relatives. Becoming a proper Muslim can be a way of resisting parental expectations. "To be a Muslim," said Sitara, "you're supposed to *think*." By this she meant that it is not enough to simply adopt the practices of one's parents and grandparents because many of these are local customs that either have nothing to do with Islam or are actually un-Islamic. Yet people in Pakistan and other parts of South Asia mistakenly think that these customary practices are a part of Islam.

The theme of children educating their parents is a common one:

> It's up to us kids—my sister and I constantly sit my parents down and we're like, "this and this you do, did you know, it's actually culture, it has nothing to do with the religion." And they're like, "oh, really?" The kids are educating their parents about religion.

This was a frequent topic in the halaqa for young women at the IAR mosque. In a discussion of proper gender relations and modesty, one girl asked, "Is it all right for grandfathers to pat their granddaughters on the head?" The girls smiled at the question and laughed at the group leader's answer: "Yes," she says, because "really, really old people don't matter in that sort of thing." When another young woman questioned the propriety of an uncle's regular attempt to shake her hand, the group reasoned that such contact is improper. In this case, there was a strongly expressed sentiment that the young woman's uncle ought to know that himself: as one girl said adamantly, "people should *know* their own religion!"

The girls laughed when the group leader, Sitara, described her own father: "He refuses to clean up after himself. He leaves banana peels on the coffee table, and then calls the four women in the house to throw them away for him. That's definitely *not* the way of the Prophet." "That sort of behavior," volunteered a girl sitting opposite Sitara, "is all cultural." The other young women resoundingly agreed. In this case, they were implicitly arguing that a Western or American cultural practice of gender equality in which women should not serve men is actually closer to the Prophet Muhammad's practice and Islam than a South Asian one is. The girls at the halaqa may have a sense of gender relations that is closer to one dominant in American discourse than their parents' perspective, but they consciously locate the roots of this model in Islam.

At one evening's meeting of the halaqa, titled "The Role of Women in Islam," discussion focused on practical guidelines for determining which cultural practices are consistent with Islam and which are not. Many of the questions raised were specific: When and with whom should a woman cover herself? Not in front of a stepson, but certainly in front of a stepfather. Is it appropriate to marry a stepbrother? Yes. A stepfather? No. Are piercings allowed? In cartilage, but not in flesh (unless it is done to please one's husband, in which case body piercings are "controversial but okay"). Sitara, the instructor, reminded the young women that they must never show anyone "the area from the belly button to the knees." They must not be naked, unless alone with their husbands or in the bathroom. Why is it okay to show breasts and not the belly button? For convenience in breast feeding, among other reasons.

There were also more general lessons about proper gender relations, especially between spouses. In the same evening's meeting, Sitara emphasized the freedoms afforded to Muslim women. She stressed that there is nothing in Islam that prevents women from being educated. Sitara told the girls circled around her: "We can keep all we earn. The man of the house must pay the bills." The Muslim wife also has recourse in instances of domestic abuse. If she is mistreated by her husband, a Muslim woman can leave a marriage with impunity: "She shouldn't be scorned as a result." Sitara told the group that, although marriage is "a very important part of life," it should not be their "whole life." Women should never be judged on the "number of children [they] have, or on the best dish [they] can cook." For the most part, Sitara's interpretations of Islam emphasized principles consistent with current Western ideas of gender equality.

But some women questioned going too far in the direction of Western gender practices. Aziza, for instance, said: "Many Muslims only have Western ideas of equality. Who's to say that's right? In Islam, the woman follows her husband, but the child follows the mother. It's a delicate, intricate balance." Other young women criticized Western gender roles in much the same way that Western feminists do. In her interview, Sara disparaged the New Jersey neighborhood in which she passed her elementary school years. She likened it to 1950s Pleasantville suburbia, referring to the film *Pleasantville* (Ross 1998), in which the women played the "traditional role" of "staying at home, baking cookies, and planning birthday parties." She felt that women should have careers, as her own mother, a physician born and trained in India, did.

Though sometimes these youth were critical of their parents' traditional ways, at other times the disagreement was over the parents' more secular orientation. Mariam, for example, described how she refuses to wear makeup, even when her mother asks her to. She explained, "If we go out, they really want us to look nice," but she feels that her "life is more simple in terms of going out and buying make up and hair products and clothes. We don't have to worry about that." Other young women described how their mothers were on occasion upset at their decisions to wear hijab and could not understand why they would choose to take up something that would stigmatize them or mark them as unmodern. Most of these young women come from conservative families, whose members pray five times a day and fast during the month of Ramadan, yet reported encountering resistance from their parents when they chose to wear hijab.

The fact that many of these young women's primary religious role models do not cover suggests that their reasons for doing so extend beyond piety as learned within the family. Sara's mother, for instance, insisted that her daughters read the Qur'an in its entirety before the ages of five and six. Yet she does not wear a headscarf. More often than not, the young women we spoke with were either the only ones in their extended family to wear a headscarf, or had been the first to do so. As one young woman said, in America, "parents [mothers] tend not to wear it as much as the kids [daughters]." Another remarked that when she first began covering in high school, her older sister did not: "My older sister didn't start wearing it until she was in college. I was the only one in the family wearing it. My mother [still] doesn't."

These women represent a transnational trend toward the conscious practice of Islam, demonstrated in activities such as the halaqa and hijab. While the decision of the young women we talked with to cover themselves reflects a growing transnational movement toward Islamic piety amongst Muslim women (see Mahmood 2005), many of these young women associated this growth with the strengthening of the Muslim community since 9/11 and indicated the effects of 9/11 as an important factor in their individual decisions.

Muslim women who keep hijab emphasize their conscious and volitional adherence to Islam. In the words of one college student of Pakistani heritage:

> It's making a statement, like, hey, I'm Muslim. That's a big motivation for me, every day. You know, when someone comes up to me and is like, hey, I'm just curious. Why are you wearing that? Oh, you're Muslim? What's that mean? That's my motivation, just to let people know who I am and what my beliefs are.

The political climate following 9/11 infused this statement of motivation with political significance that had not existed before for this generation in this place. The communicative capacity of hijab expanded beyond its significance as an enactment of proper Islam. The headscarf took on political connotations as an expression of resistance to the intolerance, misunderstanding of Islam, and racism with which Muslims were confronted after 9/11. Young women increasingly donned the headscarf in spite of the perception by some Americans (including classmates) that it signified female subjugation or support for violent acts in the name of Islam. Thus, in the minds of some Muslim American young women, it became a symbol of defiance—though not a defiance of American antiterrorist values, as it may have been read by some of their non-Muslim classmates. Rather, it was defiant of non-Muslim America's ignorance and intolerance of Islam. In one interview, three young women, recent high school graduates preparing to enter college in the fall, compared (in good humor) some of the standard questions they had received from classmates. "Do you have hair under there?" "If you take that thing [the veil] off, are you going to burst into flame?" "Your God, Allah, isn't he going to punish you right then and there [if you take off your headscarf]?" They saw their classmates' naïve questions as an opportunity to disrupt their negative and distorted impressions of Islam.

Wearing a headscarf has multiple layers of significance for each individual. Broader themes of social acceptance and stereotype rejection emerged as compelling reasons for young women to adopt hijab. Sara said, "I didn't want to be the random Indian kid. I didn't want that. I wanted to be known as Muslim." These impulses are remarkably similar to those of women in India who, by Sara's own description, cover themselves "not really as a religious thing," and not because they're "really conservative," but because it distinguishes them from Hindu women. While attending medical school in India, for instance, her own mother wore hijab "part of the time," and "sort of on a whim" because her classmates wanted to "identify" themselves as Hindus and Muslims, but not because they're "really conservative." For Sara, it is in part a tactic of self-differentiation and also one deployed to disrupt stereotypes about Muslim women: "I wanted to show that you can be open-minded, talkative like I am, as you've noticed [laughs], outgoing, crazy, and it has nothing to do with your outer appearance." Farah expressed a similar stance: "I take pride in letting people know that I'm just like any other person." Another woman said, "I wanted to show that you can respect me for who I am, just as you did before, but respect me for being Muslim, too." Islam, it seemed, did not define her, though it figured prominently in the way she defined herself. Each of these young women was aware of the stereotype that a Muslim woman wearing a headscarf is passive, quiet, and submissive, and sought to disrupt this stereotype by projecting personal identities that contradicted it. They articulated their identities in characteristically American idioms, including the importance of individuality, assertiveness, and the value of the inner self.

Although Muslim women are frequently judged by non-Muslims for their choice to wear a headscarf, Muslim adolescents deny seeing the headscarf—or lack thereof—as a basis for respect or condemnation. Shahin readily volunteered that she has friends who "don't wear a scarf, [yet] who act as better Muslims than people who do." Sara, also twenty, reiterated that sentiment. "The veil," she says, "doesn't mean that you [the wearer] are more religious than anybody else. There can be a girl who doesn't wear the veil who knows more about Islam than anyone. She can say, 'Sara, you're doing it [praying, wearing the veil, and so on] wrong,' and I'll be like, 'Oh, okay. Thanks.' " Analogously, though some young women, such as Mariam, saw wearing makeup as incompatible with being a covered Muslim woman, other young women wore makeup, even in the setting of the halaqa, indicating that the rules distinguishing proper Islamic behavior from un-Islamic cultural practices leave room for personal choice. These young women stressed that the decision to wear a headscarf or forgo makeup is very much a personal one and that there is no compulsion in Islam. These statements emphasize the principles of freedom and choice in an environment where these principles are a central aspect of public discourse.

From the perspective of anthropological usage of the concept of culture, these young women's understanding of the true practice of Islam is a cultural practice. It is clear, for example, that Saudi resources have been poured into Islamic education globally to promote a particular vision of Islamic practice that many Muslims today consider pure Islam. Other devout Muslims actively resist the hegemony of this rather austere form that forbids many practices such as celebrations of the Prophet's birthday, and certain prayers, associated with Sufi practice, from being recited in the mosque. So in this sense, the declaration that Islam is not a culture is an exercise in power and influence that, at least in some contexts, is associated with the promotion of a culturally specific form of Islam.

However, the act of distinguishing culture from Islam draws on a conceptual distinction between locally variable, plural *cultures* and *universals* that is part of a modern global discourse. A similar contrast forms the basis for ethical debates in the academy over where to draw the line between cultural rights and human rights. The assertion that "Islam is not a culture" is based on the proposition that Islam cannot be relegated to the merely cultural in this debate about universals. It is thus a form of resistance to a Western discourse that claims for itself a status as universal, thereby marginalizing Islam and other universalizing discourses while failing to recognize its own cultural particularly (see Asad 1993; Mahmood 2005).

SOCIAL INTERACTION AFTER 9/11

The sense of threat associated with the war on terror generated a number of changes in the social relationships of Muslim youth, not only their relationships with non-Muslims, including other South Asians, but also those with other Muslims, including members of the opposite sex. The rejection of South Asian cultural practices in favor of a purer Islam has its most obvious manifestation in social relationships with other South Asians, especially in school, as Muslim youth intensified their investments in a Muslim identity. Among the youth we interviewed, shared religious identity as Muslim has increasingly come to underpin their friendships. Furthermore, in the context of discussing friendships and social groups, interviewees' sense of being American as the basis for commonality or identity becomes less salient than it is when thinking in the abstract. According to one young woman:

> We don't have their [our parents'] culture, and we don't have this [American] culture. The only thing we have in common with other Muslims in this area is the religion. That's what we're kind of bonding over, that's what we'll discuss. The thing we can discuss very openly is religion. And it's all from direct sources. If we're going to talk about it, we go straight to the Qur'an or to the Prophet's life. It's nothing about culture.

A young woman of Indian parentage described her relationships with non-Muslim South Asians: "With Indians and the Desi—which is Indian, Pakistani, Bangladeshi, all South Asian people—we can say, 'hey, did you watch that Indian movie?' But it only goes so far." As she described it, the common ground between South Asians of different religious backgrounds extended no further than the movies they were apt to have seen. Another young woman described the situation in heavier terms: "Try hanging out with a non-Muslim of the same country. You can't do it. You feel like your soul is sinking." This is a political statement, an articulation of the process of drawing group boundaries that is consistent with Islamic teachings that are discussed in the halaqa. It may reflect, too, the broader penetration of religious affiliations as a basis for group identity in schools, where Protestant prayer meetings are held on school grounds after hours, especially in the South.

Among South Asian Muslim youth, tension exists between their voluntary involvement in the Muslim community and the sense that they have been relegated to that community and excluded from non-Muslim social circles. This sense of exclusion increased after the September 11 attacks. In the words of one male college student, September 11 taught him the extent to which "negative impressions of Islam can be damaging to friendships." As a result of the prejudices and questions he has confronted since 9/11, this young man's "primary, priority social circle has evolved into a very Muslim circle." It used to be "easier to hang out with non-Muslims" than it is now; it is no longer something which he is willing to do on a regular basis. Another young woman was on the verge of tears as she expressed a similar sentiment: "When people first meet me, they can't get past the fact that I look and dress differently. It's kind of hard for me to make new friends. If it's someone who's not Muslim, then a lot of times they have preconceived notions. Of course there are several exceptions, but that's—that's the hard part." She seemed to see no way of building friendships outside of the Muslim community, because non-Muslims displayed little or no interest in getting to know her, the individual behind the headscarf. In her experience, this social exclusion intensified after 9/11. Others expressed a similar sense of intensification, though it is likely that youth expressed similar social concerns before 9/11. The aftermath of 9/11 has become an idiom for articulating and accounting for many of the anxieties associated with navigating the complex dynamics of groups in high school and college, made more difficult by stigmatization associated with the intensified othering of Muslims.

The sense of danger and threat also affected gender relations among Muslim youth. Young people reported that before 9/11, they had had very little social contact with members of the opposite sex in the Muslim community due to a number of factors. Gender segregation both characterizes the South Asian cultural practices of their families and is prescribed in Islam. In an American context, there are few settings where young men and women would be in the same place, except the classroom. (Although women attend mosques, as they would not have done in South Asia, they are generally screened off from the men.) Furthermore, young women, operating in terms of a model of gender equality, feel quite independent and self-sufficient, and are free to move about the area on their own, usually without male escort. Paradoxically, the practice of gender segregation seems to have been reinforced by the emphasis that most young Muslim women growing up in the United States place on self-sufficiency, equality, and independence. Being self-sufficient, they have felt no need for male protectors, contrasting their lives with what they imagined gender relations to be like in South Asia.

But the sense of threat that the community experienced in the wake of the highly publicized local violence after 9/11 brought to the fore another aspect of gender relations that has certainly been an aspect of Islamic practice but has been contested by some Islamic feminists—the obligation of men to protect "their" women. The threat posed by 9/11 intensified a cultural practice that many young women had not previously felt was necessary in their social environment. As one university woman said, "We had to have our brothers walk us to classes because people would try to tear our scarves off." When all Muslims in the community are categorized as brothers and sisters, then this obligation extends to all Muslim women, creating a boundary between us and them. Even men of Pakistani background who were not actively practicing Muslims reported that they became protective of Muslim women in this way after 9/11.

When young Muslim men took on this role of protecting the young women at high schools, universities, and other settings, it often resulted in the creation of new interactions and relationships. Women who had seen themselves as autonomous and independent, such as Sara, acquiesced to the wishes of the young men to protect them:

> This totally was their [the brothers'] initiative. They saw what was going on. We were like, we can protect ourselves, but they were like, "yeah, I'd feel sooo much better if I knew you got to class on time". I know if I had a [biological] brother he'd try to do those things. They're our protective older brothers. That's just the way that was: they took that initiative. The guys at [the university] told our Imam to make an announcement that if we couldn't find a guy to walk us to our car, to at least walk in groups. We were all unified at that moment. Guys that I never talked to in my life would say, "hey, do you need to go to your car?" and I'd be like, okay—even if it was totally out of their way.

There are any number of reasons why these young women, who had previously cultivated autonomy and independence, accepted the protective gestures of young men from their religious community. It is likely that they truly did fear for their safety at times. But is also possible that they appreciated the opportunity to better get to know members of the opposite sex, and to do so without breaching Islamic rules. Sara commented on changes in intergender relationships:

> It was really interesting. You kind of finally got to know what this relationship that you have [with guys] is. The guy-girl relationship in Islam is kind of—it's very separate, except for business. We talk to them if there's a necessity—an MSA event or a homework assignment. We're very discouraged from flirting and unnecessary talk with guys who are unrelated. So for that reason we never really got to know who they were. We had been like, oh they're the brothers and they knew, oh, we were the sisters. But it [9/11] really brought us together and we were very unified in that. We didn't break any of the bounds, or anything, but it helped us to get to know each other.

Certainly, the practice of Islam usually does deter many of the gendered interactions expected and encouraged of adolescents in the West—chatting, flirting, and the like. This can be confusing and difficult for Muslim youth. Shahin, for instance, has had to learn to appreciate male distance not as a social snub, but as a gesture of respect. Nonetheless, it seems that in the war on terror, Islam also created a context for meaningful and even intimate interactions with the opposite sex.

The sense of threat thus opened a new venue for social interaction between young men and women that was not dating in the Western sense, which most of their parents opposed and has been explicitly declared un-Islamic by Islamic authorities. These youth expressed the feeling that social distance between girls and boys had in the past been so great that they didn't even know each other. The sense of being strangers is generated by the contours of the American diaspora, where many families from far-flung parts of South Asia as well as other parts of the world have found themselves in this particular corner of the United States. These families have come together within the mosque community but lack the depth of kinship relationships that would have allowed young men and women to know each other in other contexts. This new situation, in which men escorted young women to protect them after 9/11, was consistent with what they understood to be proper gender relations within Islam.

CONCLUSION

The middle class Muslim youth of this study felt that the events of 9/11 and their aftermath have created significant changes in their community and shaped their lives and identities. In the post 9/11 context, the expression of Islamic values and Muslim identity was subject to intensified suspicion. Young people saw themselves becoming more consciously Muslim, a process they were encouraged in through activities at the mosque and, for those in local universities, at meetings of the Muslim Students Association. Although there have been other historical moments such as the Iranian Revolution and the first Iraq war that brought Muslims into public awareness and triggered a consciousness among Muslims of their status as Other, the United States' response to 9/11 was unprecedented in the scale of surveillance, detention, and its relentless positioning of Muslims as stigmatized Other. The adolescent impulse to present and define oneself in a more public context was met with the post-9/11 imperative that American Muslims define and demonstrate a nonterrorist Islam to both Muslims and non-Muslims. In this process, religious identification in young South Asian Muslim Americans became part of a broader shift from a private to a public Islam.

These actively practicing Muslim youth see no basic incompatibility between most American cultural practices and Islam, but the war on terror has generated more self-contained social networks that rest on the distinct but mutually reinforcing processes of increasingly conscious Muslim identity practices and the experience of anti-Muslim discrimination. The sense of being culturally American does not seem to carry over into social relationships, even on the basis of shared ethnicity, especially within a high school context.

Though the war on terror and the experience of discrimination has created some ambivalence about being a Muslim in the United States, self-conscious adherence to Islam—as a practice that transcends local cultures and politics—allows many young diasporic Muslims to distance themselves from the cultural practices of their parents and thus to feel fully a part of the place in which they live, yet retain a certain cosmopolitan flexible citizenship. That is, despite a challenging cultural and political climate, they identify themselves as fully American.

NOTES

1. Following Stuart Hall (1990), we understand identities to be negotiated positionings within specific cultural, historical, and political narratives.

2. In interpreting the significance of this tension in the lives of the people we met with, however, the process of research as a social context must be taken into account. We were talking to them because they had identified themselves to us as Muslims, and they knew that the project was a study of the effects of 9/11 on their lives. Given the salience of public perceptions of Muslim as Other, and the fact that the issue of the compatibility of a Muslim identity and an American identity was, therefore, already in the air and even articulated in some of the discussions we initiated, the tension was reinscribed in the research process itself,

recreated in the space between us (Crapanzano 1985). In other spaces, it is likely that such tensions are not salient. This also means that in describing, for example, their social relationships at school, they were more likely to recall and stress events and perspectives that paralleled what they were experiencing in the interview situation (see Ewing 2006). This problem is one of the reasons that sustained participant observation, in which research is conducted across multiple social contexts, is important for accurately addressing the question of how self-conscious interview responses are related to the interviewee's views and experiences in other contexts.

3. There have been other events, such as the Iranian revolution and the first Iraq war, that had similar effects on a previous generation, though the precise reconfigurations of identity were somewhat different. It is also important to keep in mind that other youth chose to downplay their Muslim backgrounds, maintaining the American tradition of marking religion as private and irrelevant to one's public identities.

4. Sally Howell and Andrew Shryock link the rise in donations to local mosques to the difficulties in making overseas charitable donations overseas after the government's actions to regulate and shut down a number of Islamic charitable organizations (2003, 454).

5. Accessed at http://www.islam1.org/iar/services/archives/2006/01/30/youth_programs.php.

6. Marguerite Hoyler attended these meetings over the course of several months.

7. The introduction of humor to disrupt stereotypes can also be seen in a new television sitcom about Muslims, *Little Mosque on the Prairie,* which the Canadian Broadcasting Company first aired on January 9, 2007. As one viewer said, "There's this image you have of frowning, bearded mullahs, and that's not what Muslims are all about" (Dube 2007). Muslim convert Baba Ali also uses comedy to edify in a series of short videos, "The Reminder Series," produced by Ummah Films and aired on YouTube (accessed at http://ummahfilms.blogspot.com/).

8. The concept of cultural citizenship, as framed by Renato Rosaldo (1994) and taken up by Aihwa Ong (1996) and other anthropologists within the context of diasporic and minority communities, refers to "the right to be different and to belong in a participatory democratic sense," with a stress on specifying the conditions that make individuals and groups feel like first- or second-class citizens (Rosaldo 1994, 402). In chapter 2 of this volume, Sunaina Maira focuses on the issue of cultural citizenship among South Asian Muslims in the United States.

9. All names have been changed to protect confidentiality.

10. Andrew Shryock has noted that well into the third generation, people in marked immigrant communities use the term *American* to mean *not us.* He describes witnessing in his own research among Arab Americans the break point, where people start to object to this usage in conversation (Personal communication).

11. Research for this study was done before the escalation of sectarian violence in Iraq.

12. But in striking contrast to similarly positioned Muslims in Germany, who do not easily claim a German identity (Ewing 2008).
13. Hybridity has been both used as an analytic term and critiqued in studies of the cultural adaptations of diasporic communities (see, for example, Werbner and Modood 1997; Ewing 2006).
14. This perspective can be traced back to theorists such as Herder and Humboldt in Germany, through whom it made its way to American cultural anthropology through Franz Boas (see Stocking 1996).

REFERENCES

Abraham, Nabeel. 2005. "From Baghdad to New York: Young Muslims on War and Terrorism." *The Muslim World* 95(4): 587–99.

Asad, Talal. 1993. *Genealogies of Religion: Discipline and Reasons of Power in Christianity and Islam.* Baltimore, Md.: Johns Hopkins University Press.

Crapanzano, Vincent. 1985. *Tuhami: Portrait of a Moroccan.* Chicago, Ill.: University of Chicago Press.

Dube, Rebecca Cook. 2007. "Muslim Comedy Debuts in Canada." *USA Today,* January 10, 2007. Accessed at http://www.usatoday.com/news/world/2007-01-10-muslim-comedy_x.htm.

Erikson, Erik. 1959. *Identity and the Life Cycle: Selected Papers.* New York: International Universities Press.

Ewing, Katherine Pratt. 1990. "The Illusion of Wholeness: 'Culture,' 'Self,' and the Experience of Inconsistency." *Ethos* 18(3): 251–78.

———. 2006. "Between Cinema and Social Work: Diasporic Turkish Women and the (Dis)pleasures of Hybridity." *Cultural Anthropology* 21(2): 265–94.

———. 2008. *Stolen Honor: Stigmatizing Muslim Men in Berlin.* Stanford, Calif.: Stanford University Press.

Hall, Stuart. 1990. "Cultural Identity and Diaspora." In *Identity: Community, Culture, Difference,* edited by Jonathan Rutherford. London: Lawrence and Wishart.

Howell, Sally, and Andrew Shryock. 2003. "Cracking Down on Diaspora: Arab Detroit and America's War on Terror." *Anthropological Quarterly* 76(3): 443–62.

Mahmood, Saba. 2005. *Politics of Piety: The Islamic Revival and the Feminist Subject.* Princeton, N.J.: Princeton University Press.

Maira, Sunaina. 2004. "Imperial Feelings: Youth Culture, Citizenship, and Globalization." In *Globalization: Culture and Education in the New Millennium,* edited by Marcelo Suárez-Orozco. Berkeley: University of California Press.

Naber, Nadine. 2000. "Ambiguous Insiders: an Investigation of Arab American Invisibility." *Ethnic and Racial Studies* 23(1): 37–61.

———. 2005. "Muslim First, Arab Second: A Strategic Politics of Race and Gender." *The Muslim World* 95(4): 479–95.

Nair, Mira, director. 1991. *Mississippi Masala.* Culver City, Calif.: Columbia Tristar.

Ong, Aihwa. 1996. "Cultural Citizenship as Subject Making: Immigrants Negotiate Racial and Cultural Boundaries in the United States." *Current Anthropology* 37(5): 737–62.

———. 1998. *Flexible Citizenship: The Cultural Logics of Transnationality.* Durham, N.C.: Duke University Press.

Rosaldo, Renato. 1994. "Cultural Citizenship and Educational Democracy." *Cultural Anthropology* 9(3): 402–11.

Ross, Gary, director. 1998. *Pleasantville.* New York: New Line Cinema.

Stocking, George W., Jr., editor. 1996. *Volksgeist as Method and Ethic: Essays on Boasian Ethnography and the German Anthropological Tradition.* History of Anthropology, vol. 8. Madison, Wisc.: University of Wisconsin Press.

Werbner, Pnina, and Tariq Modood, editors. 1997. *Debating Cultural Hybridity: Multi-Cultural Identities and the Politics of Anti-Racism.* London: Zed Books.

PART II

THE CHANGING SHAPE OF COMMUNITIES AND INSTITUTIONS

CHAPTER 5

MULTIPLE IDENTITIES AMONG ARAB AMERICANS: A TALE OF TWO CONGREGATIONS

JEN'NAN GHAZAL READ

THE TERRORIST attacks of September 11, 2001, introduced a new era in our society, one that will likely have long-term effects on Americans of all religious and ethnic backgrounds. Since the attacks, Arab and Muslim communities in the United States have been especially vulnerable to racial profiling and discrimination, which raises important questions about the effects of September 11 on their identity and welfare. There is some evidence that Muslim Arab Americans (Muslims) are more susceptible to racial profiling and discrimination than Christian Arab Americans (Christians), in part due to their greater visibility and more recent immigrant status. There are also indications that Christians have greater latitude than Muslims in choosing their ethnic identities (Zogby 2002). These, however, are empirical questions that require further examination, which is the goal of this essay.

Specifically, I assess the impact of September 11 on Arab American identity and well being and examine whether and how the consequences differ for Muslims and Christians—that is, the role of religion in the adaptation experiences of Arab Americans after September 11. I use a comparative approach to answer the following questions: What does it mean to be an Arab in America today, and how does this vary by religious affiliation? What effect, if any, did September 11 have on the ethnic and religious identities of Arab Americans? Did it strengthen identification with other Arabs, with other Americans, with other Muslims or Christians, or a combination of these? What are the ethnic options available to Muslims and Christians, and to what extent do their options depend on situational context and sociodemographic characteristics? For example, are Christians able to assert their national identities in some contexts but pass as non-Arab in others? Are these options more available to Christians than to Muslims? If so, to what degree does this reflect differences in national origin, generational status, and social class?

I draw on ethnographic, interview, and survey data that I collected at an Arab church and Arab mosque in central Texas in the year following September 11, 2001. This approach is useful because it allows for the triangulation of survey data with in-depth interviews and participant observation to get at both general patterns and meaning and process. As a research design that compares a church and a mosque, it is also valuable because it allows Arab ethnicity and Islamic religion—so often collapsed into synonymous components of culture in studies of Middle Eastern communities—to be separated. The design further provides meaningful variation in Arab ethnic identity, which might be obscured in a more aggregated study of Muslims in the United States that includes diverse ethnic (for example, Pakistani, Indian, Arab) and racial groups. A limitation of the design is the exclusion of secularized Arabs (for example, non-churched), which is often unavoidable in studies of this population since there are no available, representative lists from which to draw comparable samples of Arabs of Muslim and Christian origin.

The chapter is organized in three sections. The first section provides the historical context for contemporary diversity in Arab American identity (i.e., Muslim and Christian), and offers a framework for theorizing about identity formation since September 11, 2001. The next section details the research questions and methodology, followed by empirical evidence on similarities and differences in Muslims' and Christians' religious and ethnic identities and experiences of discrimination. The chapter concludes by discussing the implications of the findings for the future incorporation and well being of Arabs in American society.

BACKGROUND AND SIGNIFICANCE

Research on the economic and social adaptation of immigrants occupies a substantial area in social science literature (for a review, see Foner, Rumbaut, and Gold 2000; see also Portes and Rumbaut 1996). In the past decade, scholars have increasingly recognized the importance of religion in defining the experiences of immigrant populations (Ebaugh and Chafetz 1999; Warner and Wittner 1998). Studies of newer and more established ethnic communities find that religious traditions provide secure anchors of meaning in an environment of social change. Ethnic religious institutions sustain these traditions and strengthen group identity by giving members an arena to share ideological, moral, and ethical beliefs (Haddad and Lummis 1987; Bankston and Zhou 1996).

Despite a growing literature on this topic, little is known about the influence of religion on the assimilation experiences of Arab Americans (Bozorgmehr, Der-Martirosian, and Sabagh 1996). This oversight is striking because Arab

Americans are at the intersection of ethnicity and religion—of the estimated 3 million today, approximately 65 percent affiliate with Christianity and 30 percent with Islam. Most contemporary studies focus exclusively on the Muslim population, given their increased visibility in the United States over the past two decades (Haddad 1991a). Research on the Christian Arab population is mainly limited to historical accounts of their immigration and assimilation experiences before World War II (Hitti 1924). Consequently, we know very little about the role of religion in the development and maintenance of group identity within these two communities today.

Although comparative studies of Arab Americans are limited, existing research on other immigrant populations in the United States provides a theoretical framework for understanding differences in identity construction among Christians and Muslims. In particular, earlier studies establish the importance of historical and situational circumstances in defining immigrants' ethnic and religious orientations (Chong 1998). Group identity is not automatically assumed on the basis of social category, but is an emergent form of social organization that develops in response to external forces in society, such as host hostility and racial inequality. Societal conditions have likewise shaped the identity formations of Christian and Muslim Arab Americans.

In general terms, Arab Americans immigrated in two distinct waves, the first predominantly Christian and the latter mainly Muslim. The first began at the end of the nineteenth century and continued through World War I (Naff 1994; see also Shakir 1997). The majority of these early arrivals were working class Christians from Greater Syria seeking better economic opportunities for their families. Like other immigrant sojourners of that era, most believed their immigration would be temporary and devoted little effort to assimilating into American life. Their Eastern Christian heritage served as a primary source of identity, and they built ethnic churches to provide a sense of solidarity and sustain cultural traditions unique to that heritage (Kayal and Kayal 1975). Though ethnic identity was an important part of individual identity, it was less salient than religious affiliation for these early Arab immigrants, a hold over from the Ottoman classification system that identified subjects by religious affiliation (Hooglund 1994).

Ultimately, sharing the religious tradition of the majority population facilitated their cultural and structural assimilation into American society, with many today living in communities indistinguishable from other middle and upper class white neighborhoods. Their religious practices did not greatly distinguish them from mainstream Christianity, and intermarriage with other Christian ethnic groups became common, especially for Arab men (Samhan 2001). Simultaneously, encounters with U.S. immigration policies helped solidify their position as members of the white majority population—to avoid exclusionary Asian laws, they traced their Syrian ancestries to their Arab heritage, which gave them Caucasian racial status and eventually led to their being classified with European whites on the U.S. census, a practice that continues today (Samhan 1999).

The historical context was markedly different for the second wave. In the three decades following World War II, roughly 500,000 Arabs came to the United States from twenty-two countries in North Africa and Southwest Asia. Although Christians continued to migrate, most of the arrivals were educated Muslims escaping political turmoil in the Middle East, such as the 1967 and 1973 Arab-Israeli wars. Others came as students to American universities and extended their stay permanently, often unable to return to their countries of origin for fear of political persecution (Suleiman 1994). These newer immigrants were more ethnically conscious and had stronger attachments to their nations of origin, arriving in the United States during an era of pan-Arab nationalism unknown to earlier immigrants (Suleiman and Abu-Laban 1989).

The process of assimilation was more complex for Muslim immigrants than for their Christian predecessors (Bilge and Aswad 1996). On the one hand, their educational achievements encouraged integration into the American middle class. On the other, their status as a religious minority militated against easy acculturation. Their religious traditions and practices visibly set them apart, and many chose to settle in ethnic communities for social and psychological support. United States foreign policies in the Middle East and American attitudes toward Islam left many Muslim immigrants feeling alienated in their new homeland (Suleiman 1999).

Although such diverse immigration patterns would seem to work against the development of a cohesive ethnic community, there is evidence of increased ethnic solidarity among Arab Americans in times of heightened conflict and tension. In the aftermath of the 1967 Arab-Israeli war, for example, strong American support of Israel helped forge Arab American unity (Haddad 1991b). For the first time, Christian and Muslim Arab Americans consciously chose to assert their common ethnicity by creating national organizations such as the National Association of Arab Americans to act as a political lobby and advance common Arab American interests, and the American Arab Anti-Discrimination Committee to combat negative images of Arabs and Muslims in the mass media (Majaj 1999).

Although host hostility has generally increased group solidarity, it has periodically sharpened religious and ethnic boundaries among Arab Americans. Negative stereotypes of Muslims and Arabs have encouraged Christians to dissociate from their ethnic heritage to avoid prejudice and discrimination. Similarly, the establishment of separate Muslim organizations in the United States has offered Muslim Arabs alternative methods for expressing collective grievances. Nonetheless, Christian and Muslim Arabs continue to demonstrate ethnic cohesion. For example, a nationwide poll of Arab Americans in 2004 found that the overwhelming majority of Christians and Muslims, more than

110

90 percent of each group, said that their ethnic heritage was important in defining them as individuals (Zogby 2004). Similarly, membership in national Arab American organizations remains high for Muslims and Christians of multiple generations.

Less is known, however, about identity processes among Christian and Muslim Arab Americans in the aftermath of September 11, 2001. The fact that the tragic events happened in the United States, rather than in a removed region in the Middle East, has propelled anti-Arab sentiment to unprecedented heights and turned the spotlight from Arabs abroad to Arabs in America. Thus the question remains, "What does it mean to be an Arab in America today, and to what extent does this differ for Muslim and Christian Arab Americans?"

OBJECTIVES

To more fully unpack these questions, I focus on several objectives. First, what effect did September 11 have on the religious and ethnic identities of Muslim and Christian Arab Americans? Did it strengthen identification with other Arabs, other Americans, other Muslims, other Christians, or with a combination of these groups? Some evidence in the race and ethnicity literature points to increased solidarity in times of conflict and tension, whereas other studies find that religious and national diversity diminishes group cohesion (for a review, see Bozorgmehr 2000). For Arab Americans, host hostility has typically led to increased ethnic solidarity, at least in terms of political organization. But to what extent do we see similar patterns emerging in the aftermath of September 11? To what extent are religion and ethnicity competing or compatible identities? For example, does Arab identity subsume religious identity, or is it a distinct association that undermines ethnic solidarity?

Second, to what extent do ethnic options vary for Muslims and Christians? Mary Waters argues that stereotypes about ethnic groups affect whether people identify with that group; people choose ethnicities when the benefits outweigh the costs. These choices, however, are made within societal constraints—white ethnic groups have more ethnic options than their racialized counterparts, who are assigned identities based on physical attributes (Waters 1990). As newer immigrants from diverse, more phenotypically distinct regions in the Middle East, Muslims may have fewer ethnic options than their Christian peers, many of whom are second- and third-generation descendants of émigrés from the Levant region of the Middle East and are physically indistinguishable from white Americans.

A third objective is to examine the role of religious institutions in maintaining identity and well-being among Arab Americans. Ethnic religious institutions are among the most stable of cultural forms and are known to have a profound impact on group identity (Ebaugh and Chafetz 2000). Accordingly, to what extent do the church and mosque sharpen ethnic and religious boundaries? Does church membership, for example, strengthen identification with other Arabs, or does it facilitate assimilation into American society? Does belonging to a mosque promote a pan-ethnic solidarity with other Muslims? In addition, to what degree have the church and mosque mediated the effects of September 11th on Arab American well being? For example, have they participated in community-sponsored events aimed at educating the general public on Arabs and Muslims? To what extent have they provided psychological and economic support to victims of hate crimes and racial profiling?

DATA AND METHODS

The data for this study derives from ethnographies of two Arab communities in Houston, Texas, in the year following September 11, 2001. The first is an Arab mosque, and the second is an Arab church. The Arab American population in Houston provides an excellent opportunity to examine the research questions previously outlined. Houston is one of the largest immigrant ports of entry in the United States and home to the largest Arab community in the South, ranking ninth among Arab communities nationwide. In the ten years spanning 1990 and 2000, the Arab American population grew by 13 percent, from 14,000 to 19,000 (U.S. Bureau of the Census 2000). However, many scholars and community leaders estimate that the population is much larger, perhaps 54,000 (Samhan 1999; Zogby 1990). The reasons most often cited for the underestimation include: limited collection of ancestry data (that is, only on the long form of the census sent to one in six households); placement of the ancestry question (item 10 on the long form); wording of the ancestry question (confusing terminology and examples); exclusion of groups considered by some to be Arab (for example, Sudanese); and low response rate due to general community distrust toward governmental data collection.

Regardless of size, the composition of the Arab population in Houston is very heterogeneous, made up of Muslims and Christians, immigrants and older generations, affluent professionals and working class laborers.[1] As Mae Ghalwash reported in the *Houston Chronicle* late in 2002, there are more than forty churches and mosques and hundreds of Arab-owned businesses, many of which were targeted for vandalism after the terrorist attacks ("Strangers in their Own Country," December 16, A1). Currently, there is a dearth of research on this community, both in literature on Arab Americans and in mainstream scholarship on immigration, ethnicity, and religion. For example, the Pew Charitable Trusts identified Houston as a gateway city for new immigrants, and funding from their initiative resulted in an insightful comparison of thirteen immigrant religious congregations in the Houston Metropolitan area (Ebaugh and Chafetz 2000). However, the study examined only one Muslim congregation, and it was predominantly non-Arab (85 percent Pakistani and Indian). Moreover, because the study was interested in the experiences of newer immigrants, it did not examine the more established Arab Christian population.

The two congregations for this project were selected based on their similar ethnic compositions (predominantly Arab), sizable memberships (300 or more active families), and demographic makeup (variations in social class, national origin, and generational status). The Arab churches in Houston are primarily Coptic, which is Greek for Egyptian, or Antiochian, an ancient Roman city in Greater Syria. Because membership at the Coptic churches is almost exclusively Egyptian, I focused on an Antiochian church that was more nationally diverse, comprising members from Syria, Lebanon, Palestine, and Jordan (previously part of Greater Syria).

The Muslim community in Houston is estimated at 60,000 and consists mainly of non-Arab ethnic groups, such as Pakistanis, Indians, African Americans, and white converts. Arab Muslims make up about 25 percent of this community. There are approximately thirty mosques in Houston, the majority connected to the Islamic Society of Greater Houston (ISGH), which was founded in 1968 to service the growing number of Muslim immigrants in the Houston area. They developed the first U.S. zonal mosque system to provide convenient access to mosques throughout the city for the required five daily prayers. Currently, there are six zones, each containing one or more mosques. Although ISGH does not officially acknowledge ethnic divisions within the organization, it is well known that most Arab Muslims attend different mosques than Pakistani and Indian Muslims do. Cultural differences, such as language and food, along with differences in religious practices contribute to these patterns. The mosque for this study was comprised predominantly of Arab congregants.

The ethnographies involved nine months of participant observation and in-depth interviews with religious leaders and congregants in the two religious communities. The in-depth interview schedule covered a variety of topics, concentrating specifically on the effects of September 11 on Arab American identity and well being. The questionnaire included several measures on ethnic and religious identity, economic welfare, physical and mental health, experiences of discrimination, along with standard demographic measures. The interviews consisted of open-ended and closed questions and took approximately one hour to complete.

The sample size for the in-depth interviews is thirty-eight adults, ten men and nine women from each community. For various reasons, such as scheduling conflicts, we were unable to interview an additional woman at each location. This number is a feasible size for data collection and analysis and large enough for variability on important measures, such as generational status, national origin, educational attainment, occupation, gender, and age. The sampling strategy was purposive to obtain representation on each of the aforementioned characteristics. Because there are non-Arab members in both religious communities, I screened interview participants with a standard question on Arab ancestry. A trained interviewer of female descent conducted interviews with female participants, and a male interviewer with similar qualifications interviewed male respondents. I interviewed church and mosque leaders and conducted participant observation in each of the religious communities over the course of the project. This included attending religious services, social events, and holiday celebrations.

I also administered a survey questionnaire to a sample of congregants at each location (n = 155 at the church and n = 180 at the mosque). The instrument consisted of sixty-five closed and open-ended questions that concentrated on the effects of September 11 on Arab American identity and well being, similar to the in-depth interview schedule. The questionnaire included several measures of ethnic identity, religious identity, and experiences of discrimination before and after 2001, along with standard demographic measures, such as age, gender, and social class. The surveys were pre-tested on several groups of men and women at the church and mosque, and changes were made to the questions based on their feedback. The final survey was administered after prayer services at each location and took approximately twenty minutes to complete.

ACCESSING ARAB AMERICAN COMMUNITIES
IN THE POST-9/11 ERA

One of the most difficult tasks of this study was approaching the communities a year following September 11, 2001, and asking them to allow me to conduct a study on Arab American identity and well being. I began by arranging individual meetings with the leaders of the church and mosque to introduce them to the research project. It quickly became clear that I could not introduce the project as a comparative study of Muslims and Christians due to heightened suspicion within the communities. Christian Arab Americans wanted to distance themselves from anything they felt linked them with the actions of radical Muslims, and Muslim Arab Americans wanted to have their experiences acknowledged in their own right. Interestingly, both groups felt that the term *Arab* was particularly prone to discrimination because the American public viewed it as synonymous with Islamic extremism. The leaders in each community correctly noted that the American media had at least attempted to dispel myths about Islam after September 11, but that little attention had been paid to separating Arab ethnicity from Islamic religion.

Thus, I described the project as an examination of ethnic and religious identity in the specific communities, rather than as a comparative study. For example, I first met with the priest and introduced the project as an examination of religious and ethnic identity among Christian Arab Americans. Had I described it as a comparative project with Muslims, the church would never have agreed to participate. The same is true for the mosque. The priest was very receptive to the project and invited me to present it to the parish council for a formal vote. Members of the parish council were eager to help in any way possible. They felt that Christian Arabs had long been overlooked in American society and were pleased that I was interested in examining their experiences. One or two members were somewhat skeptical because they did not like the term *Christian Arabs*. They preferred to be called *Christians of Arab descent* or *Americans of Arab descent*. I expected this response, given that one of my hypotheses is that Christian Arabs will be more assimilated into American society than Muslim Arabs. I reassured them that one of the project's aims was to examine variations in ethnic identity, thus they would have the opportunity to express their individual identities during the course of the project. At the end of the meeting, the parish council enthusiastically agreed to the project.

My initial reception at the mosque was equally positive. The leadership structure at the mosque was slightly different than the church and was run by administrators rather than the imam (equivalent to the priest). The imam was responsible for leading religious services but had little or no authority over bureaucratic matters within the mosque. Three professional businessmen ran the mosque, and all shared my national heritage (Libyan), which made introducing the project much easier. I met with two of the three administrators, who readily approved the research. I spoke with the absent member several times by telephone, but he was not interested in getting involved in the project and said that he supported his two colleagues' decision to approve the research. As I was to learn in the ensuing months, the one absent member has the final authority in the mosque, which eventually proved challenging for the research.

COMPARATIVE PERSPECTIVE

Before examining the in-depth interviews, it is useful to compare the basic sociodemographic characteristics of the Muslim and Christian respondents. Table 5.1 provides detailed information on the thirty-eight interviewees' characteristics, and table 5.2 describes the profiles of the Muslim (n = 180) and Christian (n = 155) survey respondents at the two congregations. As seen in table 5.1, the women we interviewed range in age from twenty-one to sixty-one and the men range from twenty-one to fifty-nine. All but nine of the thirty-eight interviewees are married, and most have children in the home. We avoided interviewing anyone under the age of twenty-one because it is difficult to assess identity processes during this phase of the life cycle, a time when identity is fairly malleable.

As seen in both tables 5.1 and 5.2, Muslim respondents are much more likely than Christians to be first-generation immigrants, which follows known patterns of immigration from the Middle East. Most (82.8 percent) of Muslim

Table 5.1   Interview Characteristics of Respondents (n = 38)

	Generation	Education	Age	Marriage	Employment	Children
Muslim women						
Amina	2	BA	21	Single	—	—
Mona	2	BS	22	Single	X	—
Fozia	1	BS	23	Married	—	X
Maha	2	BA	26	Married	—	—
Amna	1	BS	27	Single	X	—
Rabia	1	HS	32	Married	—	X
Najat	1	MD	34	Married	—	X
Hala	2	BS	34	Married	—	X
Najwa	1	MA	47	Married	X	—
Christian women						
Hannan	1	HS	23	Married	—	X
Layla	2	HS	24	Single	X	—
Jenna	4	BA	26	Married	—	X
Laura	1	HS	38	Married	—	X
Samia	1	HS	43	Married	—	X
Carolyn	2	MA	47	Married	X	—
Suzanne	1	HS	49	Married	—	X
Helen	1	HS	51	Single	—	X
Camilla	3	HS	61	Married	X	—
Muslim men						
Marwan	1	BS	21	Single	—	—
Mahmoud	1	BS	22	Married	X	—
Saad	1	BS	35	Single	X	—
Abdullah	1	HS	36	Married	X	X
Amir	1	BS	36	Married	X	X
Ammar	1	MA	45	Married	X	X
Ramsey	1	PhD	48	Married	X	X
Mack	1	MA	48	Married	X	X
Ali	1	BA	52	Married	X	X
Mustafa	1	PhD	59	Married	X	X
Christian men						
Aden	2	BA/LAW	31	Married	X	—
Sami	2	MA	33	Single	X	—
George	3	MA	34	Married	X	—
Randall	1	HS	35	Married	X	X
Steven	1	BS	35	Single	X	—
Camille	3	MA	36	Married	X	X

Table 5.1   Interview Characteristics of Respondents (n = 38) (*Continued*)

	Generation	Education	Age	Marriage	Employment	Children
Robert	1	MS	37	Married	X	X
Salem	2	MA	41	Married	X	X
Jim	1	HS	47	Married	X	X
John	1	PhD	56	Married	X	X

Source: Author's compilation.

survey respondents are foreign-born, versus 45.8 percent of Christians. Among the interview respondents, all of the Muslim men and most of the Muslim women are immigrants, though many have lived in the United States their entire adult lives. Despite our efforts, we were unable to include second-generation Muslim men in the interview sample because most of the second-generation men who attend the mosque are under eighteen. We were more successful in obtaining diversity in generational status among the Christian interview respondents, in part because the community has a longer history in Houston and is more diverse by nativity.

Reflecting their longer residency in the United States, Christians are more likely than Muslims to subjectively identify as either American (17.6 percent to 3.4 percent) or hyphenated American (listed in the Other category). These results parallel those of the Detroit Arab American Study, where Christians were less likely than Muslims to accept the Arab American label. Muslims, on the other hand, are more likely to identify themselves as Arab (59.0 percent) or Asian (28.7 percent), though it is worth noting that roughly an equal number of Christians consider themselves Arab (56.8 percent). Not surprisingly, Muslims have stronger ties to their ethnic identity, as evidenced by their greater frequency of cooking ethnic meals and contact with friends and family in the Middle East. These results indicate that Christians are more assimilated than their Muslim counterparts, both in terms of attitudes and behaviors.

In a telling question on perceived racial category, 30 percent of Christian respondents report that other people consider them white, compared to only 5.2 percent of Muslims. Specifically, the survey question asked, "What group do you think other people think you belong to?" The response categories derived from the pretests included: whites, blacks, Asians, Hispanics, Arabs, don't know, and Other. An additional one-fifth of Christians report that they are unsure of their racial categorization, which may indicate that race is less salient than other aspects of their identity, or at minimum, that race is not a defining characteristic of their everyday experiences. Muslims, on the other hand, are much more

Table 5.2   Survey Characteristics of Muslim and Christian Respondents
(n = 335)

	Christian (n = 155)	Muslim (n = 180)
Background		
Nativity		
Foreign-born	45.8%	82.8%**
U.S.-born	54.2	17.2
Duration of U.S. residence		
Less than five years	3.3	12.7**
Five to fourteen years	26.3	41.8
Fifteen or more years	70.5	45.5
Education		
Less than high school	2.6	6.9
High school graduate	8.5	3.4
Some college	23.5	17.8
College and higher	65.4	71.3
Not applicable	0.0	0.6
Father's education		
Less than high school	39.7	26.0**
High school graduate	23.2	14.5
Some college	9.3	12.1
College and higher	24.5	45.6
Not applicable	3.3	1.7
Mother's education		
Less than high school	38.2	36.5*
High school graduate	35.5	24.1
Some college	12.5	13.5
College and higher	10.5	23.6
Not applicable	3.3	2.4
Family income		
Less than $39,999	17.7	22.8*
$40,000 to $79,999	28.2	37.8
$80,000 or higher	43.0	30.0
Not applicable or did not work	11.3	9.6
Married	70.6	67.6*
Mean age	47.1	37.3**

Table 5.2   Survey Characteristics of Muslim and Christian Respondents (n = 335) (*Continued*)

	Christian (n = 155)	Muslim (n = 180)
Religious identity		
Religious background		
Christian	96.1	3.9**
Muslim	0.0	94.4
Other	3.3	1.1
None	0.7	0.6
Religiosity		
Not very religious	3.3	4.5
Somewhat religious	38.8	50.0
Very religious	57.9	45.5
Family religiosity during youth		
Not very religious	13.0	17.9**
Somewhat religious	39.0	52.2
Very religious	48.1	29.8
Attend Sunday or Friday services		
Never	3.3	5.1**
One to three times a month	48.0	27.6
Every week	48.7	67.4
Attend other religious activities		
Never	31.2	14.2**
One to three times a month	53.2	47.7
More than once a week	15.6	38.1
Ethnic identity		
Ethnicity		
American	17.6	3.4**
Arab	56.8	59.0
Asian	1.4	28.7
African American	0.7	2.8
Hispanic	0.0	1.1
Slavic or Romanian	7.4	0.0
Ethiopian or Eritrean	0.7	0.0
Other	15.5	5.1

(continued)

Table 5.2   Survey Characteristics of Muslim and Christian Respondents
(n = 335) (*Continued*)

	Christian (n = 155)	Muslim (n = 180)
Perceived racial category		
White	33.8	5.2**
Arab	25.2	54.3
Asian	0.7	13.3
Hispanic	17.9	16.8
Black	1.3	2.9
Don't know	21.2	7.5
Ethnic friends		
None	12.3	5.0*
One or two	25.3	17.9
Three or more	62.3	77.1
Ethnic meals per week		
None	16.1	5.1**
One or two	29.5	18.0
Three or more	54.3	77.0
Ethnic neighbors		
None	41.8	36.3**
Some of them	32.0	48.6
Most of them	7.2	7.3
All of them	0.0	1.1
Unsure or not applicable	19.0	6.7
Contact with Middle East		
Never	32.9	5.6**
A few times a year	28.3	36.9
More than once a month	25.0	53.1
Not applicable	13.8	4.5
Ethnic versus religious identity		
Ethnicity more important	9.3	8.8
Religion more important	34.0	43.9
Both equally important	52.0	44.4
Neither	4.0	2.3
Don't know	0.7	0.6

Table 5.2   Survey Characteristics of Muslim and Christian Respondents (n = 335) (*Continued*)

	Christian (n = 155)	Muslim (n = 180)
Discrimination		
Discrimination before 9/11		
Never	55.9	31.8**
Rarely	28.9	51.4
Fairly often	3.9	10.6
Very often	3.3	2.8
Don't know	7.9	3.4
Discrimination after 9/11		
Never	52.7	18.6**
Rarely	31.3	38.4
Fairly often	8.0	26.0
Very often	4.0	11.9
Don't know	4.0	5.1
Ethnic discrimination		
Yes	31.6	58.9
No	68.4	41.1
Religious discrimination		
Yes	2.6	58.9**
No	97.4	41.1
Discrimination of family or friends		
Never	39.5	11.4**
Rarely	27.9	38.1
Fairly often	10.9	33.0
Very often	3.4	8.5
Don't know	18.4	9.1

Source: Author's compilation.
*p = < .05; **p = < .01

likely to report that others perceive them as Arab (54.3 percent), Hispanic (16.8 percent), or Asian (13.3 percent), with only a small fraction (5.2 percent) feeling that they pass as white Americans.

Corresponding to these differences in ethnic and racial identification, Muslims are also more likely than Christians to have experienced discrimination before 9/11 (13.4 percent to only 7.2 percent), though a sizable number of Muslims report having rarely or never experienced it (83.2 percent). This is in marked contrast to after September 11, where the number of Muslims who experienced discrimination doubled and tripled respectively for the categories fairly often (26.0 percent) and very often (11.9 percent). Christians only experienced a slight increase in discrimination after 9/11, and the vast majority (84.0 percent) still report rarely or never experiencing discrimination. An equal number of Muslims feel that the discrimination is on the basis of their ethnicity and religion, in part because they feel that Americans confuse the terms Arab and Muslim.

Also striking in tables 5.1 and 5.2 is the high level of educational attainment among the respondents, especially among Muslim men and women. Nearly three-fourths (71.3 percent) of Muslim and two-thirds (65.4 percent) of Christian survey respondents have a college degree or higher, and all but two of the Muslim interviewees had a bachelor's degree or higher. Although the Christian respondents are well educated compared to the average American, they are less so compared to the Muslim respondents and are more likely to come from lower social class backgrounds than Muslims, evidenced by educational attainments of their mothers and fathers. The overall higher attainment of these two communities relative to other Arab American communities (for example, Dearborn, Chicago) reflects differences in migration histories of Arabs to different geographic locales throughout the country. Arab émigrés to Houston have been drawn by the oil industry and tended to come from middle to upper class backgrounds.

INTERSECTING AND DIVERGING IDENTITIES

One central objective in this chapter is to examine identity processes among Muslims and Christians in the post-September 11 era. The in-depth interviews and ethnographic field notes are particularly useful in this regard because they provide insight into the complex negotiation of multiple, competing identities among Arab Americans. They also reveal several interesting points of convergence and divergence between Muslim and Christian Arab Americans. First, the interviews find that both Muslims and Christians identify strongly with multiple cultural identities, including religion, ethnicity, and national origin. Both groups also share a strong sense of American identity and credit their ability to enjoy these overlapping identities to being American. When asked what being American meant to them and to what extent they felt American, nearly all of the interviewees, Muslim and Christian, reported feeling very American because they have freedoms that they did not or would not have in their countries of origin. As a thirty-four-year-old second-generation Muslim woman put it, "I'd rather disagree with a country's politics [U.S.] and be free than live in a Muslim, Arab country and have no rights." A twenty-four-year-old Christian immigrant man from Palestine agrees, "America means that I have individual rights and free choice."

Universal attachment to American identity is one of the more surprising findings from this study. Regardless of religious affiliation, generational status, gender, social class, or age, nearly all of the interviewees responded that they felt very American because they had freedom—freedom to practice religion, freedom to engage in politics, freedom of speech. As one twenty-six-year-old, first-generation Muslim woman said, "I've always seen myself as American and post-September 11 has strengthened that feeling." Another says, "Being American means I can wear the hijab and stay in school—I have freedom and choices." Christian Arab Americans voiced similar sentiments. For example, a first-generation thirty-one-year-old woman said, "Being American gives me rights and freedom . . . like the right to work."

These strong attachments to American identity coexist with equally strong ties to ethnic and religious identities. One forty-year-old Christian woman said succinctly, "because I'm an American, I can state my Arab ethnic identity even more forcefully. Multiculturalism is embraced in the U.S." Even Muslim women who wear the veil feel that their American identities are compatible with their Arab identities, contrary to widespread belief that Islam is incompatible with Western values. One second-generation Muslim woman started wearing the veil after September 11 to show that there are "good Muslims, too." She attributed her ability to make this decision to the fact that she was American.

At the same time, both Christians and Muslims emphasize their religious identities more forcefully than their ethnic ones because they feel that the word *Arab* has become pejorative since September 11. When asked how they would respond if a neighbor asked about their ethnic heritage, both Christians and Muslims responded with a variety of labels that infused religion into their ethnic backgrounds: Palestinian Muslim, Orthodox Arab American, Lebanese Christian, Muslim of Arab descent, and so on. Further, many of the Christian respondents expressed their desire for the American public to understand that not all Arabs are Muslim. As one Christian woman observed, "Where does everyone think Jesus came from anyway? It was the Middle East. But now the Middle East is synonymous with Muslim and Arab."

Beyond attachment to multiple cultural identities, Muslim and Christian Arab Americans have little in common since September 11. The terrorist attacks and ensuing war in Iraq have resulted in Muslims experiencing more difficulties than Christians in negotiating multiple identities, and many feel that the ongoing conflict between their American, Arab, and Muslim identities will jeopardize their futures in American society. When asked if there had ever been a time in their lives when being Arab was in conflict with being American, many Muslims commented that they were living through such an era. For example, a thirty-eight-year-old Muslim immigrant man said, "I see myself as an American, as an Arab, and as a Muslim. I need to support the troops but they're killing Arabs and Muslims." A forty-seven-year-old second-generation Muslim woman said much the same thing, "Being American means being free. I'm an American, but since September 11, I've lost my freedom . . . I hide who I am in public, which isn't free at all."

In contrast, Christian respondents reported feeling generally less affected by the events of September 11. For example, a forty-nine-year-old Christian immigrant woman from Syria said, "I'm an Arab American but I don't feel like 9/11 has anything to do with me because I'm not involved." She went on to explain, "My identity hasn't really changed since 9/11 because I'm an American and a Christian, and I had nothing to do with it." A thirty-nine-year old second-generation Christian man explained it this way, "I'm proud of my Arab heritage and am actually more forceful about being of Arab descent since 9/11. You know, it's really terrible what happened, but I'm not responsible."

These individual-level responses are situated within institutional contexts that shape and reflect real differences in how Muslims and Christians experience American society. The racial and religious hierarchies in the United States provide more wiggle room for Christian Arabs to distance themselves from the events of September 11 by allowing them to use their religious and racial identities (Christian and white) as a bridge to the American mainstream. Muslims, on the other hand, are finding that their Islamic identity and physical appearance (darker phenotype) are increasingly serving as a barrier to their social and political integration. Their economic mobility has been less affected, in part because high levels of educational achievement among the Muslims in this study have largely buffered them from the economic sanctions Muslims in other parts of the country experienced. The institutional characteristics of the mosque and church reinforce these general differences. The mosque is architecturally distinct from mainstream places of worship, and in the days following September 11, the mosque administrators were forced to hire security to ensure the safety of its congregants from protestors. The church, by contrast, is indistinguishable from other American churches and went largely unnoticed in the aftermath of September 11. The church officials refused interviews with local media because they did not want attention brought to the church, and when some of the congregants suggested hiring security, the church's response was, "Hiring security will only give the appearance that we have done something wrong, and we have not. We have nothing to do with terrorists."

CONCLUSION

Based on the evidence presented here, it appears that the events of September 11, 2001, created a cultural wedge that factionalized the Arab American community along religious lines, with important political implications. Christian Arab Americans are able to emphasize cultural aspects of their Arab identity (for example, celebrating Arabic holidays) and play down political aspects (for example, being active in Middle Eastern politics) to distance themselves from the events of September 11 and demonstrate that they are neither terrorists nor terrorist sympathizers (that is, boundary work). In other words, they can disassociate from aspects of their heritage that are seen as threatening to American society, thereby maintaining their secure statuses within the mainstream.

Muslim Arab Americans, on the other hand, are newer immigrants with stronger cultural and political ties to their homelands and, as such, are unable to maintain such boundaries given their religious, ethnic, and racial out-group status. Despite having strong attachments to American identity, Muslim Americans are at risk of further disenfranchisement from mainstream society in view of the ongoing war in Iraq, the turmoil in the Middle East, and the global fight against terrorism. The implications are particularly dire for second-generation children of Muslim immigrants, whose incorporation and well being in American society may depend more on their Muslim heritage than on their rights as American-born citizens.

NOTES

1. Estimated population compiled by the Arab American Institute Foundation in Washington, D.C., in conjunction with Zogby International in Utica, New York.

REFERENCES

Bankston, Carl L. and Min Zhou. 1996. "The Ethnic Church, Ethnic Identification, and the Social Adjustment of Vietnamese Adolescents." *Review of Religious Research* 38(1): 18–37.

Bilge, Barbara, and Barbara C. Aswad. 1996. "Introduction." In *Family and Gender Among American Muslims: Issues Facing Middle Eastern Immigrants and their Descendants,* edited by Barbara Aswad and Barbara Bilge. Philadelphia, Pa.: Temple University Press.

Bozorgmehr, Mehdi. 2000. "Does Host Hostility Create Ethnic Solidarity? The Experience of Iranians in the United States." *Bulletin of the Royal Institute for Inter-Faith Studies* 2(1): 159–78.

Bozorgmehr, Mehdi, Claudia Der-Martirosian, and Georges Sabagh. 1996. "Middle Easterners: A New Kind of Immigrant." In *Ethnic Los Angeles,* edited by Roger Waldinger and Mehdi Bozorgmehr. New York: Russell Sage Foundation.

Chong, Kelly H. 1998. "What it Means to be Christian: The Role of Religion in the Construction of Ethnic Identity and Boundary Among Second-Generation Korean Americans." *Sociology of Religion* 59(3): 259–86.

Ebaugh, Helen Rose, and Janet Saltman Chafetz. 1999. "Agents for Cultural Reproduction and Structural Change: The Ironic Role of Women in Immigrant Religious Institutions." *Social Forces* 78(2): 585–612.

————. 2000. *Religion and the New Immigrants: Continuities and Adaptations in Immigrant Congregations.* New York: Altamira Press.

Foner, Nancy, Rubén G. Rumbaut, and Steven J. Gold, editors. 2000. *Immigration Research For a New Century: Multidisciplinary Perspectives.* New York: Russell Sage Foundation.

Haddad, Yvonne Y. 1991a. "Introduction." In *The Muslims of America,* edited by Yvonne Y. Haddad. New York: Oxford University Press.

————. 1991b. "American Foreign Policy in the Middle East and Its Impact on the Identity of Arab Muslims in the United States." In *The Muslims of America,* edited by Yvonne Y. Haddad. New York: Oxford University Press.

Haddad, Yvonne Y., and Adair T. Lummis. 1987. *Islamic Values in the United States: A Comparative Study.* New York: Oxford University Press.

Hitti, Philip K. 1924. *The Syrians in America.* New York: George H. Doran.

Hooglund, Eric J., editor. 1994. *Crossing the Waters: Arabic-Speaking Immigrants to the United States Before 1940.* Washington: Smithsonian Institute Press.

Kayal, Philip M., and Joseph M. Kayal. 1975. *The Syrian-Lebanese in America: A Study in Religion and Assimilation.* Boston, Mass.: Twayne Publishers.

Majaj, Lisa Suhair. 1999. "Arab-American Ethnicity: Location, Coalitions, and Cultural Negotiations." In *Arabs in America: Building a New Future,* edited by Michael W. Suleiman. Philadelphia, Pa.: Temple University Press.

Naff, Alixa. 1994. "The Early Arab Immigrant Experience." In *The Development of Arab-American Identity,* edited by Ernest McCarus. Ann Arbor, Mich.: The University of Michigan Press.

Portes, Alejandro, and Rubén Rumbaut. 1996. *Immigrant America: A Portrait,* 2nd ed. Berkeley, Calif.: University of California Press.

Samhan, Helen Hatab. 1999. "Not Quite White: Race Classification and the Arab-American Experience." In *Arabs in America: Building a New Future,* edited by Michael W. Suleiman. Philadelphia, Pa.: Temple University Press.

————. 2001. "Arab Americans." Grolier Multimedia Encyclopedia. Accessed at http://www.grolier.com/gi/products/reference/gmeol/docs/gmeol.html.

Shakir, Evelyn. 1997. *Bint Arab: Arab and Arab American Women in the United States.* Westport, Conn.: Praeger.

Suleiman, Michael W. 1994. "Arab-Americans and the Political Process." In *The Development of Arab-American Identity,* edited by Ernest McCarus. Ann Arbor, Mich.: University of Michigan.

————. 1999. "Introduction: The Arab Immigrant Experience." In *Arabs in America: Building a New Future,* edited by Michael Suleiman. Philadelphia, Pa.: Temple University Press.

Suleiman, Michael W., and Baha Abu-Laban. 1989. "Introduction." In *Arab Americans: Continuity and Change,* edited by Baha Abu-Laban and Michael W. Suleiman. Belmont, Mass.: Association of Arab-American University Graduates.

U.S. Bureau of the Census. 2000. "Census of Population and Housing." Public Use Microdata Samples. Washington: U.S. Department of Commerce.

Warner, R. Stephen, and Judith G. Wittner, editors. 1998. *Gatherings in Diaspora: Religious Communities and the New Immigration*. Philadelphia, Pa.: Temple University Press.

Waters, Mary C. 1990. *Ethnic Options: Choosing Identities in America*. Berkeley, Calif.: University of California Press.

Zogby, John. 1990. *Arab America Today: A Demographic Profile of Arab Americans*. Washington: Arab American Institute.

———. 2002. *Arab American Institute/Zogby Group Poll*. Washington: Arab American Institute.

———. 2004. *Arab-American Telephone Poll*. New York: Zogby International.

CHAPTER 6

OVERSTRESSING ISLAM: BRIDGEVIEW'S MUSLIM COMMUNITY SINCE 9/11

CRAIG M. JOSEPH, MELISSA J. K. HOWE,
CHARLOTTE VAN DEN HOUT, BARNABY RIEDEL,
AND RICHARD A. SHWEDER

EVEN BEFORE 9/11, a debate had simmered for some time in the United States about the ability and willingness of Muslims to become full participants in American society and the compatibility of Islam with democracy and modernity. The debate was sometimes framed as a general philosophical and normative question about the character of our liberal and pluralistic society; it raised provocative questions about the extent to which our political and legal institutions are premised on "thick" versus "thin" notions of citizenship and can accommodate immigrant minority groups who hold divergent views of gender, religious practice, civic participation, communal in-group loyalty, authority relations, and so forth.

At a more specific and less theoretical level, however, the debate quickly, even if quietly, became a discussion about whether "there is something in Islam" that makes Muslims resistant to tolerance, respect for pluralism, and other features of contemporary liberal democracy, with an emphasis on "there is something in Islam." That stress was not just a matter of linguistic emphasis; it also revealed certain recurrent anxieties in the mainstream non-Muslim population, even among secular liberals, about the place of Muslim immigrants in American society. Undoubtedly many non-Muslim mainstream Americans have never been overly stressed by the "something in Islam" thought. Nevertheless, a range of popular anxieties, some mild, some extreme, can be identified.

In the eyes of some non-Muslim American observers, Muslims, and especially Muslim immigrants, are a potentially indigestible minority, one resistant to assimilation because of values or practices or beliefs that are incompatible with America's modern, individualistic, progressive, tolerant way of life. Others have viewed Muslims even more darkly, as a fifth column, a community that at least passively supports terrorist violence against the United States.[1] Lately, as some civil libertarians may have feared, discussion of internment has been explicit, though not so much as a concrete proposal for dealing with a current threat as a reconsideration of earlier episodes of internment.[2] Quite apart from this discussion is the constant stream of Islamophobic rhetoric, often equal parts ignorant bigotry and religious fanaticism, from some evangelical Christian leaders, such as Franklin Graham, and their followers.

This essay, and that in chapter 7, emerge from the Russell Sage Foundation project "The Qur'an and the Constitution: Islamic Adaptations in the United States" and focus on the life of Muslim youth and adults (predominantly Arab Palestinian, Syrian, Egyptian, Moroccan, and Sudanese) in Bridgeview, Illinois, a suburb of Chicago. The essays might be viewed as a call for a skeptical critique of one kind of polarizing discourse, in which exaggerated or overstressed majority group fears of so-called difference are matched against real or imagined minority group fears about mainstream bigotry, pressures toward assimilation, or a loss of a meaningful collective identity. Such debates often work to the detriment of a realistic and more moderate appraisal of the mutual accommodations, internal disagreements, and creative cultural and religious transformations that may be taking place both within and between Muslim and non-Muslim groups in a liberal, pluralistic, and somewhat decentralized, democracy such as our own. We thus approached the Russell Sage Foundation conference as an opportunity to take stock of some of the ways that developments in one particular Muslim Arab community do not readily fit in the something about Islam mold.

Our portrait of the community is partial (space considerations alone make that necessary) and provisional (we are still in data analysis mode).

Generally speaking, how are Bridgeview's Muslims doing in the aftermath of September 11? This is obviously not a question with a simple answer, and we explore some of the complexities of this community's experience. One of the striking aspects of Bridgeview is the degree to which it has been able to maintain both lively diversity of opinion and lifestyle within the community and peaceful—and sometimes collaborative—relationships with non-Muslim communities. Indeed, although it is important to maintain constant awareness of the challenges and threats the community faces on a daily basis—not least of which are ongoing government scrutiny and arrests and prosecutions of residents and instances of hostility from non-Muslims—it is fair to say, we think, that one of the dominant themes of the Bridgeview story is resilience, the failure of the 9/11 attacks to derail the community's ongoing effort to find a workable accommodation with life in the United States.

In this respect, at least, the Bridgeview community is not anomalous. A number of researchers have remarked on the surprising failure of the terrorist attacks to destroy the progress Muslims have made in integrating into American life. Diana Eck recently explained it this way:

> On the whole, we would have to say that these incidents of backlash unleashed by the terrorist attacks ultimately revealed something more complex, and more heartening, about American society. The response evoked by each ugly incident made clear that the multireligious and multicultural fabric of the U.S. was already too strong to rend by random violence. Despite new fears of "sleeper cells" of Muslim terrorists and "assimilated terrorists" lounging by the condominium pool, Americans would not condone indiscriminate violence against neighbors of any faith or culture. The Palestinian bookstore owner in Alexandria, Virginia, stunned by the shattered glass and its message of hatred, soon discovered hundreds of supportive neighbors he did not know who sent him bouquets of flowers and cards expressing their sorrow at what had happened. In Toledo, Cherrefe Kadri, the woman president of the Islamic community, reflected on the September 11 rifle fire: "That small hole in the dome created such a huge outpouring of support for our Islamic community," she said. "A Christian radio station contacted me wanting to do something. They called out on the airwaves for people to come together at our center to hold hands, to ring our mosque, to pray for our protection. We expected three hundred people and thought that would be enough to circle the mosque, but two thousand people showed up to hold hands around the mosque. I was amazed!" In Plymouth, the Iraqi pizzeria owner whose shop had been burned out was inundated with flowers, trays of brownies, and offers of financial support. In Mesa, Arizona, where one man shot and killed a Sikh, hundreds of people left flowers at the gas station where he had died, and thousands of people who had never met him or any other Sikh came to the civic center for a public memorial service. By early 2002 his family had received more than ten thousand letters and messages of condolence. Statistically, one would have to say benevolence outweighed the backlash. (2002, xv–xvi)

If resilience is one of the themes suggested by the Bridgeview experience, another is diversity. Bridgeview, like many communities—Muslim or not, is characterized by a great deal of internal diversity, on many dimensions— national origin (Palestinian, Syrian, Egyptian, Moroccan, Sudanese), political attitudes, opinions regarding Islamic belief and practice, historical experience, socioeconomic status, and so on.

Previous research has detected a growing diversity and pluralism within Muslim communities in America. Some have argued that 9/11 actually acted as a catalyst to internal diversity. Karen Leonard, for example, noted that since 9/11 there

> may be greater openness about conflicts among Muslims and perhaps a higher level of comfort with this pluralism. Despite the brave show of unity and support

for the nation by the national Muslim political organizations, there are signs that divisions among various African Americans, other converts, and immigrant Muslim groups may be widening. . . . Yet American Muslim media and organizations have become more open about divisions among Muslims and more comfortable with their own diversity and pluralism. (2003, 137)

Along the same lines, Marcia Hermansen has written that "subsequent to the terrorist attacks of September 11, 2001, the Muslim community, like the larger American society, has become increasingly polarized along ideological lines" (2003, 307).

One of the effects of September 11 and subsequent events has been to turn public attention much more intensely—and often, for Muslims themselves, much more uncomfortably—to the conflicts among Muslims over religious doctrine, social attitudes, stances toward non-Muslims and non-Muslim societies, political engagement, and other things. In 1992, the philosopher Akeel Bilgrami wrote of a "conflict *within* the hearts of moderate Muslims themselves, a conflict made the more excruciating because it is not always explicitly acknowledged by them" (Bilgrami 1992, 824). Not only that kind of conflict but also emerging varieties of opinion, belief and attitude among Muslim immigrants and their descendants have come to be seen as matters of great relevance to non-Muslim Americans.

We would not want to make too much of the idea of America's "special providence," though some points of distinction are worthy of note. One is how different the situation of Muslims in the United States seems to be from that of Muslims in other Western countries, especially Denmark, France, Germany, and the Netherlands. Compared with contemporaneous Muslim communities in European countries, for example, American Muslims are the targets of much less general hostility, are the objects of much less scrutiny by and interference from national governments, and suffer much less from poverty and alienation. This is even more remarkable when one considers the diversity of Muslim immigrant communities to the United States. Although Somali immigrants (for example) are despised by many in Italy (including intellectuals like Oriana Fallaci, who published the pathologically racist screed *The Rage and the Pride* in 2002), they are, despite a few widely publicized minor explosions of hostility or anxiety, relatively well tolerated on a day-to-day basis in unlikely host communities like Lewiston, Maine. Arabs, Pakistanis, Turks, Moroccans, Bosnians, and Ethiopians—all of these groups have largely flourished in the United States, and have continued to do so since September 11.

Without in any way minimizing the concerns of all defenders of our civil liberties or the understandable worries of multiculturalists, all this suggests that one of the most interesting questions about the post-9/11 period in the United States is why there has been so little reaction, especially on the part of ordinary citizens.

Similarly, despite the fact that the 1944 United States Supreme Court's ethnically based (some would say racist) internment precedent in *Korematsu v. United States* (323 U.S. 214) looms large in the nightmare scenarios imagined by many liberal Americans, one should probably be very cautious and circumspect about asserting historical parallels to the current situation of Muslims in the United States. Despite the understandable worry that Muslims might be rounded up like Japanese Americans in World War II, there are important differences between the national and global situations of the United States now and then. For example, the historian Gary Gerstle has noted that the oppressive treatment of Japanese citizens and immigrants during World War II and German citizens and immigrants during and after World War I was part of a more comprehensive campaign to suppress their cultures and assert a thick core American cultural identity. Such were the times after World War I that, at one point, the city of Boston prohibited playing Beethoven at Symphony Hall; the state of Oregon passed legislation to abolish all private schools and gain control of a common public school curriculum so as to assimilate immigrants to a local mainstream standard of citizenship and civic responsibility (*Pierce v. Society of Sisters,* 268 U.S. 510); and the state of Nebraska prohibited teaching all modern foreign languages to children under the age of twelve, with the aim of making sure that only English was the language of thought for American children in the state of Nebraska (*Meyer v. Nebraska,* 262 U.S. 401, 402). To speak German was to think like a German, they thought, and to think like a German or any other foreigner was to think in ways that were alien to the political culture of the United States.

Those two infamous ethno-national convulsions and attacks on so-called aliens in our midst (Germans and Japanese) occurred during a historical epoch that had, with the advent of World War I, witnessed the total collapse of the last great period, begun in 1870, of globalization, free trade, and transnational labor migrations. As the world went to war, national borders were reinforced, identities became more fixed and bounded, and outsiders were quickly distinguished from insiders and viewed as a potential threat. That early twentieth century worldwide retreat from a transnational vision, a time when the boundary corroding forces of internationalism and globalization came to an abrupt halt and went dormant, lasted a relatively long time, but it came to an end starting in the mid-1960s.

In contrast, the September 11 attacks were met, not with a mass mobilization of the populace against Islam or our Muslim neighbors (despite all too many instances of violent hate crimes, acts of discrimination and intimidation, and enduring anti-Muslim discourses), nor by a campaign of suppression on the part of the government, but, at least publicly, by swift exhortations to tolerance and solidarity and a rush to learn more about Islam and Muslims (in the form of sales of the Qur'an, enrollment in Arabic language and Islamic studies classes, and so on). This does not mean that it is impossible that we will see something like a replay of the earlier Japanese and German episodes, but it is worth thinking about why that has not happened so far, and why it did not happen even in the immediate aftermath of September 11, which provided an opportunity to those prepared to advocate such a dreadful thing.

THE IMPACTS OF 9/11

The Bridgeview, Illinois, community is perhaps one of the most visible Muslim communities in the United States. Just after the September 11 attacks, Bridgeview was one of the most common datelines for wire service and newspaper stories. The anti-Muslim demonstrations, marches, vandalism, and rhetoric, along with reactions from Muslim residents of the community, were reprinted in newspapers around the country and abroad. Local and national newspapers have written profiles of the community and of some of its members and leaders. The PBS show "Frontline" made Bridgeview the centerpiece of its segment on Muslims in the United States.

IMMEDIATE IMPACT

Bridgeview's Muslims reacted to the attacks of September 11 with a mixture of disbelief, outrage, revulsion, and fear. The fear was largely about the possibility of reprisals against Muslims, and that, of course, was quickly borne out. The earliest mentions of Bridgeview in the media coverage depicted the community's institutions—particularly the mosque and the two Islamic schools—as among the many sites being secured in the confusion triggered by the attacks. One of the first newspaper articles, in a late edition of the *Chicago Tribune* on September 11, mentioned the closure of Universal School and Aqsa School between a list of university and college closures and the evacuation of a Jewish girls' school. The next day saw a *Tribune* article with the headline "Muslims Brace for Misplaced Blame: Area Communities Pray for Victims and for Tolerance." Among the events it reported was a van festooned with American flags circling the complex in which the mosque and schools are located, and the removal by Bridgeview police of signs reading "Kill all Arab terrorists."

The succeeding days brought further pressure and intimidation on the community. On the evening of September 12, in an incident widely reported in the national media, a crowd of 300 "young people" attempting to march on the Mosque Foundation had to be turned back by more than 100 police officers.[3] The demonstration, featuring marchers chanting "USA! USA!" lasted until past midnight. One nineteen-year-old demonstrator was quoted as saying, "I'm proud to be American and I hate Arabs and I always have." Muslim residents and business owners reported many incidents of vandalism, harassment, and assault representative of those that swept the United States in the days after the attacks.

133

There were also, among the non-Muslim community and by leaders at all levels, expressions of solidarity with Muslim neighbors. Governor George Ryan, State's Attorney Richard Devine, and Chicago Mayor Richard Daley echoed President Bush in condemning acts of violence and intimidation and calling for calm. In Bridgeview, a man who had lived in the city for fifty years and was a veteran of World War II said he was disgusted with what he was seeing, saying, "the Muslims are great neighbors." Members of churches of various denominations formed human chains around area mosques, bearing signs reading "Peace" and "Unity."

Some of the scenes were startling in their juxtaposition of Muslim anxiety and non-Muslim anger. On Thursday night several Muslim youth, twenty-one-year-old Yusuf Ghori and his Arab American friends, decided to join a demonstration taking place twenty blocks from the mosque. According to the *Tribune,* the men nervously "waded into the crowd, waving their own American flags. [The] group received plenty of dirty looks. Eventually, though . . . the hostility greatly decreased. 'We defused their anger,' said Ibrahim Abusharif, forty-two, who said he had joined Ghori and other Muslims Thursday night. 'They were stunned. It did better than what the National Guard could do' " (Stephen Franklin and Don Terry, "Muslims Battle Fear, Frustration: Children Become Targets of Anti-Arab Anger," September 16, 2001, 14.).

MEDIUM-TERM IMPACT

As the immediate fears of additional terrorist attacks subsided, intelligence and law enforcement agencies shifted their efforts and sought to identify possible associates of the perpetrators and organizations that might have been involved in fundraising and other forms of assistance to terrorist networks. Bridgeview quickly became a focus of these investigations.

In late September, Nabil al-Marabh, a resident of the nearby town of Justice, was arrested on suspicion of complicity in the 9/11 attacks. A New York Times article noted that "the Chicago area in which Mr. al-Marabh was arrested has long been a hub of militant Islamic activity, revolving around an Islamic charity and several members of a mosque in Bridgeview" (Jodi Wilgoren and Judith Miller, "The Nation Challenged: The Hunt; Trail of Man Sought in 2 Plots Leads to Chicago and Arrest," September 21, 2001, accessed at http://nytimes.com). Reactions among Muslim residents ranged from "throwing the book at him" to worrying about the effect the arrest would have on the already tense relations between communities.

The investigations soon centered on two Islamic charities headquartered in Bridgeview: the Holy Land Foundation for Relief and Development, and the Global Relief Foundation. These charities had been under scrutiny even before the attacks, suspected of being conduits between American Muslims and Hamas, which Washington has named as a terrorist organization. In 1993, a Bridgeview resident named Muhammad Salah was arrested in Israel on charges of raising funds for Hamas, and spent five years in an Israeli prison before returning to Chicago. Many Bridgeview-area Muslims regard his case as a prime example of the unjust stigmatization and persecution of Muslim activists, particularly those who oppose American policy in the Arab-Israeli conflict.

The charges against Islamic charities, many of which had their U.S.-based assets frozen by the government, naturally caused consternation among members of the Muslim community, many of whom saw and used the charities as a primary means of discharging the obligation of zakat (almsgiving)—one of the five pillars of Islamic belief and practice. Such charities served to connect American Muslims not just economically but also morally and spiritually to fellow Muslims around the world, including in conflicts in places like Palestine, Chechnya, and Kashmir, and were a major component of a transnational feeling of solidarity and community among Muslims. Many Muslims, including many Bridgeview residents, were upset and angry at the closure of the charities. There were also some who were worried by the possibility that their charitable donations might have been diverted to terrorist organizations like al Qaeda and to help pay for similar violent attacks. In the years since, Muslim communities and national organizations have increasingly been working with government agencies, particularly the Treasury Department, to create ways of verifying the uses to which their donations are put by charitable organizations.

LONG-TERM IMPACT

It is not possible here to give a complete history of the Bridgeview community's response in the three to four years immediately following the 9/11 attacks. Looking at the community today, in many respects there has been a return to normalcy, at least in day-to-day life. People go to work or to school, they go to the mosque to pray and to socialize, they engage in many of the same communal activities they always have. Less visible but no less certain is the undercurrent of anxiety and resentment over the ongoing government and media surveillance of their community and of Muslims in general. Bridgeview Muslims are frustrated and in some cases humiliated by the heightened scrutiny of their actions, their travels, their associations, and their beliefs.

According to many members of the community, the media attention on Bridgeview and some of its leaders has been especially painful. In 2004, the *Chicago Tribune* published a series of lengthy articles under the umbrella title "Struggle for the Soul of Islam," at least two of which shone a partially critical light on the community. In the fall of 2003, a local newspaper, the *Daily Southtown,* reported that federal agencies were investigating the Bridgeview mosque for potential ties to terrorist organizations, which mosque leaders denied. Mosque leaders even requested a public meeting with the FBI and the United States attorney, Patrick Fitzgerald, to raise questions about the reported investigations. The federal officials agreed, citing a need for expanding the dialog between the government and the Muslim community (Chris Hack and Allison Hantschel, "U.S. Investigating Mosque Foundation," September 21, 2003, accessed at http://www.dailysouthtown.com). Despite this incremental progress, the newspaper report—which proved premature and inadequately researched—left lingering resentment among community residents and confirmed their feeling that Muslims and Islamic institutions are fair game, and that media and law enforcement treat them with a lower standard of care and cooperation than other communities.

Some members of the Bridgeview-area community have also been caught up in the government's campaign, which often uses secret evidence and other questionable tactics, against alleged security risks. One prominent case involved Sabri Samirah, a resident of Orland Park and founder of the United Muslim Americans Association. A resident of the United States since 1987, Samirah's wife was a teacher of Arabic and Islamic studies at the Universal School in Bridgeview, and the couple had three children, all American citizens. On returning to Chicago from a visit to Jordan in January of 2003, Samirah was informed by an immigration officer that his "advance parole authorization"— his permission to travel outside the United States while his permanent residency application was pending—had been summarily revoked on the ground that he had been determined to be a security risk. He was forced to return to Jordan, where he has been ever since, despite some inconclusive victories in American courts.

Samirah's case has become something of a focal point for area Muslims' frustration over their treatment by the government. Perhaps more important, it has alienated many Muslims who might otherwise be inclined to cooperate with the authorities in their investigations of terrorist groups and their sympathizers. One community leader made the point especially chillingly: "Here is a man, he said, who has done everything right: advanced degrees in economics and public policy from Chicago-area universities, a community leader, with a thoroughly American suburban family life, and yet he is in effect lured out of the country (by the promise that he would be able to return from his trip with no problems), and then shut out, leaving his family behind without a father." "What," this community member asked rhetorically, "is this man's motivation now for being loyal to the United States? Would he not be an easier target for recruitment by radical or anti-American groups? What is the logic of this kind of treatment?" (Since then, of course, the Bush administration has gone even further in the apparently arbitrary shutting of America's doors, revoking the visa of Tariq Ramadan, an internationally-respected Muslim progressive scholar, on the flimsiest of pretexts.)

Behind all this is a pervasive anxiety among community members about the long-term future of Muslims in the United States. In particular, there is a constant, low-key dread of the next attack. (This dread, one might add, is shared by most civil libertarians, who are acutely aware of the power of national and personal security concerns to override concerns about individual liberty rights and rights to equal treatment and due process before the law.) One community leader expressed his fears about the future this way:

> once you are a threat it doesn't matter how good you are, how peaceful you are, all . . . all the other side has to do is do one horrendous thing and then demonize you and then it—it—it sells. And so that's my worry now . . . I heard some of the Christian right's, you know, rhetoric, and some people described some of the meetings during this convention. And how people were, it was so . . . fervent, and people were like crying about, about the horrendousness of Islam and Muslims and how terrible they are, worse than the Nazis, worse than . . . whatever, they are God's curse on this earth, that kind of atmosphere. You have that, and then, then I feel like I don't need an Osama bin Laden to come and do bad to this country, cause you're gonna find people who are gonna say, okay, we know that the Congress has gone this far as a result of 9/11, and then a lot of things we didn't even dream of, we know now the laws are targeting those people *specifically,* they are not general laws anymore, they are targeting only the Egyptian and the Syrian and the Jordanian, and leaving every other . . . criminal on earth roaming in America, so really all we need is another thing, similar, close, whatever, and that's my worry. And I believe there's enough fanatics within Hinduism, within Is . . . within Christianity, within Judaism that will do just like what Os . . . they will justify in the same manner.

STUDENTS' REACTIONS

In the context of our research in the Bridgeview community junior and senior students at the Universal School completed a survey assessing their social, political, and religious views. The self-administered version took about two hours on average. The data reported here were collected in January 2005. The questionnaire contains 160 questions, most of which are closed-coded, asking respondents to circle answers that reflect their views most accurately. Some questions, however, are open-ended, asking respondents to write out responses in their own words. Among them are the 9/11 impact questions.

We focus here on responses to five such questions asking them to describe how the attacks affected their and others' experiences:

1. When a major historical event occurs, it is common for people to remember vividly where they were, what they were doing, what they were feeling, and so on. Do you have specific memories of this kind regarding the September 11, 2001, terrorist attacks? What were you doing when you found out about the attacks? What did you do once you found out? What

137

feelings did you have? What thoughts went through your mind? Please be as specific as possible.

2. How do you think September 11 has affected relations between Muslims and non-Muslims in the United States?

3. How do you think September 11 has affected the attitudes of Muslims in your community?

4. Overall, have your feelings about the future of Muslims in the United States changed after September 11? Do you feel more optimistic or pessimistic?

5. How has your life been specifically affected by September 11, if at all?

Space limitations prevent a more detailed question-by-question analysis. However, in the context of the general theme of this essay we wish to emphasize the following findings. Students at Universal School painted a quite mixed picture of their post-9/11 situation. It was not black and white and it was not purely negative. Especially when referring to themselves and their own experiences, there was a clear acknowledgment of both positive and negative outcomes. Some non-Muslims had treated them with contempt (and they had felt victimized) while others seemed to have reached out, curious to know more about their faith. Students were saddened and made to feel angry about discriminatory practices and unfair representations of Islam in the media but they also felt hopeful about their future in the United States and the ability of their fellow Muslims to positively represent the faith. Although non-Muslims were seen as perpetrators of violence and negativity, they were also depicted as both victims and as potential friends, suggesting that post-9/11 there were various frames of mind in the Bridgeview community. The general mood was not one of clear and certain pessimism about the future.

THE STUDENTS

Of the fifty-seven respondents, thirty-three (58 percent) were girls and twenty-four (42 percent) were boys. Students' ages ranged from fifteen to nineteen (see table 6.1). Thirty-five (61 percent) were juniors and twenty-two (39 percent) were seniors (see table 6.2).

All fifty-seven respondents answered our question about birthplace (see table 6.3). Fifty (88 percent) reported the United States; forty-three (75 percent) were born in Illinois. Only seven students (12 percent) indicated that they had immigrated to the United States after birth. Of these, two identified Kuwait as their birthplace, one Jordan, one Ramallah, Palestine, one Karachi, Pakistan, one Jerusalem, Israel, and one Basel, Switzerland. Only one reported that she was not a citizen of the United States.

138

Table 6.1   Respondent's Birth Year by Sex

Birth	Male	Female	Total (1 missing)
1986	2	2	4
	3.6%	3.6%	7.1%
1987	7	21	28
	12.5%	37.5%	50.0%
1988	13	9	22
	23.2%	16.1%	39.3%
1989	2	0	2
	3.6%	0.0%	3.6%
Total	24	32	56
	42.9%	57.1%	100.0%

Source: Authors' compilation.

To gain an impression of students' linguistic backgrounds, we asked them to state the language or languages they speak at home most often, second most often, and third most often. As table 6.3 shows, of the fifty-five students who responded, only three students (5 percent) reported speaking just one language, English. No students reported that English was never spoken at home. Most students, forty-three (78 percent), reported speaking two languages, and nine (16 percent) reported speaking three (see table 6.7). Forty-three (75 per-

Table 6.2   Respondent's Grade in School by Sex

Grade in School	Male	Female	Total
11th grade	19	16	35
	33.3%	28.1%	61.4%
12th grade	5	17	22
	8.8%	29.8%	38.6%
Total	24	33	57
	42.1%	57.9%	100.0%

Source: Authors' compilation.

Table 6.3   Respondent's Birthplace

		Frequency	Percent
Illinois	Chicago	24	42.1
	Oak Lawn	5	8.8
	Bridgeview	4	7.0
	Summit	2	3.5
	Brookfield	1	1.8
	Burbank	1	1.8
	Orland Park	1	1.8
	Skokie	1	1.8
	Bolingbrook	1	1.8
	Justice	1	1.8
	Palos Park	1	1.8
	Hickory Hills	1	1.8
Total Illinois		43	75.4
Other U.S.	Parma, OH	2	3.5
	Athens, OH	1	1.8
	Philadelphia, PA	1	1.8
	Pullman, WA	1	1.8
	Miami, FL	1	1.8
	Brookings, SD	1	1.8
	Total other states	7	12.2
Total U.S.		50	87.7
Immigrated to U.S.	Kuwait	2	3.5
	Jordan	1	1.8
	Ramallah, Palestine	1	1.8
	Karachi, Pakistan	1	1.8
	Basel, Switzerland	1	1.8
	Jerusalem, Israel	1	1.8
Total immigrated		7	12.2
Total		57	100.0

Source: Authors' compilation.

cent) reported that they speak English at home most often, eight (8 percent) reported Arabic, and five (7 percent) reported Urdu. Overall, fifty-four students (98 percent) spoke English, thirty-eight (69 percent) spoke Arabic, and twelve (22 percent) spoke Urdu. One student reported speaking Albanian, Bengali, Gujarati, German, Hebrew, Kurdish, and Punjabi as well (see tables 6.4, 6.5, and 6.6).

Table 6.4   Language Spoken Most Often at Respondent's Home

	Frequency (55 out of 57)	Percent (n = 57)	Valid Percent (n = 55)
Arabic	8	14.0	14.5
English	43	75.4	78.2
Urdu	4	7.0	7.3
Total	55	96.5	100.0

Source: Authors' compilation.

Table 6.5   Language Spoken Second Most Often at Respondent's Home

	Frequency (55 out of 57)	Percent (n = 57)	Valid Percent (n = 55)
Arabic	30	52.6	57.7
English	11	19.3	21.2
Urdu	7	12.3	13.5
Bengali	1	1.8	1.9
Albanian	1	1.8	1.9
Gujarati	1	1.8	1.9
German	1	1.8	1.9
Total	52	91.2	100.0

Source: Authors' compilation.

Table 6.6   Language Spoken Third Most Often at Respondent's Home

	Frequency (9 out of 57)	Percent (n = 57)	Valid Percent (n = 9)
Urdu	1	1.8	11.1
Spanish	5	8.8	55.6
Hebrew	1	1.8	11.1
Kurdish	1	1.8	11.1
Punjabi	1	1.8	11.1
Total	9	15.8	100.0

Source: Authors' compilation.

Table 6.7   Number of Languages Spoken at Home

Only English	Only Non-English	Two Languages	Three Languages
3	0	43	9

Source: Authors' compilation.

REFLECTIONS ON SEPTEMBER 11

Our average response rate to the five open-ended questions about 9/11 was fifty out of fifty-seven possible responses (88 percent). Four students did not answer any of these questions, and seven wrote responses to some, but not all, of the five questions. Responses ranged from single-word responses to mini-essays that took up the entire page provided.

The first question asked students to share their memories of what they experienced and how they felt on September 11, 2001. Of the five questions, this one generated the lengthiest, albeit the fewest (forty-nine), responses. Louise Cainkar's description of Bridgeview Arab Muslim experiences following 9/11 is worth noting:

Table 6.8   Number of Respondents per Language Spoken at Home

Languages	Frequency	Percent (n = 55)
English	54	98.2
Arabic	38	69.1
Urdu	12	21.8
Spanish	5	9.1
Albanian	1	1.8
Bengali	1	1.8
Gujarati	1	1.8
German	1	1.8
Hebrew	1	1.8
Kurdish	1	1.8
Punjabi	1	1.8

Source: Authors' compilation.

For three days after the attacks, the large mosque and the surrounding Arab residential community in Bridgeview—a predominantly white, working- and middle-class suburb southwest of Chicago with a large Arab residential and commercial population—were threatened by mobs of angry whites. More than 125 local police officers were called in to keep the peace (Cainkar 2004, 227).

Sharing the same parking lot with the Bridgeview mosque are two private Islamic schools, the Universal School and the Aqsa School. Such marches on the mosque would thus inevitably spill into students' educational space in the days following 9/11.

Written responses from students, most of whom attended Universal School that day, color in that outline. Most respondents reported that they arrived to the Islamic school the morning of the 9/11 attacks with little or no awareness of the first plane crash into New York's Twin Towers. Here we have recollections from two students:

Basically it was a normal regular day of school, got up took a shower and headed off to school. Not knowing what had happened. During assembly a friend came up to me and said that a plane had crashed into the world trade center, I didn't think anything big. As we headed off to our classes slowly students were being called to go home. All students including me were worried cause we didn't know what was going on until we got home. As the days passed by it started to affect me more and more cause our classroom doors were locked and we had police cars surrounding the Mosque and the school. It wasn't great at all cause all including me were scared realizing that the rest of our lives are going to change.

I was at school and the whole day I was confused and didn't know what to think. That day, for fear of security, the school sent its students home. I then watched the news and comprehended somewhat of what exactly happened. Now, I recall my grandmother praying it wasn't an Arab or Muslim because she feared other people's reactions. It was at that time that I realized how extremely harmful the situation could be for innocent Muslim American citizens like me. I was somewhat frightened but when I went to school (like a week later) I was reassured and felt safe when I saw policemen standing guard at the schools front doors!!

One after another, parents retrieved their children from school. Uncertainty about what was happening coincided with student, teacher, and parent concern for their safety. Students recall tearful and worried teachers, as well as their principal, who announced the news of the attacks during assembly and promptly dismissed students from school. Information about the first and then second crash diffused throughout the school, eliciting mixed reactions of confusion, disbelief, sadness, and fear.

Some students expressed fear for family members, friends, and other unknown victims in New York. Others recall fearing that a Muslim might have committed the atrocities and that all Muslims would receive blame as a result.

> I was in school when I heard. I was surprised and I felt sorry for all those people that had no choice but to jump outside the building. When I heard it was Arabians I knew that we were going to get criticized. I left the school that day early. When I walked out there were people screaming at us. I felt horrible and Americans think that there was only Americans in that building but there was Muslims also.

> It was first period and I was in my history class. One by one, every student was being called downstairs, and parents were picking up their kids. Our teachers came in and told us what happened and said that we all have to call home because some angry people might come and harm the students in our Muslim school. Soon enough I was called down and my dad picked me up. Our school was closed for a week because angry people from around different neighborhoods were getting ready to come into the neighborhood and may do something. My friends and family didn't leave our houses for a week because we were uncertain of what may happen to us.

Other students, like these, recall anticipating that the attacks would turn non-Muslims against Muslims. The imagined threat soon became real when a group of non-Muslims marched on the mosque, targeting verbal and physical assaults at their Muslim neighbors. A number of students recalled retreating into their homes for days in order to avoid public hostility. A bomb threat on the school precluded attendance for the rest of the week and warranted a police presence at the schools and mosque throughout the following year.

Nearly four years later, a number of students report experiencing lasting negative effects of 9/11 on their lives, while others seem to have put the event and its aftermath behind them. The four remaining questions, listed above, asked students to describe how they feel today: to comment on the impact of 9/11 on relations between Muslims and non-Muslims, on Muslim attitudes generally, on whether they feel optimistic or pessimistic about the future of Muslim Americans, and on how they think 9/11 has affected their lives specifically. We present the results to these questions first according to a schema we developed to gain a general sense of the data, and second by giving a brief qualitative overview of responses to two of the questions.

OVERVIEW OF YOUTH RESPONSES TO POST-9/11
MUSLIM LIFE IN BRIDGEVIEW

For the first quantitative analysis, students' responses to all the open-ended impact questions were broken up into separate statements, which were then coded for five characteristics:

- the subject of the phrase, either self (S), other Muslims (O), or non-Muslims (NM);

- whether the phrase referred to external actions or events (E) or internal events (I), such as feelings or beliefs;

- whether the subject was the passive recipient (PA) or active producer (A) of the actions;

- the valence of the events or actions referred to in the statement, whether positive (P), negative (N), mixed (M), or neutral (0); and

- whether the actions were described as occurring in the short (SH) or long-term (L).

A few examples will elucidate how this coding scheme worked to capture the varying responses of the subjects. One subject said, "Non-Muslims are accusing Muslims of supporting terrorism and plotting against the U.S. government." This statement was coded NMEANL: (NM) because it is about non-Muslims, (E) because it is about an external action (making an accusation), (A) because the subject was an active producer of the action, (N) because the valence of the action was negative, and (L) because the negative accusations about Muslims occur over a duration of time (L). Alternatively, one subject said, "Non-Muslims received negative images from the media about Muslims and stereotypes about Muslims." This statement was coded NMEPANL: (NM) because it is about non-Muslims (NM) being the recipients (PA) of images (E) which are bad (N) over a duration of time (L). Lastly, the statement, "Muslims are being treated unfairly by the government and the general public" was coded OEPANL because it refers to other Muslims (O) passively receiving (PA) a negative (N) external treatment (E) over a period of time (L). A statement such as, "Obviously, since 9/11 Muslims have been attacked in the media for almost everything" received the same code.

The frequency distribution of these codes, summarized in figure 6.1, creates a picture of the diversity of reactions and experience of Muslim youth post-9/11. We will examine the findings in relation to each of the subjects—self, other Muslims, and non-Muslims—respectively.

Perhaps the most noteworthy finding of this analysis is that statements reflecting the long-term internal experience of the self showed a mixed response

Figure 6.1   Quantitative Analysis of Q156–Q160

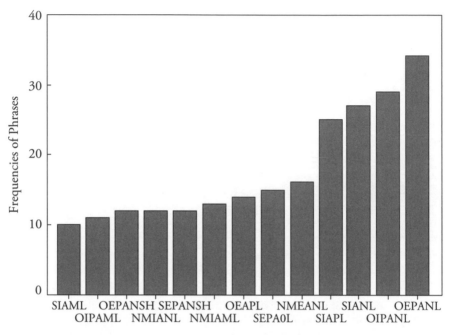

Student Responses to 9/11 Questions

SIAML: mixed thoughts or feelings over the long-term coming from self
OIPAML: mixed thoughts or feelings over the long-term received by other Muslims
OEPANSH: negative external events over the short-term received by Muslims
NMIANL: negative thoughts or feelings over the long-term coming from non-Muslims
SEPANSH: negative external events over the short-term received by self
NMIAML: mixed thoughts or feelings over the long-term coming from non-Muslims
OEAPL: positive external events over the long-term produced by other Muslims
SEPA0L: neutral external events over the long-term received by self
NMEANL: negative external events over the long-term produced by non-Muslims
SIAPL: positive thoughts or feelings over the long-term coming from self
SIANL: negative thoughts or feelings over the long-term coming from self
OIPANL: negative thoughts feelings over the long-term received by other Muslims
OEPANL: negative external events over the long-term received by other Muslims

Source: Authors' compilation.

overall. Negative internal experiences (SIANL = 7) were balanced by positive ones (SIAPL = 25), and a number of statements were explicitly mixed (SIAML = 10). When referring to external experiences of the self, experiences in the short term were decidedly negative (SEPANSH = 12), principally reflecting the post-9/11 rally held outside the school, while experiences in the long-term were cast as primarily neutral (SEPA0L = 15), occasionally negative (SEPANL = 9), and less frequently mixed (SEPAML = 4), or positive (SEPAPL = 3).

In contrast to statements about the experiences of the self, statements referring to other Muslims showed them to be the recipients of negative feelings (OIPANL = 27) and actions (OEPANL = 34). Stereotyped and prejudiced depictions by the media were coupled with discriminatory actions by the government and a general air of mistrust. Interestingly, in contrast to what they received from non-Muslims, Muslims were discussed as responding to these negative experiences with positive actions (OEAPL =1 4), for instance by taking responsibility for raising awareness about Muslims, building bridges with non-Muslims, and involving themselves in politics.

When statements referred to non-Muslims, the picture was more mixed. Emphasis was placed on their actively negative behavior (NMEANL = 16) and they were described as having either mixed (NMIAML = 13) or negative feelings (NMIANL = 12) toward Muslims. But non-Muslims were also discussed as victims, having been made to harbor negative (NMIPANL=9) or mixed (NMIPAML – 9) beliefs and feelings as a result of the media or the 9/11 attacks in particular. Also, some non-Muslims were clearly acknowledged as having expressed both favorable feelings (NMIAPL = 8) and positive actions toward Muslims (NMEAPL = 7) since 9/11.

Turning to an examination of the particular responses to two of the questions one finds a fair amount of disagreement among the students about whether 9/11 has had positive, negative, or mixed effects on relations between Muslims and non-Muslims. Of 52 students who answered the question about how September 11 affected relations between Muslims and non-Muslims, forty-nine provided responses that could be coded into better, worse, or mixed effects of 9/11 on relations between Muslims and non-Muslims in the United States. Only three (6 percent) believed that 9/11 has affected interfaith relations positively, twenty (41 percent) described interfaith relations as deteriorating since 9/11, and twenty-six (53 percent) gave mixed responses. The twenty-eight girls who responded tended to give more positive answers than the twenty-one boys. Eleven percent of the girls but none of the boys stated that Muslim relations were better since 9/11, 61 percent of the girls versus 43 percent of the boys had mixed opinions, and only 29 percent of the girls versus 57 percent of the boys thought relations have become worse (see table 6.9).

Any hint of ambiguity in a statement earned it a mixed code, for example: "Generally, as a result of the September 11 attacks, the relation between Muslims

Table 6.9   Muslim Youth on the Impact of 9/11 on
              Muslim–Non-Muslim Relations

			Male	Female	Total
Better, mixed, or worse relations	Better	Count	0	3	3
		Percent of total	0	6.1	6.1
	Mixed	Count	9	17	26
		Percent of total	18.4	34.7	53.1
	Worse	Count	12	8	20
		Percent of total	24.5	16.3	40.8
Total		Count	21	28	49
		Percent of total	42.9	57.1	100.0
Better, mixed, or worse relations	Better	Count	0	3	3
		Percent within respondent's sex	0	10.7	6.1
	Mixed	Count	9	17	26
		Percent within respondent's sex	42.9	60.7	53.1
	Worse	Count	12	8	20
		Percent within respondent's sex	57.1	28.6	40.8
Total		Count	21	28	49
		Percent within respondent's sex	100.0	100.0	100.0

Source: Authors' compilation.

and non-Muslims weakened. However, it affected Muslims both ways." One student's indisputably mixed response unwittingly provides a fairly representative summary of the different lasting effects most students observed 9/11 as having on Muslim relations with non-Muslims.

> This event led to good and bad effects. The bad effects: false accusations blaming us; our absolute rights being affected; innocent brothers and sisters of our religion in the world are being; and affected wrongly. The good effects: unity; a sudden want for everyone to learn more about Islam; false misconceptions about Islam being cleared up; and more strength in faith of some believers.

Other students volunteered similar examples of bad effects in their responses, such as "created a barrier and hostile environment between both groups."

Of those statements depicting worsened relations, one major theme is victimization. In such cases, students position Muslims on the receiving end of non-Muslim hostility, mistrust, and violence: for example, "People looked at us as being bad, not patriotic; "people started treating us differently and meanly." One girl made it clear that she understands 9/11 to have precipitated a skeptical non-Muslim approach towards Muslims: "Although before 9/11 non-Muslims were somewhat open to Islamic religion's practices such as wearing the scarf, I feel as though they attempt to scope out people of Islam and assume something about them that is not true."

References to victimization also occur in some statements coded as mixed. One student wrote, "Some non-Muslims are ignorant and fear all Muslims believing that they had something to do with the attacks or are violent people. While others are very supportive and believe that Muslims are victims." Characteristic of "things got worse" responses is the suggestion that Muslims are the powerless victims of non-Muslims, who have the power to either sympathize or victimize.

In some of the statements coded as "things got better" there was not only a depiction of a power differential but also of strategy for empowering Muslims to escape victimization. That strategy was to raise awareness about Islam through interfaith communication. Two students claiming that relations between Muslims and non-Muslims have improved since 9/11 celebrated increased non-Muslim awareness of Islam and communication with Muslims. One wrote, "Now, everyone knows who we are. They know about Islam, and our religion. And what we believe, and they have a better understanding of us." The other echoed, "It has made Islam more known to non-Muslims. More Americans have learned about the religion of Islam and language of Islam. These practices have resulted in a more understanding communication between the two groups."

Of the fifty students who answered the question about changed feelings about the future of Muslims in the United States after 9/11, 47 (94 percent) provided answers that we could code into optimistic, mixed, and pessimistic. Of those forty-seven responses, we coded nineteen (40 percent) as optimistic, eleven (23 percent) as mixed, and seventeen (36 percent) as pessimistic. The gender gap in responses to this question was much smaller than it was for the previous two questions. In this case, twenty-three boys and twenty-four girls supplied answers. 44 percent of the boys and 38 percent of the girls wrote optimistic responses, 22 percent of the boys and 25 percent of the girls gave mixed responses, and 35 percent of the boys' compared with 38 percent of the girls' statements were coded as pessimistic. Nearly equal numbers of boys and girls were represented in each category (see table 6.10).

Table 6.10   Muslim Youth on the Future of Muslims
              in the United States

		Male	Female	Total
Optimistic	Count	10	9	19
	Percent of total	21.3	19.1	40.4
	Percent within			
	respondent's sex	43.5	37.5	40.4
Mixed	Count	5	6	11
	Percent of total	10.6	12.8	23.4
	Percent within			
	respondent's sex	21.7	25.0	23.4
Pessimistic	Count	8	9	17
	Percent of total	17.0	19.1	36.2
	Percent within			
	respondent's sex	34.8	37.5	36.2
Total	Count	23	24	47
	Percent of total	48.9	51.1	100.0
	Percent within			
	respondent's sex	100.0	100.0	100.0

Source: Authors' compilation.

Explanations for feeling optimistic included the observed increase in the number of converts to Islam, higher Muslim visibility, the sense that Muslims are strong and will persevere, and favorable comparison of Muslim immigrant experiences with those of non-Muslim immigrants. Students wrote:

> I think this is just a period of confusion which will be [gone] after a while. It hasn't changed. Optimistic, because I think there is a future for Muslims in United States.

> I honestly think optimistic because people are starting to realize Muslims for what they really are.

> I feel optimistic. With every bad there will always be good. As long as we work with the American community, show our voice in politics, and make progress, people will see what Islam is all about, not what they see on CNN, MSNBC, and FOX!

In contrast are students' expressions of feeling pessimistic. The range of reasons include fear of the government taking away their rights and of being affected by deportations, concern about being judged based on bad actions of the terrorists because they identified themselves as Muslims, and an overall sense of the persecution of Muslims, such as through negative portrayals of Islam and Muslims, particularly in the media.

> I feel pessimistic because I feel like our reputation with many Americans is going down. There is no love or care for ___. We need to increase trust.

> I feel that the future for Muslims has changed drastically. I feel pessimistic about the future because the evil-doers are still out there. For example, Osama Bin-Laden and everybody sadly believes that he is the typical Muslims when in fact he is not.

> Yes, sometimes I feel pessimistic about the future of Muslims in America. It seems like things are getting worse for us with all that we hear on the news etc.

> I feel more pessimistic. I am worried about our situation in the future and I hope that it will improve.

In addition, some students provided reasons for simultaneously feeling optimistic and pessimistic. Still others communicated a desire to be optimistic in spite of forces encouraging them to feel pessimistic. Responses indicate that feeling optimistic has been easier for some students than for others.

> I'm trying to be optimistic, but it seems that Muslims are being portrayed as horrible, violent people and [it] seems like they place the blame on Muslims. This shows me that the future of Muslims in the United States had changed after 9/11 and [it] will be difficult to succeed.

> Yes, It has changed. I have become more pessimistic about Islamic life in the United States because of the way we are treated and accused of outrageous things such as terrorism, yet still I can see an optimistic future as well because people can change and most Americans are open-minded and not against Muslims.

DISCUSSION AND SUBSTANTIVE THEMES

Our analysis of students' responses to our five questions about 9/11 reveals that purely negative statements outweigh purely positive ones, yet also, somewhat surprisingly, that many students considered 9/11 to have mixed consequences for themselves and other Bridgeview Muslims. Among the substantive themes or propositions that emerged three of the most noteworthy were an appeal for recognition that Muslims are fellow Americans, not terrorists, and that our similarities are many and deep; expression of confidence that through communication and outreach programs Muslims can gain acceptance in

America and defend themselves against victimization—in other words, faith in the power of discussion and growing awareness as correctives to false knowledge.

In addition, they offered a very negative view of the media as purveyors of false and damaging claims about Islam and the Bridgeview community. Almost without exception, the youth described the media's impact on Muslim reputations in negative terms. They expressed feelings of anger, both at the media's biased portrayal of Muslims and at its effect on growing racism against Muslims and Arabs. As one youth explained, "Some are angry at the media for giving wrong information world wide. Some are afraid to go out in public, afraid of being attacked." More generally, many emphasized the media's power to damage the reputations of Muslims and Islam in America:

> I think that after 9/11 all or most Muslims were considered as terrorist. And the media too; they poked fun at Muslims and saying things like Islam spread by the sword. Media was the most influential way to affect the people of the United States. I think non-Muslims have the wrong impression of Islam from the media.

With these observations in mind, we conducted a content analysis of post-9/11 reporting about the Bridgeview Muslim community in local Chicago newspapers. Our aim was to determine how local newspapers describe the Muslim community in Bridgeview, what themes are discussed in connection with the community, and what is stated or implied about their relationship with American society and government. More fundamentally, we aimed to determine whether local newspapers tend to present a positive or negative portrayal of Bridgeview Muslims—whether they are described as a minority eager to adapt, to participate, and to be included in larger society or, alternatively, as a group that secludes itself and disapproves of American society and government.[4] In the interest of space, we present a brief overview of the study's main results, which we intend to further elaborate in a separate publication.

Although we initially expected that our findings would corroborate the negative reactions of Bridgeview Muslims to the media, our analysis produced more complicated results. From a quantitative point of view, at least, the newspaper portrayals of the Bridgeview Muslim community are complex, diverse, and mixed in both message and evaluative tone. More than half of all articles were judged neutral in overall tone by independent coders: this means either that the overall message of an article was neutral in itself, or that the positive and negative statements in an article balanced one another out.

When the neutral messages and articles were disregarded, negative statements tended to outweigh positive ones—and particularly in statements referencing Bridgeview Muslim loyalties, appearance, values, or religiosity. On May 5,

2002, for example, an article in the *Chicago Sun Times* asserted that "with these recent charges, it becomes increasingly apparent that Chicago's near southwest suburbs may have been a significant gathering spot for individuals suspected of funneling money to terrorist groups for more than a decade" (Janet Rausa Fuller, "You Never Know About the Folks Next Door," 8). On December 2, 2001, a *Chicago Tribune* reporter said of a converted Muslim woman:

> She agreed to explain to me why a woman born in America, free to choose the way she wants to live, would convert to Islam, a religion that appears to treat women as inferior to men. Even if Muslim women in America lead less oppressive lives than they could in Afghanistan or Saudi Arabia, where a woman may be thrashed for letting her veil slip in public, or for walking to the drugstore at night without a male escort, they live by a far more strict set of rules than most of their neighbors. Why would they choose to limit their choices in dress and marriage, never again to socialize with men, run on the beach, or drink a beer? (Katherine Millett, "American by Birth, Muslim by Choice," 12)

There are exceptions to these negative portrayals, however. Many reports make an effort to describe Islam as compatible with values such as tolerance, peacefulness, freedom, and democracy. On November 18, 2001, for instance, the *Tribune* published an article entitled "Proud to be Muslim—and an American: The principal of a Muslim school preaches dignity and tolerance. He sees no conflict in praising Allah and saluting the U.S. flag" (1). The piece not only highlights a Muslim's love for America, but also argues that Islam is a peaceful religion preaching values that are not contradictory with those of American society. The individual discussed is quoted as follows: " 'I love this country,' he said. 'Despite the minority of bigots, I can practice my religion, raise my family, go to law school and dream my dreams. And so far, most of them have come true.' "

Our findings thus reveal a noteworthy discrepancy between our evaluation of newspaper articles about Bridgeview Muslims and the critical views of the media expressed by Bridgeview Muslim youth. Bridgeview youth's perceptions of the media are, of course, based on a combination of sources, such as movies, magazines, and television news stations and shows. And on a theoretical level, one must consider how a reader's subjectivity influences his or her personal interpretation of an article. We assume that articles will be evaluated by readers on the basis of their knowledge, opinions, and image of Islam and Muslims, as well as their opinions of the American government and the media in general. With so many influential factors molding a person's judgment of newspaper content, it is safe to say that the articles analyzed in this study invite a wide spectrum of possible interpretations. A non-Muslim reader who knows little about Islam and is suspicious of the Bridgeview Muslim community may see his or her fears confirmed by the media, whereas a reader who is less wary of this community and more favorable toward multicultural-ism in general may come away with a positive message of hope.

Given the spectrum of possible subjective interpretations by non-Muslims, it is not surprising that Bridgeview Muslims are sensitive to the media's failure to unequivocally portray their community in a positive way. The media exerts a significant influence on public opinion and Bridgeview Muslims have observed firsthand how widespread negative public opinion of their community can translate into a threat to their welfare.

CONCLUSION

As we have seen in the Bridgeview community, pessimistic outlooks are mixed with optimistic ones. Frustration with misrepresentations of their community and faith has prompted many Bridgeview Muslims to rally together. It has inspired some Muslims to write corrective letters to the editors of local news-papers and encouraged others to reach out to non-Muslim neighbors, such as through participation in interfaith activities with local churches. And, as the fifty-seven boys and girls who completed our questionnaire indicated, negative media coverage since 9/11 has motivated some Muslim youth to aspire to join organizations, such as media outlets, to gain a more direct impact on public opinion. So even as unfavorable news stories threaten their fragile image, many Bridgeview Muslims take measures to defend and define their collective and individual identities—both to themselves and to non-Muslims.

NOTES

1. According to Louise Cainkar, "The post-9/11 profiling of them as the 'suspected other' or as a fifth column poses a serious challenge to their inclusion" (2004, 239). One of the more florid recent examples of this is a recent season of Fox's hit series *24*, in which the main plot concerns a Muslim family that turns out to be a sleeper cell activated to help carry out a terrorist plot including the kidnapping of the American Secretary of Defense and the simultaneous meltdown of a number of nuclear reactors across the country.
2. See, for example, Daniel Pipes, "Why the Japanese Internment Still Matters," *New York Sun,* December 28, 2004, accessed at http://www.danielpipes.org/article/2309. See also Malkin (2004).
3. A number of media accounts noted that teenagers were disproportionately rep-resented at rallies and demonstrations such as this. If accurate, this is a phenom-enon worth further research.
4. To answer these questions, we analyzed the content of articles found in three local newspapers. Searching the electronic archives of the *Chicago Tribune,* the *Chicago Sun Times,* and the *Daily Southtown,* we collected all articles published between

September 11, 2001, and December 31, 2004, that pertained to the Bridgeview community. We then designed two coding systems for analysis of the eighty-nine articles thus collected—one for analysis of the overall content of an article as a whole, and one for the identification and analysis of individual statements or passages within each article—and followed up with a number of reliability tests.

REFERENCES

Bilgrami, Akeel. 1992. "What Is a Muslim? Fundamental Commitment and Cultural Identity." *Critical Inquiry* 18(4): 821–42.

Cainkar, Louise. 2004. "The Impact of the September 11 Attacks on Arab and Muslim Community in the United States." In *The Maze of Fear: Security and Migration after 9/11,* edited by John Tirman. New York: New Press.

Eck, Diana. 2002. *A New Religious America: How a "Christian Country" Has Become the World's Most Religiously Diverse Nation.* New York: HarperCollins.

Hermansen, Marcia. 2003. "How to Put the Genie Back in the Bottle? 'Identity' Islam and Muslim Youth Cultures in America." In *Progressive Muslims: On Justice, Gender, and Pluralism,* edited by Omid Safi. Oxford: Oneworld.

Leonard, Karen Isaksen. 2003. *Muslims in the United States: The State of Research.* New York: Russell Sage Foundation Publications.

Malkin, Michelle. 2004 *In Defense of Internment: The Case for 'Racial Profiling' in World War II and the War on Terror.* Washington: Regnery Press.

CHAPTER 7

ISLAMIC SCHOOLS, ASSIMILATION, AND THE CONCEPT OF MUSLIM AMERICAN CHARACTER

CRAIG M. JOSEPH AND BARNABY RIEDEL

THE TERRORIST attacks of September 11, 2001, intensified a concern many Americans have long had concerning its Muslim residents and communities. One of the forms this concern has taken is a heightened scrutiny of Muslim institutions and practices that might foster attitudes incompatible with the goal of integrating Muslims fully into American political and social life. More specifically, many Americans have become increasingly worried that American Muslims, especially Muslim youth, are being indoctrinated with anti-Western or anti-American attitudes, or with intolerance of other religious traditions.

In this context, Islamic schools abroad have increasingly become a source of concern. Immediately after 9/11, journalists and pundits became interested in the baleful effects of madrasas, or traditional forms of Islamic schooling. Islamic schools in the United States have attracted less of this kind of attention; but here too there has been a degree of alarm over the tone and content of some textbooks used in these schools. For example, a March 30, 2003, article in the *New York Daily News* revealed that a few New York Islamic schools were using textbooks containing frankly anti-Jewish and anti-Christian statements: " 'Many Jews and Christians,' the textbook says, 'lead such decadent and immoral lives that lying, alcohol, nudity, pornography, racism, foul language, premarital sex, homosexuality and everything else are accepted in their society, churches and synagogues' " (Larry Cohler-Esses, "Sowing Seeds of Hatred: Islamic Textbooks Scapegoat Jews, Christians").

Recently coverage of Islamic schools has been more encouraging. For example, a 2002 survey of Islam on the PBS documentary series *Frontline* showcased an American Islamic school and its principal. The same school—Universal School in Bridgeview, Illinois—has been profiled in several segments on National Public Radio, and most recently in an article in *Time* magazine. It is on this school that our investigation of Islamic education in the United States after 9/11 focuses. We focus on it as an acknowledged prototype for Islamic schools across the country and briefly describe it and the community surrounding it, examining in particular how it has sought to resolve the dilemma of socializing its students to be both good Americans and good Muslims. In contrast to current essentializing discourses, based on the worry that there is "something about Islam" that fundamentally conflicts with the West, the Universal School aspires to show that the two are compatible; that developing good Muslims is at once consistent with the aim of cultivating successful Americans.

As a result of 9/11 increased attention has been paid to Islamic schools in the United States, giving the impression that these schools only just emerged, perhaps even as a response to 9/11. On the contrary, Islamic private schools such as Universal School have a history that stretches back to at least the early 1990s. Reporting often contextualizes these schools as existing in the wake of 9/11 but the most interesting and neglected question is whether Islamic private schools have changed as a consequence of 9/11. Did 9/11 have an impact on the development of Islamic curricula, Islamic educational aims, or the organization of school life? Did 9/11 create factions within these communities, foster a sense of institutional alienation, or result in polarizing discourses emphasizing the incompatibility of Islam and the West? What about the effect of 9/11 on the identity, self-esteem, and academic achievement of Islamic private school students?

We cannot answer all of these questions because we focus primarily on one school, Universal School, and one stratum of institutional life, namely teachers and administrators. But, even through this small window, the story to be told about 9/11's effect on Universal School is perhaps unexpected. Our observations of this community—which began before 9/11—suggest that the terrible events of that day and their aftermath did not significantly alter the trajectory of the school or radically change school life. Grief counselors were not brought in. The school was not shut down for a prolonged period. Curricula were not revamped or overturned, and the school's philosophy remained the same. In fact, when asked about the effect of 9/11, teachers and administrators at Universal School have consistently noted the lack of change. As traumatic as 9/11 was, it did not derail the school or set it on a new course. The adaptations to American life that were already in progress at the school continued to go on as they had before.

On the other hand, it would obviously be absurd to suggest that 9/11 left no mark on Universal. Every Muslim and Islamic institution in the United States has been affected by the events of and since that day. The question is how particular institutions and individuals have dealt with the situation. In the case of Universal School, the significance of 9/11 may best be thought of in terms of its place in the broader narrative of its effort to articulate and realize a particular vision of Islamic education in the United States. Thus, we see this chapter as a reminder that, in at least some areas of American Muslim life, the events of 9/11 did not fundamentally disrupt or alter processes of assimilation already underway. If anything, they have accentuated the importance of Universal School's effort to cultivate strong and grounded American Muslim youth.

ISLAMIC PRIVATE SCHOOLS AND AMERICAN MUSLIM ADAPTATION

Muslim immigrants to the United States face two kinds of pluralism and diversity in forging individual and communal identities. On the one hand, many first-generation immigrants have come from societies that are fairly homogeneous—especially with respect to religious beliefs and practices—to one characterized by a phenomenal diversity of religions, ethnicities, lifestyles, attitudes, and so on. On the other, in the Muslim communities to which they come or which they form, they confront a plurality of ways of being Muslim, diverse beliefs, attitudes, experiences, modes of practice and worship, and self-identification. These two kinds of pluralism have had a significant impact on what it means to be a "good Muslim," but it has also given them an experience somewhat characteristic of the American experience more generally—an experience that has been shaped and reshaped by the diversifying consequences of global forces. Just as American Muslims must seek to define a common Islam in the wake of internal diversity, America has repeatedly sought to bridge its internal differences with recourse to various ideas of Americanness capable of reflecting, and being shared by, its varied citizenry.

In many respects, Islamic schools in the West face challenges similar to those of all religions and systems of religious education. A central concern of anyone committed to a religious tradition or community is how to inculcate that commitment, in the form of an identity, in succeeding generations. Another, which is in some ways in tension with the first, is how to also instill a sense of belonging with the wider society and culture, so that children (and adults) are not felt (whether by themselves or that society) to be outsiders or aliens.

One distinction that has been made in this regard, by the scholar of religion Diana Eck, is between "wall-builders," who are "concerned about the educational task of maintaining religious identity in the face of the corrosive powers of modern individualism, pluralism, relativism, and consumerism," and "bridge-builders," who are "convinced that the encounter with religious pluralism is not only inevitable, but also theologically and educationally necessary and enriching" (2002).

Data collected both ethnographically and through interviews has made it clear that Universal School has attempted to resolve issues of difference (both within and without the community) by conceptualizing Islam not just as a distinct religious tradition, but also, importantly, as a system of universal values and virtues. In doing so, the school is working both to inculcate an authentically Islamic personality and to demonstrate that this goal is consistent with authentic Americanness. The hope that this approach holds out is a critical one for the future of Islam in the United States, and perhaps for Islam in general.

In the past fifteen years, approximately 200 full-time Islamic schools have been established across the United States, catering to the educational and religious needs of some 20,000 Muslim children (Sachs 1998). At present, there are 220 such schools, a 10 percent increase in the last three years alone (Greg Krupa, *The Detroit News,* "Metro Islamic Schools See Enrollment Surge," March 14, 2005). Yet a sizable lack of academic scholarship and sustained journalistic inquiry into these schools remains. The lack of recognition of this American-born, Islamic schooling movement is both ironic and unfortunate. It is ironic because at the very moment when there seems so much anxious concern over the question "Is there something about Islam?" these schools provide a stark contrast to our stressful and, as it turns out, myopic imaginings. It is unfortunate because it allows for the persistence of *misrecognition,* and, as Charles Taylor has noted, "a person or group of people can suffer real damage, real distortion, if the people or society around them mirror back to them a confining or demeaning or contemptible picture of themselves" (1994, 1). Perhaps more important, a lack of recognition deprives both Muslim and non-American Muslims of an opportunity for productive engagement between one another. In contrast to the post-9/11 public perception of the place of Islam in American society, whereas some non-Muslims overstress (and are "stressed out" by some notion of) the unity and evils of Islam, many American Muslims are simply worried about how to become recognized as good, productive, and contributing members of American society.

The proliferation of private Islamic schools is bound up with that of mosques and mosque-based communities. Approximately two-thirds of the 1,206 mosques in the United States have been established since the 1980s, with an estimated 25 percent increase in the 1990s; and an average of 1,625 Muslims are associated in some way with the religious life of each mosque (Bagby, Perle, and Froehle 2001). In other words, Muslim communities are growing; and it is largely because of their collective efforts that Islamic private schools have flourished. Whether it is because Muslim parents stereotype public schools as morally corrupt—wracked by drugs, violence, and sexual promiscuity—or because they want to shield their children from discrimination and Islamophobia, the establishment of Islamic private schools is gaining momentum.

The recent surge in the establishment of private Islamic schools like Universal School is not an isolated phenomenon, nor is it specific to Muslim immigration. It is, rather, just the latest instance of a long-standing phenomenon, going back at least 150 years: the response of immigrant communities, especially confessional ones, to American life and the American public school system. In eighteenth and nineteenth century Europe, centrally controlled mass education in newly formed nation-states replaced the church as the primary mechanism of education. But the primacy of church schools in Europe, however diminished, was not eliminated, so that when waves of Catholic and Jewish immigrants began arriving to the United States in the first half of the nineteenth century, many were both predisposed to prefer faith-based schooling alternatives and skeptical of centrally controlled forms of education. Many Catholic immigrants, for example, found the public school system to have a Protestant bias (Protestant versions of the Bible were read daily) and therefore deemed them unacceptable as places for the education of their children (Bryk, Lee, and Holland 1993). Muslims arriving in the United States from Africa and the Middle East have been similarly predisposed, coming as they do from countries where religious institutions remain centers for education and where public education still tends to have a religious component. The so-called secular environment of American public schools is seen by many Muslims as falling short of the educational aims they have for their children. Muslim parents who choose private schooling for their children do so because they believe the dominant society, mirrored in the public school, seriously jeopardizes Islamic identity and community. As Cristillo notes in his study of a New York City Islamic school:

> In as much as a private Muslim school is meant to provide a quality education on par with the public school, its proponents see the school's "Islamic environment" as a safeguard to prevent Muslim children from drifting away from the imagined spiritual community, or Ummah, of Muslim "brothers" and "sisters." In addition, by creating overlapping networks of social relations among members of local households, mosques and businesses, the private Muslim school provides a physical locus of collective identity in an otherwise religiously plural society where Muslims are a minority. (2004, 7)

The Chicago area is home to five full-time Islamic schools, all of which are certified by the State of Illinois and teach an accredited curriculum along with Islamic studies and Arabic. All of these schools are located in the suburbs—one in a northern suburb (the Muslim Education Center), two in the western suburbs (the College Preparatory School of America and the Islamic Foundation School), and two in the southwest suburb of Bridgeview (the Universal School and the Aqsa School). Four of the five are open to both boys and girls—separated after the fifth grade—whereas the Aqsa School is exclusively for girls after the fourth grade.

UNIVERSAL SCHOOL

Universal School is one of the oldest and most prestigious Islamic private schools in the country. The Muslim presence in Bridgeview dates to the early 1970s, when a number of working class Palestinian families, many from the town of Beitunia in the occupied West Bank, began looking for property to build a mosque. Bridgeview was a small, predominantly Christian community then, with several churches and a large amount of inexpensive land. The first Muslims to settle in Bridgeview bought some of this land for a mosque but it was years before they could afford to begin construction. Only after a second wave of Muslims arrived were they able to pull funds together and begin building. These Muslims were much more politically minded and educated than those already there, not clerks and salesmen but doctors, lawyers, and engineers. They were among the hundreds of thousands of well-educated and ambitious Muslims immigrating to the United States in the 1970s. Many of these Arab immigrants, particularly Egyptians and Syrians, came to the United States after postcolonial nationalist fervor in the Middle East failed to translate into higher standards of living and access to jobs. In Bridgeview, these Muslims joined the original Palestinian community, as well as more recent arrivals from Palestine who had immigrated after Israel's 1967 takeover of the West Bank and the Gaza Strip. Finally, with strong transnational ties and a significant base of support this community was able to raise enough money for the construction of the mosque (later named the Mosque Foundation). In the fall of 1981, just before Ramadan, it held its first call to prayer (for a more extended history of the Bridgeview mosque, see Noreen Ahmed-Ullah, "Struggle for the Soul of Islam," *Chicago Tribune*, February 8, 2004).

Universal School owes its existence to the founding of the Bridgeview mosque and the Muslim community that rapidly developed around it. In the mid-1980s, three wealthy Bridgeview doctors committed themselves to establishing a model Islamic school. Construction began in 1988, and the school opened its doors on September 4, 1990, to 140 students and eleven staff members. In 1992, the school was recognized by the Illinois State Board of Education and today it is one of the largest K–12 Islamic schools in North America, with a student body of more than 600 students and more than fifty staff. It is a founding member of both the Council of Islamic Organizations in Chicago and the Council of Islamic Schools in North America.

Universal School is one of a cluster of buildings including a mosque, a youth center, the Chicago headquarters of the Muslim American Society (MAS), and Aqsa School. The school building is long, squat, and institutional in appearance. Gray concrete and mirror-tinted lengthwise windows define its facade. Inside it houses a number of classrooms, a large gymnasium, two laboratories, a library, large preschool and kindergarten rooms, and a sizable lunchroom-cafeteria in the basement, where halal hamburgers are served beside French fries (for more on the school, see Schmidt 2004).

As we have already mentioned, the reasons for establishing Islamic private schools are similar to those that motivated Jews and Catholics to establish their own schools in the early part of the twentieth century. Indeed, anti-immigrant discrimination, plus some skepticism about the melting pot presumptions of the common schools movement, provided a strong impetus for many immigrant communities of faith to establish private schools. Here, familiar structures of language, religion, and culture could be preserved and reproduced (Sanders 1977, 40; Winter 1966, 5–6). The same is true of Islamic private schools. As one administrator at Universal School stated, the original purpose of establishing Islamic schools was "to create a safe, comfortable place for Muslim students to get a solid education while retaining their identity as Muslims." And it is toward the preservation and reproduction of Muslim identity that these schools direct themselves. As a science teacher put it, the aim of Islamic education in the U.S. is "to establish an Islamic identity, an American Islamic identity, where students will come out viable and productive people of American society with their Islamic identity, kept, preserved, not destroyed, not lost."

BUILDING AN AMERICAN-ISLAMIC CURRICULUM

It is important to note that many Islamic schools promote themselves to their constituents not simply by providing an "Islamic environment" but also by promising a high-quality education by secular standards, one that can translate into high scores on the important standardized tests and acceptance into the finest colleges. At Universal School, approximately 95 percent of graduating students go on to college in pursuit of eventual employment and financial success. For religious and cultural reasons, many Muslims value both spiritual and material advancement, and signs of an emerging "Protestant" ethic among American Muslims have been documented (Abdus-Sadur 1998).

One of the foremost challenges for full-time Islamic private schools such as Universal has been to adapt the secular frameworks and core curricula of the public school system to an overarching Islamic model of schooling. The question of how to "Islamize" education has been answered variously by Muslim schools, but a gradual progression in this national movement can be observed, moving from a concern over how to Islamize knowledge to an emphasis on developing an Islamic environment based on the instantiation of Islamic character.

The project to Islamize knowledge bridges with the larger goal of developing a formal Islamic epistemology, one in which all knowledge is perceived and transmitted as sacred and given by Allah through reason as well as revelation. Although schools seem to be putting less emphasis on this project, other institutions have been established around the country and the world with this specific goal in mind (The International Institute of Islamic Thought (IIIT), The Child Development Foundation, The Muslim American Society, The Association of Muslim Social Scientists, etc.). The Islamization of knowledge project, as stated on the IIIT website, "endeavors to elucidate Islamic concepts that integrate

Islamic revealed knowledge with human knowledge and revives Islamic ethical moral knowledge." A more robust definition of the Islamization project is given by Dr. Ismail al Faruqi, former director of the IIIT:

> To recast knowledge as Islam relates to it, is to Islamize it; i.e., to redefine and reorder the data, to rethink the reasoning and relating of the data, to reevaluate the conclusions, to re-project the goals—and to do so in such a way as to make the disciplines enrich the vision and serve the cause of Islam. To this end, the methodological categories of Islam, namely, the unity of truth, the unity of knowledge, the unity of humanity, the unity of life, the telic character of creation, the subservience of creation to man and of man to God must replace the western categories and determine the perception and ordering of reality. So too the values of Islam, namely, the usefulness of knowledge for man's felicity, the blossoming of man's faculties, the remolding of creation so as to concretize the divine patterns, the building of culture and civilization, of human monuments in knowledge and wisdom, heroism and virtue, pietism and saintliness, should replace the western values and direct the learning activity in every field (accessed at http://shaukani.wordpress.com/2007/02/24).

Basic differences in the Western and Islamic worldviews strongly influence the ways in which their respective aims and philosophies of education are set forth. Islamic private schools have since their establishment been in the position of having to reconcile secular educational standards and American models of achievement with the moral and epistemological framework of Islam, often variously defined.

The shift from an emphasis on transforming knowledge to transforming environments is an interesting one, and seems to parallel the shift documented here from submission to revealed doctrine to the development of moral character through the provision of a value-based educational environment. This shift is a noteworthy feature of an emerging conception of what it means to be Muslim. Though the emphasis on differences between the "Western" and "Islamic" visions of education remains, many Islamic schools today have successfully accommodated the secular subject areas and liken themselves to Jewish and Catholic private schools.

Islamic private schools in the United States are distinguished from public schools principally by the addition of religious studies classes and the provision of a self-described Islamic environment through which an explicit emphasis on Islamic character education is implemented. In addition to the secular curriculum, these schools include Islamic studies and Arabic classes during periods that might otherwise be used for electives in public schools (such as music, home economics, shop, and so on). Religious studies at Islamic schools generally include the study of selected portions of the Qur'an, Arabic language instruction, core principles of Islamic theology and worship, and Islamic history. One of the primary difficulties of religious instruction, however, is the lack of a systematized, consensual religious curriculum. Indeed, after more than a decade of operation, Universal School still finds itself without an Islamic curriculum. The current principal of the school explained it this way:

> It's not like we have a "curriculum curriculum" where you say, "Here's this book. Finish this. Take a test. You're done." No, you know, we do have books. We change the books every year because we're never satisfied with the information that's provided in them; because it's not set up like a curriculum. That's the problem! I mean, none of the books are really written for schools to use. They're just informational books about the life of the prophet or the life of the sahaba, his companions, or about Islam the religion or about Abraham and Moses, you know. All of that. And we need to bring it together comprehensively as a curriculum and that hasn't been done yet.

The tendency of Islamic schools in the United States has been to adopt educational materials published overseas, for instance from Pakistan, Saudi Arabia, or Jordan. But American educators are often critical of these materials, because they contain nationalist and culture-specific content they feel has little relevance for American-born Muslim youth. Recently, several American-based organizations have taken the initiative to develop an Islamic studies curriculum rooted in the American experience. For instance, the International Education Foundation (IQRA) and the Islamic Foundation of North America (IFNA) now publish Islamic studies curricula, textbooks, and educational materials. In addition, the Islamic Society of North America (ISNA) holds an annual meeting of Islamic school teachers and administrators in Rosemont, Illinois, to foster collaboration in coming up with a curriculum; and the Islamic School's League of America runs a national email listserv that enables Islamic educators and administrators to support each other year round.

Without an explicit religious studies curriculum, and given the need to adapt to secular educational standards, the question of how to Islamize education has increasingly been answered through the provision of a self-described Islamic environment. At Universal School, the day begins with students filing through the front door to ensure that each student has complied with the dress code; boys wear navy blue slacks and a light-blue collared shirt; girls wear dark slacks, a hijab (enforced after the fifth grade), and a navy blue, calf-length top (much like a jilbab). Students are instructed in the appropriate use of Arabic in prayer (or salat) and in interpersonal contexts, for instance in greeting one other (as-salamu 'alaykum), giving thanks (al-hamdu lillah), referring to the future (insha'allah), and according praise (masha'allah). Religious norms are also enforced; behavior and food are classified as halal (lawful) or haram (prohibited), and boys and girls are separated in class, at lunch, and during assemblies after the fifth grade. Some scholars have noted that the maintenance of this type of Islamic environment functions as a kind of hidden curriculum constituted by the use of symbolic knowledge, language, and religious norms (Cristillo 2004).

If the Islamization of education is increasingly done through the provision of what teachers and administrators describe as an Islamic environment, then the ultimate goal of this environment is to provide a space capable of nurturing Islamic character. For a number of years, the annual ISNA Education Forum, held in Chicago, has been titled "Islamic Schools: Developing the Emerging Muslim American Character." Conference papers discuss topics such as the importance of Islamic schools in helping to promote an Islamic personality, and a standardized Islamic character curriculum, commonly referred to as the Tarbiyah Project, is being discussed nationwide. The introductory paragraphs of this curriculum include the following statement:

> Islam is founded on the principles of belief and righteous conduct. This con-nection between values and practice lies at the very heart of the Islamic way of life. Nevertheless, a crisis in values and character development exists through-out the Muslim ummah today that is working to undermine the fabric of the Islamic spiritual, moral and social system. Lacking a clear moral compass, Mus-lims today find themselves marginalized socially, disoriented spiritually and generally in a quandary about their role and responsibility in modern society. Without a proper understanding of the Islamic value system, there is little hope that the true goals, or maqasid, of Islam can be achieved. (Uddin 2001)

The word tarbiyah is derived from the Arabic root rbw (to make or let grow, to raise, rear, bring up, teach, or instruct). Tarbiyah—in contrast to ta'liim, which has more the sense of imparting knowledge—includes upbringing and raising people to have values and character (Starrett 1998). The Tarbiyah Project is thus a call to resuscitate awareness of the Islamic value system for strength and guidance, for regrouping and rearticulating an Islamic character founded on the principles of belief and virtuous conduct. If the primary aim of an Islamic school such as Universal is to preserve Muslim identity in the face of challenges from the American mainstream, then the primary means of realizing this goal is seen as issuing forth from a renewed emphasis on instantiating the Islamic value system.

The renewed emphasis on Islam as a system of values and ethics is part of a more general trend among Muslims in the West to "deculturalize" Islam. This trend goes beyond the American context, and may be seen more generally as an attempt to purify Islam in the West of any specific cultural ties. Attempts to deculturalize Islam evidence how the forces of globalization have had an impact on the articulation of Islam in the West and in American Muslim communities

165

particularly (see Roy 2004). Global trends are most apparent in the national and cultural diversity within American Muslim communities and institutions. In the context of Universal School, the global is evidenced by the high degree of student diversity. With students hailing from Palestine, Egypt, Syria, Morocco, and America itself, the school must articulate a vision of Islam that is recognizable and acceptable, a common Islam. Focusing on Islam as a system of values and ethics may be seen as one way to manage a hermeneutic process that might otherwise lead to a crisis of interpretation. Migration and uprooting seem to go hand in hand with the quest for some type of universality. As Olivier Roy notes: "The quest for authenticity is no longer a quest to maintain a pristine cultural identity, but to go back to and beyond this pristine identity through an ahistorical model of Islam" (2004, 23).

In this community's attempt to find in Islam a system of universal values and ethics, important questions have arisen regarding the relationship between religion and culture. Are prohibitions against dating and the mingling of the sexes Islamic or cultural? And if these practices are manifestations of "universal values" than are the practices themselves universally binding or relative to the Islamic tradition? We now turn to our findings of how individuals in this community are thinking about the values they espouse and how they manage to conceive of them as truly universal.

RELIGION, CULTURE, AND CHARACTER

Why have notions of character and virtue been such prominent concepts in American Muslims' attempts to adapt, especially through educational institutions, to American culture and society? One important reason is that these notions have a long history in Islam, and are embedded in its history and in its spiritual and intellectual life. Because of this, Muslim character and "Islamic personality" have a unique authenticity and authority in debates over the goals of Islamic education and socialization.

The distinction between Islam and culture has become a pervasive theme in contemporary Muslim discourse, especially in the West. Many scholars of Islam note that Muslims have become particularly adamant about separating what is genuinely Islamic, which usually means what can be found in or supported by the Qur'an and sunna, from practices and beliefs that are "cultural," meaning held over from pre-Islamic times, or more generally, devised by man as opposed to Allah. The division between what is Islamic and what is cultural is, in a sense, built into Islam and its self-concept, in that one of the explicit reasons for the revelation to Muhammad was to eliminate or reform cultural practices, such as female infanticide, usury and idolatry, that were seen as corrupt and unjust. Today, this tension is often brought to the fore in debates over controversial practices such as female circumcision, with each side citing passages from the Qur'an and hadith to support its position.

The tension between religion and culture reflects Islam's aspiration to be a universal religion, one that speaks to all of humanity, not just certain peoples or cultures. One way in which this aspiration is expressed through morality is in the assertion that the virtues professed by Islam are universal. When we asked, in our interviews of teachers and students at Universal School, whether there are specifically Islamic virtues, we were often corrected by interview subjects who told us that Islam has not brought any new virtues to mankind. Rather, what it has done is to reaffirm virtues and other moral norms that have always been recognized but that either have ceased to be practiced or have been forgotten entirely. For these subjects, there is no question that the virtues are universal, and that they have a rational basis in revelation and human nature.

Another way in which this point was articulated for us was in this somewhat surprising statement from a young Egyptian-born woman, Aminah:

> The akhlaq [ethics or character] we are talking about are not strictly . . . they're not *Arab,* they're not Islamic. They're everybody's. So I could be dealing with a Christian or Jew, or Hindu, or Zoroastrian, one has akhlaq and one doesn't have akhlaq. And we can observe people, and say, "Wow, his akhlaq are so Islamic, he might as well convert," you know? Or he *thinks* he's Muslim, but look at his akhlaq, he might as well just be an atheist or something. You know, Muhammad Abduh . . . a great writer, in the late nineteenth and early twentieth century, he went to France, actually, and he had a correspondence with Tolstoy. [And he] said, in Europe, I saw Muslims without Islam, and here back home, I see Islam without Muslims. In other words, the essence of Islam is sometimes to be found in the land of the infidel. He was just being general, talking about people in the West who were impressive to him, in other words, [when they say] "I will be there at three," they're there at three. "No, I can't do it" means no, I can't do it. "Yes I can do it" means yes, I can do it. He was a reformer, he wanted to purge society, whatever you want to call it, he wanted to make society more Islamic. And, but you know what, Islam is not a word, it's a practice, it's a way of life, and that way of life seemed to him to be more alive in . . . ironically, outside the borders of the world of Islam. And very lacking in the so-called Islamic world. So people always quote him, and, you know, look at the essence of a human being, not at the external.

Aminah is here expressing a very strong form of universalism, but one that is not controversial among Muslims. For, just as Muslims see Islam as a religion and way of life with universal appeal, they also believe, as a corollary, that in a sense all human beings are Muslim when they are born, but that some are led away from Islam. Islam, many Muslims say, is natural for human beings, and when a non-Muslim becomes a Muslim, the change is most often described as a *reversion,* rather than a *conversion.*

One of the contexts in which this shift from Islamized knowledge and Qur'anic learning to Muslim personality or Muslim character has to be understood is in the Islamic conception of morality, which, as in all religions, is highly complex. As in other religious traditions, especially monotheistic ones, morality in Islam includes principles, duties, divine commands, and other familiar categories. But, very significantly, Islam places much greater emphasis on character and virtues than the other monotheistic traditions, and this emphasis is shown, in part, by the concept of akhlaq. For the vast majority of Muslims, morality or ethics *is* akhlaq. Among the many people we have interviewed and observed, akhlaq was almost universally the translation offered for both morality and ethics.

This is significant for a study of virtue concepts in Islam because of the etymology of akhlaq and its cognate words. Akhlaq comes from the Arabic root kh-l-q, which means to create, shape, make, form, or mold. Akhlaq is the plural form of khuluq, which denotes an innate peculiarity, natural disposition, character, or nature. The Arabic translation of "ethics" in the sense of a philosophical discipline is 'ilm al-akhlaq (science of akhlaq). Thus, though there are several Arabic words that translate morality, the predominant one reflects an identification of morality and ethics with mankind's nature as created, and thus with a specific telos. In our interviews with Muslims at Universal School (both teenagers and adults), the use of akhlaq to translate "morality" was nearly universal, as was the justification of moral standards in terms of man's nature as a created being.

The use of akhlaq to denote the moral domain has a long history in Islam. In the Qur'an (68:4), for example, God tells Muhammad, through the angel Gabriel, "thou (standest) on an exalted standard of character" (innaka la'ala khuluqin 'adheemin).[1] There are also many references to akhlaq in general and to specific virtues in the hadith and in stories about the Prophet. For example, many interviewees related how Muhammad, even before he became a prophet, was known as al-Amin, or the Trustworthy, because of his reputation as an honest man and businessman. Others quoted the following ahadith, among others:

Usama bin Shareek narrates: We were sitting in the presence of Allah's messenger [that is, the Prophet] so quietly as if birds were perched on our heads. Nobody had the courage to open his mouth. In the meanwhile a person came and asked the Prophet, "among Allah's slaves who is the dearest to Him?" The Prophet replied: "One who has the best moral character [akhlaq]."

Abdullah ibn Amr narrates: I have heard the Prophet saying, "Shall I not tell you who among you is the most likeable person to me and who will be the nearest to me on the Day of Judgment?" He repeated this question two or three times. The people asked him to tell them about this person. The Prophet said, "he among you who has the best moral character [akhlaq]."

The predominance of akhlaq as the object of morality and ethics is also reflected in Islamic theology (kalam) and philosophy (falsafa). For example, one classic work of Islamic ethics is Ibn Hazm's eleventh century book *Al-akhlaq wal-siyar* (*Character and Conduct*). And the Islamic emphasis on character and virtue manifests itself in the myriad philosophical works focusing on the development of character and virtuous dispositions, such as al-Ghazali's *Criterion of Action* and *Revival of the Religious Sciences*.

Akhlaq is so important to Muslim moral thinking that many interviewees, in discussing it, made the point that the perfection of people's character, their akhlaq, is the fundamental purpose of Islam. Those who argued this pointed to a well-known hadith, in which the Prophet is reported to have said "Innama bu'ithtu yutammima makarim al-akhlaq." Mustafa translated and explained this hadith in this way:

> When the Prophet one time was asked about the purpose of his message, he said, I was sent for nothing but to perfect or complete the moral character or the high moral character of humanity or individuals or people. . . . That was the purpose of his message, according to him.

As we have just noted, it is in a sense incorrect to speak of specifically Islamic virtues, if that phrase means virtues that are necessarily tied to local social or cultural circumstances, or traits that are thought of by Muslims as culturally distinctive. However, there are certain virtues which are more difficult to translate neatly than others, and they are seen as similar by Muslims (for a more detailed empirical study, see Joseph 2001).

The Muslim students and teachers being interviewed for our research perceive a very clear hierarchy among the virtues; for example, there are mandatory and discretionary virtues. The idea that the virtues differ in how important, fundamental or necessary they are for human flourishing was reflected in interviews and discussions with many informants. Aminah articulated this distinction explicitly:

> Another virtue . . . I mean, there are lots of kind of virtues that you can do without . . . that you don't have to have, but are good to have. . . . There are the virtues that you have to have, like sidq [honesty, truthfulness] and amana [trustworthiness] and not to be a munafiq [hypocrite], and to have taqwa [fear of God, God-consciousness]. Those are the main ones that you actually have to have.
>
> Q: So those three would be the core . . .
>
> A: Yeah. And then, the ones that it's nice to have are shaja'a, courage; 'adala, justice . . .

Aminah's specification of sidq (truthfulness) as a core virtue was echoed by most informants. By any measure it emerges as the most salient and central virtue for Muslims. 'Umar, a truck driver in his twenties, in fact observed that sidq, as well as sincerity and humility, is so important that it is in a sense not even a virtue (fadila, plural fada'il, is the word used in the passage):

> So sincerity is one of them. Humbleness. Truthfulness. Honesty. And all of these what we might call evidence of manners . . . are described to be stages or levels of iman [faith].
> Q: So would these be what you would call in Arabic fada'il [translation]?
> A: No, these are not fada'il. These are stuff everyone should be doing. Fada'il is things like, you are doing something more.

'Umar goes on to cite a well-known hadith on the subject of honesty and dishonesty, which is somewhat more clearly expressed by the account of another informant, 'Ali:

> There's probably eighty different hadith, eighty different times in his life that he [the Prophet] uttered that. So it has been submitted or transmitted to us through totally different chains of people until the time it was written down. That represents a lot more moral authority than for him to say the following, what I'm going to tell you. It is reported that he was asked, Would a mu'min commit adultery? And he said, yes. And he was asked, Would a mu'min steal? And he said, "Yes." And there was like four or five questions of things that are very serious, and . . . then they asked him, Would a mu'min lie. And he said, no, he would not. And so he said a faithful [person] would not lie. But he may commit the others. And the idea is that the others all are . . . can be indicative of a human weakness. And that nobody is free of that, again, apart from prophets. That . . . nobody's free from that, but lying is a conscious decision, and you should be free of that.

This hadith shows, in a different way, the centrality of truth-telling in Islam. It is, in a sense, a fundamental criterion for iman (genuine faith), in that someone who lies cannot, almost as a logical matter, be said to be a believer.

Informants also ranked justice and fairness as highly important, or mandatory, virtues. Despite apparently classifying 'adala as a discretionary virtue in the passage cited above, for example, Aminah went on to describe it as a central virtue:

> To be fair is so important. Because once you're not fair, you're creating . . . in Islam, the worst state of being is anarchy. Throughout Islamic political theory, the state that was being avoided was anarchy. Not war. War is part of life. Anarchy.

Anarchy is when you have no . . . rules whatsoever. And whatever causes that had to be nipped in the bud. Anarchy was worse than war. Because war had rules. It had motivations, it had rules. Once your goals were achieved, that was it. But anarchy is the worst thing. So to be fair is very important in Islam because it is one of the preventive measures to that kind of anarchy.

For Aminah, justice or fairness is important primarily because God has enjoined it on human beings and because it preserves communal harmony and social order, not because it is a self-constructed universal ethical principle, as in some contemporary Western ethical theories.

We have already mentioned another virtue concept, that of taqwa. Along with sidq (honesty) and amana (honesty-trustworthiness), it is perhaps the foundational virtue for Muslims. Indeed, it is perhaps not even accurate to include taqwa with the other virtues, because it is really the source of virtue and the primary motivation for the cultivation of all the other virtues. As Ahmad, a Syrian man, put it:

We believe that we should be striving, and the more we know God, because His name is al-haqq, for example—that means the Truth—the more we know Him, we become better and more truthful people. And His name is also al-'adl, the Just. And the more we know Him, the more we become conscious of Him, and the more he's present in our life, we will be more just in our life. And so on. And we will never get to fully understand these names. We strive to get as close as possible, but with our life, with our body here, we are to look at these attributes and strive to be there. Try to be as good as possible, but [we will] never be there, because only God is like that.

Ahmad's explanation of taqwa echoes, in a surprisingly direct way, one of the central themes of Iris Murdoch's *The Sovereignty of Good* (1970), namely, the necessity of shared "objects of attention" for moral development on an individual level and moral progress on a communal level. One function of taqwa is to keep one's attention focused on the names and qualities of God, and on the character of the Prophet, as a means of self-improvement; simultaneously, attention to these qualities increases taqwa by increasing one's understanding of God.

While virtues and associated concepts are by no means the only moral concepts to be found in Islam, they have a centrality and importance for Muslims that is quite different from the other monotheistic faiths, in which, though the virtues are valued, they are simply not as thoroughly woven into sacred texts, popular literature, and religious practice. At least for the informants we encountered in our fieldwork, the virtues are necessary not only for being a good person, but for being a good Muslim in general. The point, however, is that virtue concepts in the moral consciousness of Bridgeview Muslims are ones that

Westerners would readily recognize as being constitutive of character. We now turn to how this fact is reflected in Islamic education at Universal School.

BUILDING BRIDGES THROUGH VALUES AND CHARACTER

As the name suggests, the values taught at Universal School are not seen in contrast to American or Western values, but are instead seen as shared and universal. Just in the past year, Universal School made a switch from the Tarbiyah curriculum to the Character Counts! curriculum used in many American public schools. Initiated by the Josephson Institute of Ethics in 1992, the Character Counts! Coalition represents perhaps the most significant character education movement in the United States. Inspired by the problem of moral decline in America and the need to teach values to the young, this coalition has affirmed six "core ethical values rooted in democratic society" that "transcend cultural, religious, and socioeconomic differences." The Character Counts! curriculum, according to the program's website, "is a non-profit, non-sectarian, non-partisan character-education framework that rests on the six pillars of character: trustworthiness, respect, responsibility, fairness, caring, and citizenship." In 1999, the coalition formed a national partnership of over three hundred different organizations, including church groups, teachers' and principals' unions, youth organizations, charities and foundations. Together these organizations claim to reach "more than 40 million young people." As a coalition, they are "united in one overriding mission: strengthening the character of America's youth" by "integrating character education into new and existing educational programs" (see http://www.charactercounts.org).

When asked how this switch made sense from an Islamic perspective (aside from its practical benefits), one administrator explained:

> We've adopted the program available in public schools and then we've put an Islamic twist to it where we teach the same values but then we just give them the Islamic perspective of how this is common with Islam as well. So rather than teach to the students, which we already do, that this is an Islamic value but it's also an American value, now we're doing it the other way around also, to complement that, to say, "This is an American value. But you know what? It's an Islamic value too." It's one and the same.

With a renewed focus on Islam as a system of values and ethics, the essence of Islam is increasingly conceived among Islamic private schools as residing in the virtuous person, rather than, for instance, in the person who has vast amounts of religious knowledge. At least in contexts like Universal School, Islam is less and less defined in terms of a set of beliefs based on a revealed book, a culture linked with a historical civilization, or an inherited legacy based on a common origin. Islamic education in the United States is about teaching students how to be good people, and this is viewed in contrast to the traditional emphasis on strictly Qur'anic learning. As one teacher noted:

> Our purpose is not to have students who have memorized the entire Qur'an. . . . The purpose is really simple, just, you know, be good role models, be good practicing Muslims where you follow basic values about maintaining your family, taking care of each other, contributing to the community, helping the community to grow, be an asset to society and making sure that Islam is there helping to do that. Which is their duty. And that's just the sense and at the basis of it. So you know its not technical stuff about you have to learn so much of the Qur'an or they have to know so much of the Sunnah. It's not that.

Defining Islam in these terms carries with it consequences for how Islam is taught and transmitted. Because the emphasis is on values and ethics, the teaching of Islam and Islamic character occurs primarily through the staff's own religiosity, their own embodiment of virtue, and their own moral exemplarity. Likewise, the Islamic environment is constituted by sociomoral norms of conduct upheld by all who participate in the school, particularly staff. As both the current and former principals at Universal School noted:

> *It's about example and modeling.* I mean that's what the emphasis is on. It's the practical approach, you know, and how it, we can see it . . . how we can see the results of that, the direct results of that.
>
> [I: How does the school foster an Islamic environment?] "I mean, this is our daily struggle to tell you the truth. And *there's no way around authentic experiences from the adults around the children.* And we fail and succeed to the degree that we fail and succeed in projecting a good role model into the kids. I mean there's no way around it."

The ecumenical vision of values that Universal School staff profess naturally leads to ambivalence over the claim that they have been Westernized, Americanized, or Protestantized. For teachers and administrators, such a narrative of adaptation slights Muslim agency and the symbolic capital of Islam and Islamic traditions. Instead, they invoke a more empowering narrative that sees the turn towards values as a rediscovery of what is already essentially a part of Islam. As another administrator put it, "non-Muslims will say, 'Well that's because of the effect of the West on Islam.' To me, no, that is already part of Islam. It's just something that is rooted in the Western experience and it happens to bring out that part of Islam."

CONCLUSION

Teachers and administrators at Universal School strive to show that Islam is not necessarily Other to American society, that it is, to use a somewhat banal metaphor, one river leading to the common ocean of shared, self evident human values. This emphasis on human commonality is likely motivated by a collective narrative that sees diversity and difference as a threat to both the cohesion of the community and the community's ability to garner support and legitimacy from the outside; that is, in a political environment that's sensitive about its Muslims, and in a communal environment that's Muslim but sensitive to its cultural differences, the emphasis on human commonality makes good sense.

It is increasingly apparent that many American Muslims feel trapped by an essentializing discourse, one in which its upholders (culturalists, Islamophobes, and fundamentalist Muslims) overstress the relevance of Islam to present social and political conflicts. From the essentialist perspective, there is "something about Islam," some fixed and codifiable quality that makes it analytically distinguishable from the social and cultural context in which it takes root. Teachers and administrators at Universal School, however, argue that Islam is not monolithic, homogeneous, or necessarily Other to American society. Islam is conceptualized as universal in its values but particular in its manifestations. One administrator expressed it this way:

> Look at the cultures in those countries and Islam is completely distinct. From Kenya to Nigeria to Indonesia . . . and you have a totally, in a way, different Islam. I mean the only thing that brings it together with the rest is just a general core set of values; but the way they go about it, the practice of it, a lot of things are different.

Though the problem of Muslim adaptation is readily framed as a conflict of values, teachers and administrators at Universal School argue that an essentialist analysis of Islam neglects the terrains of solidarity and fluidity that exist between Muslims and non-Muslims; that is, the ways in which communities of various sorts (religious, cultural, political) have depended on the cross-fertilization of ideas and practices.

> Human civilization is not . . . first of all it's not isolated nor is it the credit of anyone by themselves. So what I find in this civilization, two-thirds of it fits just fine with my religion. It's not something . . . I'm not all of a sudden being Westernized. It's just I'm recognizing those things within this civilization that have been taking from all the others and rightly so.

Once this type of ecumenical vision of Islam gets emphasized, then the enormous amount of literature that stresses an essential conflict between Islam and the West begins to seem misguided. Muslims in this context define the problem not in terms of different values but in terms of different value *commitments*. Indeed, it is the non-committal attitude of the American mainstream to basic shared values that teachers and administrators at Universal School find reprehensible and dangerous. A study conducted by the Council on American-Islamic Relations (CAIR), *The Mosque in America,* found that 99 percent of Muslims polled in the United States agreed that America is technologically advanced. Seventy-seven percent agreed that freedom and democracy in America is an example to be learned from. On the other hand, 67 percent agreed that "America is an immoral corrupt society" (2001). One might suggest that all of the ambivalence of American Muslims is embodied in these figures.

This paper suggests that the lines of conflict assumed by the "culture wars" worldview have given way to other battle lines. Indeed, the post-1965 return of the globalization project, with its increasingly free flow of goods, money and peoples, and the blurring of boundaries, is resulting in unexpected lines of affiliation. By focusing on the provision of a values-based education and the cultivation of character, Muslims at Universal School join other socially conservative Americans in this country—Protestants, Catholics and Jews—who feel themselves vulnerable to a growing moral crisis.[2] Ironically, where Muslims and Christians in this country are being discussed as increasingly different from one another, some of them (the socially conservative ones) are in fact looking more similar. The turn to character education affiliates American Muslims with an emerging neotraditionalist sector of American society, a sector that encourages the preservation of religious commitments and the agency made possible by such commitments. Overstressing Islam obscures these mixed genres of religious and cultural life in America and the themes that bind them together. Interestingly, in joining this sector of American society, many American Muslims in the Bridgeview community have appropriated a powerful voice of resistance that is at once quite germane to the American experiment and critical of where that experiment might be headed.

The authors would like to thank the Russell Sage Foundation for the generous funding which supported both the research described in this paper and the paper itself.

Authors are listed alphabetically. Craig Joseph's work focuses primarily on Islamic moral concepts and much of his contribution to this chapter comes from his ongoing fieldwork in the Bridgeview community, particularly the mosque. Interviews related to moral concepts in Islam that are presented here were conducted with mosque members, some of whom were also teachers and administrators at Universal School. Barnaby Riedel's work focuses primarily on Islamic education in the United States. His contribution to this chapter comes from his ethnographic fieldwork at Universal School and his interviews with teachers and administrators over the course of the 2005 to 2006 school year. Collectively the two authors have a view of Universal School that spans before and after 9/11, allowing them to make observations about the impact of 9/11 on the community and on Universal School in particular.

NOTES

1. In quotes from the Qur'an, the English comes from the translation of 'Abdullah Yusuf 'Ali. In the references, the number before the colon refers to the surah, or chapter; the number after the colon refers to the ayah, or verse within the surah.
2. The evidence thus supports the recently developed notion of segmented assimilation, referring to the fact that immigrants assimilate to particular sectors of American society (Portes 1995; Portes and Zhou 1993).

REFERENCES

Abdus-Sadar 1998. "A Muslim School's Response to the Dilemma of Ghetto Life." Ph.D. dissertation. Curry School of Education, University of Virginia.

Ali, Abdullah Yusuf 1987. *The Holy Qur'an: Texts, Translation and Commentary.* New York: Tahrike Tarsile Qur'an.

Bagby, Ihsan, Paul M. Perle, and Bryan T. Froehle. 2001. *The Mosque in America: A National Portrait.* Washington: Council on American-Islamic Relations.

Bryk, Anthony S., Valerit Lee, and Peter B. Holland. 1993. *Catholic Schools and the Common Good.* Cambridge, Mass.: Harvard University Press.

Council on American-Islamic Relations (CAIR). 2001. *The Mosque in America: A National Report,* Washington: CAIR.

Cristillo, Louis F. 2004. " 'God Has Willed It': Religiosity and Social Reproduction at a Private Muslim School in New York City." Ph.D. dissertation. Columbia University.

Eck, Diana L. 2002. *A New Religious America: How a "Christian Country" Has Become the World's Most Religiously Diverse Nation.* San Franciso Calif.: HarperOne.

Joseph, Craig. 2001. "The Virtues as a Cultural Domain: A Study of Arab Muslims." Unpublished Ph.D. dissertation. Committee on Human Development, University of Chicago.

Murdoch, Iris. 1970. *The Sovereignty of Good.* London: Routledge & Kegan Paul.

Portes, Alejandro, editor. 1995. *Children of Immigrants: Segmented Assimilation and its Determinants.* New York: Russell Sage Foundation.

Portes, Alejandro, and Min Zhou. 1993. "The New Second Generation: Segmented Assimilation and its Variants Among Post-1965 Immigrant Youth." *Ethnic and Racial Studies* 15(1): 74–96.

Roy, Olivier. 2004. *Globalized Islam: The Search for a New Ummah.* New York, Columbia University Press.

Sachs, Susan. 1998. "Muslim School in US: A Voice For Identity". *New York Times,* November 10, 1998, A1.

Sanders, James W. 1977. *The Education of an Urban Minority: Catholics in Chicago, 1833–1965.* New York: Oxford University Press.

Schmidt, Garbi. 2004. *Islam in Urban America: Sunni Muslims in Chicago.* Philadelphia, Pa.: Temple University Press.

Starrett, Gregory. 1998. *Putting Islam to Work: Education, Politics, and Religious Transformation in Egypt.* Berkeley, Calif.: University of California Press.

Taylor, Charles. 1994. "The Politics of Recognition." In *Multiculturalism: Examining the Politics of Recognition,* edited by Amy Gutman. Princeton, N.J.: Princeton University Press.

Uddin, Sommieh. 2001. "Implementing the Tarbiyah Project In Your School: Resources and Reasons Why." *Islamic Schools League of America.* Accessed at http://www.4islamicschools.org/tarbiyah.htm.

Winter, Nathan H. 1966. *Jewish Education in a Pluralist Society: Samson Benderly and Jewish Education in the United States.* New York: University of London Press Limited.

CHAPTER 8

FAITH IN THE FORM: ISLAMIC HOME FINANCING AND "AMERICAN" ISLAMIC LAW

BILL MAURER

A CASUAL observer of Muslim American social life after September 11, 2001, might assume that visible practices that mark someone as Muslim—the headscarf is perhaps the most commented upon example—would decline in prevalence if Muslims newly feared being singled out for discriminatory treatment or harassment. At the same time, however, one might also assume that the prevalence of such practices would increase, as a sign of political assertion, or a testament to Muslim Americans' presence in and importance to the American social fabric. The same assumptions have been made since September 11 about Islamic banking, a less visible practice, and one linked in the popular imagination to terrorist financing. When Islamic charities were suspected of having played a role in the financing of the 9/11 plotters, Islamic banking was thrust into the spotlight. One might assume that Muslim Americans who had been using Islamic financial alternatives for their banking and borrowing might have quietly transferred their assets and debts to conventional alternatives.

The evidence does not bear out any of these assumptions, however, and, perhaps more than anything else, demonstrates the continual development of Islamic institutions in the United States, despite events like those that took place on September 11 and their aftermath. That development may have taken a few unexpected detours, as we will see here, particularly with respect to Muslim Americans' understanding of Islamic jurisprudence. But those detours ultimately had little to do with September 11 and much more to do with an American faith in bureaucratic rationality and the market, specifically, the faith that, with the correct formal procedures, any group can be turned into a niche market, and that this is a kind of equality offered by the United States to all its inhabitants. Additionally, the evidence on the effect of 9/11 on Islamic banking demonstrates that Muslim Americans' understanding of Islamic jurisprudence owes much to their understanding of law generally, and a specifically American legal consciousness that assumes that the law consists of forms and procedures which one may not understand but the very formality of which indexes its legitimacy. September 11 did have a measurable impact on American Islamic banking and finance. But in several key respects this had much less to do with the Islam part and much more to do with the banking, finance, and American parts.

Islamic banking and finance begins from the Qur'anic injunctions against riba. Riba literally means increase but is often translated as usury or interest, and occurs twenty times in the Qur'an.

Those that live on usury [riba] shall rise up before God like men whom Satan has demented by his touch; for they claim that trading is no different from usury. But God has permitted trading and made usury unlawful. He that has received an admonition from his Lord and mended his ways may keep his previous gains; God will be his judge. Those that turn back [turn again to riba] shall be the inmates of the Fire, wherein they shall abide for ever. (2:275)

God has laid His curse on usury and blessed almsgiving with increase [yurbi, root: RaBa]. God bears no love for the impious and the sinful. (2:276)

Believers, have fear of God and waive what is still due to you from usury, if your faith be true, or war shall be declared against you by God and his apostle. If you repent, you may retain your principal, suffering no loss and causing loss to none. (2:278–79)

Believers, do not live on usury, doubling your wealth many times over. Have fear of God, that you may prosper. (3:130)

That which you seek to increase by usury will not be blessed by God; but the alms you give for His sake shall be repaid to you many times over. (30:39)[1]

The last verse brings two forms of increase together so that they cancel each other out: riba and alms (also literally increase).

Islamic banking and finance consists of experiments taking place around the world to create financial products and banking institutions that do not rely on interest. Much of the activity is taking place in Malaysia, Indonesia, the United States, the United Kingdom, the Arabian peninsula, the Indian subcontinent, and, to a lesser extent, west and east Africa. In other words, this activity has not just taken place within the financial systems of nation-states that have officially at one time or another Islamized their economies, such as the Sudan, Brunei, Iran, and Pakistan. The broadest definition of Islamic banking and finance includes all activities understood to be financial or economic that seek to avoid riba—itself a term of considerable definitional anxiety—generally through profit-and-loss sharing, leasing, or other forms of equity- or asset-based financing.

This chapter distills the findings of two years of research into Islamic home financing in the United States, the complete results of which are documented in the book *Pious Property: Islamic Mortgages in the United States* (Maurer 2006). Islamic home mortgages are a relatively recent Islamic financial innovation. I attempt here not only to provide a history of the development of Islamic home financing, but also to convey a sense of the wider conversation about Islamic mortgages that is taking place in the United States today, and the effects of 9/11 on those conversations. My research involved ethnographic, interviewing and quantitative methods, focusing on Muslim Americans in southern California who were interested in Islamic mortgages, as well as the creation of a data set on demographic features of all applicants for Islamic home mortgages to two main Islamic financing companies in 2002 and 2003 (the first years for which such data were available; n = 2507). I also conducted face-to-face, email and telephone interviews and conversations with professionals involved in creating and marketing Islamic mortgage products, as well as archival research on the development of Islamic home financing, including mass media stories, legal documents, religious and regulatory rulings and the proclamations of prominent individuals in the field.

Classical Greek and medieval Christian injunctions against usury are echoed in contemporary Islamic financial practice, although there is considerable debate over whether the Qur'anic riba can in fact be simply translated as interest or usury (see El Gamal 2000a, 2000b; Saleh 1986). The Aristotelian objection to money's fecundity is found in the Pasadena, California-based American Finance House LARIBA's statement of its organizing concepts: "Money is not a commodity. It is a measuring scale. It also does not reproduce. It only grows when used in an economic activity. Money is man-made."[2] The American Finance House LARIBA was one of the earliest entrants into the Islamic mortgage market. The medieval Christian concern that a contract should be clearly bound to a physical, tangible asset is echoed in the *Guide to Understanding Islamic Home Finance,* a booklet published by Lightbulb Press and introduced by Shaykh Yusuf Talal DeLorenzo, who sits on the shariah supervisory board of the Guidance Financial Group, which offers a competing Islamic home mortgage product:

A conventional mortgage loan is a loan of money secured by a lien against property. A halal [lawful, Islamically acceptable] home acquisition agreement, on the other hand, is either a partnership in property, a loan of property, or a sale of property. In other words, the essential difference between a Shariah-compliant method of home finance and a conventional loan is the difference between:

An acceptable transaction that involves acquiring something of tangible value—in this case, real estate—for cash.

An unacceptable transaction that involves borrowing cash and promising to repay that cash plus an added amount. (Morris and Thomas 2002, 3)

Finally, the medieval Christian concern that the lender should not be insulated from the risks of business is found throughout the Islamic banking literature (for example, Vogel and Hayes 1998) and is embedded in the profit-and-loss sharing contracts that animate a good deal of Islamic financial activity (see Maurer 2005). The American Finance House LARIBA mortgage model explicitly invokes risk sharing.

Before September 11, 2001, Islamic home financing had just begun to achieve some national prominence and reach. After September 11, it expanded considerably. There are a number of reasons for this. First, Islamic investment companies that had been focusing on developing mutual funds and other investment vehicles for devout Muslims suffered from the same economic shocks as all other investment companies after the market reacted to September 11. To put it bluntly, Americans in general, Muslims included, took their money out of the stock market after 9/11 and started investing in real estate, buoyed by historically low interest rates. Second, Islamic mutual funds had been able to maintain their Islamicity in part by contributing a portion of their profits to charity in order to religiously cleanse the funds; as charities came under governmental suspicion for being a possible route for terrorist money laundering, many Muslims withdrew their investments. It is unclear from my research, however, whether people's claims that they took their money out of Islamic mutual funds for fear of government scrutiny merely provided a religious veneer to an essentially economic decision to get out of the market. Third, Muslim Americans' desires to "own a piece of the rock," as one put it, and claim a stake in American society only seem to have increased after September 11, as a form of political assertion and claim to national belonging. Home financing, people told me, is the cornerstone of the American dream, and they were eager to demonstrate their commitment to that dream. Mortgage financing has also taken on such prominence in the American Islamic banking scene compared to other countries because of the manner in which American tax policy subsidizes home ownership through incentives like the mortgage interest income tax deduction. One might just as well ask, therefore, whether 9/11 spurred the mortgage and real estate markets generally, not just for Islamic mortgages or Muslim homebuyers.

The American Finance House LARIBA (American Finance House) wrote the first Islamic mortgage in 1987 for the purchase of a home in Madison, Wisconsin (see generally, Abdul-Rahman and Abdelaaty 2000; Abdul-Rahman and Tug 1999; Ebrahim and Hasan 1993). The mortgage contract followed a cost-plus model (murabaha)[3] according to which the finance company purchased the house and the client paid the cost of the house plus a pre-set and unchanging markup over a period of time. It is the pre-set and unchanging amount of the markup that distinguished this contract from a conventional interest-based mortgage, from the point of view of Islamic finance. Later mortgage products developed by the American Finance House used lease-to-purchase agreements based on ijara (leasing contracts) from classical Islamic jurisprudence, or hybrid ijara-musharaka contracts in which the lender and the borrower form a joint partnership (musharaka) which holds the leads and which the borrower buys from the lender over a period of time.

Two Middle Eastern financial companies had attempted to offer Islamic financial services in the United States as well, but with limited success, as did a small financial services company based in Houston, Texas. The Saudi firm Dallah al-Baraka opened a subsidiary in California in 1988, only to move to Chicago shortly thereafter and to shift its emphasis from consumer finance to real estate and industrial investment. The United Bank of Kuwait (UBK) opened a mortgage company, al-Manzil, in 1998, but closed shop in 2000. In its two years of operation, it provided loans for sixty households. The Ameen Housing Cooperative in Palo Alto, California, has been helping Muslims buy homes using ijara contracts since 1998. MSI, an outgrowth of the Islamic Circle of America, offered various loan products to consumers based on lease-to-purchase and co-ownership models in the Houston area, but never achieved the visibility or scale of the American Finance House. Unlike MSI and the American Finance House, UBK and al-Baraka lacked a constituency in the communities in which they attempted to operate, and, as a result, could not mobilize the networks into which the other two companies had tapped through community connections, mosques, and political and social organizations. Significantly, however, UBK's brief foray into Islamic home finance sparked an interpretive ruling from the Office of the Comptroller of the Currency (OCC) that has had enduring significance for the field. The OCC issues interpretative rulings on banking and financial activity in the United States. It issued two rulings in the 1990s that determined that because mortgage-replacement products were functionally equivalent to mortgages, they could be understood as extensions of a bank's financing powers, not as a bank's acquisition of real property or leasing. This functional equivalence of Islamic and conventional mortgages remains a point of debate among professionals and laypeople alike, many of whom see Islamic mortgage alternatives as a smokescreen for interest-based activities or a clever marketing ploy with no real Islamic content.

In March 2001, the Federal Home Loan Mortgage Corporation (Freddie Mac) signaled its support for American Finance House's Islamic mortgages by investing $1 million in existing American Finance House contracts.[4] By 2005, it had invested a total of $45 million. Freddie Mac support has been hailed as an incredible milestone in the growing visibility and legitimacy of Islamic mortgage alternatives. Before September 11, Freddie Mac had begun to expand its purchase of Islamic mortgage alternatives. In August 2001, it invested $10 million to purchase lease contracts from Standard Federal Bank and United Mortgage of America in Detroit.[5] Freddie Mac support has been crucial to the success and expansion of the Islamic mortgage alternative sector. In 2003, the Federal National Mortgage Association (Fannie Mae) also agreed to purchase $10 million in Islamic financing contracts.[6]

Since Freddie Mac got involved in Islamic home finance, Islamic and conventional banks have devised a number of new home financing options for American Muslims. The most significant new entrant into the field is Guidance Residential, incorporated in 2002, which entered into an agreement with Freddie Mac for an initial commitment of $200 million.[7] It quickly established a national reach and has emerged as American Finance House's chief competitor nationally. The multinational bank HSBC (formerly, the Hong Kong and Shanghai Banking Corporation) opened its Amanah Islamic finance window in 2003 and began offering a home finance product based on the murabaha contract. In 2004, SHAPE devised a lease-to-own home ownership program it calls MALT™ (Mortgage Alternative Loan Transaction) based on an ijara contract; it offers a mortgage-alternative calculator on its website (http://www.shapefinancial.com) so that potential borrowers can compare its product with a conventional mortgage. In 2004, University Bank in Michigan hired a specialist in Islamic mortgage financing to implement the MALT™ model under its community banking division.[8] In Minnesota, the Federal Reserve Bank of Minneapolis, seeking a way to serve the financial needs of Somali Muslim immigrants, began exploring home financing alternatives together with a consultancy firm called Reba-Free, the St. Paul Neighborhood Development Center, the Northside Residents Redevelopment Council, and other community organizations (Tyndall 2001; Bennett and Foster 2002; Minnesota Housing Finance Agency 2002, 9). The Neighborhood Development Center began offering both murabaha and ijara based mortgage alternatives for business financing. Devon Bank in Chicago also began offering murabaha and ijara based mortgage alternatives in 2003, and has grown considerably since 2005.

These new entrants into the field of Islamic home finance have helped to address one of the chief shortcomings of Islamic mortgage alternatives: long waiting lists for financing. Before Freddie Mac and Fannie Mae, potential clients might wait as long as five or six years to get an Islamic mortgage,[9] because the lender's capital would be bound up in its currently held properties and it could not attract depositors without violating the separation of commercial from investment banking that was mandated by national banking laws until the 1999 Financial Services Modernization Act. Furthermore, the National Bank Act and state-by-state banking charters generally treat mortgages as liens against the collateral of the property, rather than as the actual holding of the title to the property (see Bennett and Foster 2002).

For Freddie Mac, investing in Islamic mortgage alternatives fell under its mandate to expand opportunities for underserved populations to gain access to home ownership.[10] Freddie Mac's commitment has endured, unchanged, since September 11, 2001. Indeed, among mortgage professionals, according to one interviewee, the only change brought about by September 11 has been "a new sense of resolve that what we're working on is more important now than it was on 9/10."[11] Indeed, Islamic financial institutions offering mortgage alternatives saw an increase in business and inquiries since 2001. Some attribute this increase to the general turn away from the stock market and into real estate. Others, however, attribute it to a feeling that American Muslims after September 11 want more than ever to assert their position as full members of American society. They also see a sort of political progression or evolution growing from Muslim home-ownership. As one Islamic mortgage professional remarked:

> The most intangible thing is that, when you take puritan Muslims who refuse to participate in interest, and have lived in apartments and so on, and put them in decent neighborhoods, they will start mixing with the American community and become responsible American citizens and this will grow in the neighborhoods and develop relationships and friendships and so forth.

At the same time, however, it is difficult to know whether professionals' faith in Muslims' newfound political assertion is actually pointing to an economic phenomenon that has little to do with political identity and more to do with identity-based niche marketing, and the developing realization among Islamic finance professionals that there is a wide untapped market. Both Islamic and conventional banking professionals see incredible economic potential in home financing alternatives:

> At this point we're dealing with a sleeping giant. But . . . it's about to hit in a big way. And the reason for that is the appearance very shortly of home acquisition programs. . . . The home acquisition programs, they address an essential need, and they basically put something in people's pockets, whereas the other programs, I mean the investment things, the different funds that are developed, those are either aimed at high net-worth individuals or institutions, or, at the retail level, they're for people with *extra* money.

In other words, where Islamic mutual funds or more exotic instruments like derivatives may appeal to the Muslim investor with a lot of room for experimentation in their portfolio, Islamic home financing has the potential for a much wider and ultimately more profitable reach. If September 11 made Islamic finance professionals aware of that potential, it was because of the stock market's failures at least as much as it was Muslims' possibly newfound sense of political assertion.

The role of Freddie Mac cannot be understated. Freddie Mac also spurred the Islamic home financing community to begin to conceptualize the securitization of Islamic mortgage alternatives for the purposes of selling Islamic mortgage paper on the secondary market to investors seeking Islamically acceptable investment vehicles. An interviewee remarked that this created an incentive for "organizations with the deep pockets" to step in. Securitization also made Islamic mortgage alternatives scalable in a way they had not been before, when they were primarily local or regional affairs backed by small and often local or regional investors.

In addition to providing liquidity, stability, and scalability, the support of Freddie Mac generated competition among Islamic financial service providers. Islamic banking professionals pride themselves on their civility and collegiality, and the spirit of cooperation, mutual trust and inquisitive experimentation that underpins their activity. When debate gets heated, it usually occurs in private and over very technical matters of the interpretation of fiqh (jurisprudence). Increased business for Islamic mortgage providers since 9/11 has led Islamic banking to take on the qualities associated with other forms of competitive enterprise. Professionals are actively involved in marketing their products and emphasizing the benefits (financial, spiritual, or otherwise) of their products over those of their competitors. There has also been increasing market differentiation and fragmentation, with different products being marketed to different communities of Muslims.

Ijara is an Islamic finance company that offers a mortgage replacement product that can be used for a home purchase as well as a refinancing loan.[12] Ijara prides itself on a carefully articulated product modeled on an ijara contract from classical Islamic jurisprudence. Its product also has a clear exegetical basis; that is, it has a clear basis in Islamic traditions of jurisprudence and interpretation. An ijara contract is essentially a lease-to-own contract. The client and company enter into a partnership agreement whereby the client agrees to pay back a pre-determined amount of the principal every month, plus a proportion of the property's fair market rental value. That proportion is determined by the client's share of the ownership of the property. Over time, the rent paid decreases as the client's ownership share increases. In other words, if Bilal wants a mortgage with Ijara for a house worth $100,000 and has the money for a 20 percent down payment (Ijara's standard until recently, which may account for its higher than expected frequency of wealthier applicants), he becomes a 20 percent co-owner and Ijara becomes an 80 percent co-owner of the property. In the first month, he will pay back a predetermined amount of the principal together with 80 percent of the monthly fair market rental value of the property. In effect, he pays the remaining 20 percent of the rent to himself. The next month, his share ownership of the house has increased, and so the proportion of the monthly rent due to Ijara decreases.

Searchlight is Ijara's main competitor, and its mortgage-replacement model is quite different. Based on a musharaka contract from Islamic jurisprudence, the mortgage replacement product looks on the surface like a conventional mortgage because it appears to include a rate-based interest payment. It functions rather differently, however. A musharaka contract is a co-ownership contract without any specification as to whether or how ownership might change over time. Searchlight and the client enter into a corporate partnership and form a limited liability company (LLC) together. The object of the contract they create is that LLC, not specifically the property the client seeks to purchase. The LLC owns the property, and the company and the client re-calculate their percentage share in the partnership—not the property—over the term of the contract (fifteen, twenty, or thirty years). Searchlight also invites other potential investors to share in the ownership of the LLC. This provides a mechanism for Freddie Mac, for example, to add capital to the Islamic mortgage market. Freddie Mac can first purchase a share in several LLCs held jointly between Searchlight and its clients, and then can create securities in its co-owned assets for trade on the secondary market. As with Ijara, Searchlight's relationship with Freddie Mac has required the use of standardized mortgage application and disclosure forms; those forms include terms like *loan, interest, lender,* and *borrower.* Searchlight's Sharia supervisory board has determined that such usages do not invalidate the essential nature of the diminishing musharaka contract at the heart of Searchlight's mortgage alternative model.

Searchlight's model consists of a musharaka partnership grafted onto a declining balance component, whereby one owner (the client) gradually buys out the other owner (the company). This makes it look similar to an ijara contract, but with one exception: where in ijara a monthly rent is assessed based on market values, and this rent determines the monthly markup (which takes the place of an interest payment in a conventional non-Islamic loan), in Searchlight's diminishing co-ownership model the monthly markup is an administrative fee added to Searchlight's profit from the co-ownership arrangement. It is arbitrarily set by Searchlight. It may resemble rent, and may be described as rent, but it is not necessarily set by rental market values and is not technically speaking a payment for the enjoyment of the property. Searchlight calls this portion of the monthly payment the profit payment. The portion of the monthly payment for the client's additional shares in the LLC it terms the acquisition payment. The occupant-client is responsible for all applicable property taxes and maintenance costs, as these are considered to benefit the occupant because he or she maintains sole enjoyment of the property.

Searchlight explicitly states that it seeks a profit payment that is competitive with interest rates available in the broader home finance market. It also states that its profit payments might be linked to an interest rate index (such as LIBOR, the London Interbank lending rate). The profit payment is not technically interest because it is not based on the capital Searchlight extends to the client but rather based on the business partnership that the company establishes with its clients.[13]

For the following analyses, a data set was created from the 2,507 applications to both companies in 2002 and 2003 from data collected by the Federal Financial Institutions Examination Council (FFIEC) for compliance with the Home Mortgage Disclosure Act (HMDA). The data set includes all applications for conventional loans and refinancing loans, whether they were accepted, denied, or withdrawn.[14] Data for Ijara and Searchlight seem on the surface to be of better quality than HMDA data for other lenders, although there is a substantial degree of nonreporting of race as well as some other glitches in the reporting (for example, missing or incomplete data for some census tracts). From the point of view of fair lending concerns, which usually have to do with differential denial rates, it is striking that Ijara and Searchlight have not had much of a denial rate. In 2002, Searchlight did not reject any applications for either conventional loans or refinancing out of a total of twenty-nine and 116, respectively. Ijara rejected one conventional loan application of a total of 251; four applications were withdrawn, for a total denial rate of 2 percent. It rejected none of the seventy-seven refinancing applications. In 2003, there were more denials overall, but not significantly so when compared with national averages. Searchlight rejected seventeen of 475 refinancing applications (4 percent) and eighty-nine of 890 conventional loan applications (1 percent). Ijara rejected three of 201 refinancing applications (1 percent) and thirteen of 253 conventional loan applications (5 percent). The denial rate nationally for all lenders is about 18 percent.

In what follows, I use the terms *conservative* and *progressive* to refer to some mortgage applicants, but am not comfortable with these terms because they seem inadequate to describe the complexity of emerging Islamic legal norms in the United States. When I first presented an overview of the patterns in this quantitative data to a non-Muslim colleague, she had assumed that when I referred to conservative Muslims I meant women who dressed modestly, covered, and keep silent, and men who make their wives walk three paces behind and don't listen to what they have to say. In using the term, I am aware that I may call up this stereotype in the minds of some readers. In addition, the proxy measure for conservatism here—whether a person is listed as a male instead of a joint applicant despite marital status—may have more to say about belief (or aspiration) than actual practice. A man who wishes to be or thinks he is in charge of a household's finances, of course, may be living a fantasy. Furthermore, a strict interpretation of the sources of Islamic law may, ultimately, warrant what many in the United States would consider a progressive politics, a commitment to social justice, and a strong belief in gender equality. And this kind of

187

strict interpretation of Islamic law, when wedded to American minority struggles for political recognition, may even further confound the stereotypical assessment of conservative Islam. As one young woman explained to me, "I am Muslim, I am a woman, I wear hijab, but I am a woman of color."

Both companies have a wide geographic distribution of lending activity. Ijara, an older company with licenses to operate in all states except New York, has a broader national scope than Searchlight. Searchlight, in business only since 2001, operates in eleven states and the District of Columbia.[15] In 2002, though there was overlap in the regions in which each operated, the companies only seemed to be in direct competition in two MSAs: the Chicago area and the Baltimore area. In 2003, the two companies were in direct competition in Ann Arbor, Baltimore, Chicago, Detroit, the states of California, Florida and New Jersey, and the Washington, D.C., metropolitan area. Table 8.1 lists the states from which applications originated in 2002 and 2003. One of the striking things about the geographic data is the extent to which Ijara has a presence even in smaller, southern and central states, compared to Searchlight, whose activity is concentrated in states with large urban centers. Because Ijara has a longer history and has relied on word of mouth and the Internet, whereas Searchlight advertises mainly through Muslim organizations, Ijara has been more successful in reaching isolated Muslims who may not have a large community around them. The geographic data suggest that Searchlight, which has had a tightly focused marketing campaign since its founding, has concentrated on reaching areas with potentially large Muslim communities and thus a potentially large market. Ijara, by contrast, has concerned itself since the beginning with reaching out to Muslims anywhere who seek an interest-free alternative.

The two companies have virtually opposite profiles in terms of the types of loan applications they receive. For both years combined, Ijara received more than one and a half times as many conventional loan applications as refinancing applications; Searchlight received twice as many refinancing applications as conventional loan applications. Searchlight better approaches the national statistics: in 2002 and 2003, 26.5 percent of all loan applications nationally were for conventional mortgages and 73.5 percent were for refinancing loans. This reflects the period of historically low interest rates. Searchlight's initial business model and marketing campaign focused on encouraging Muslim homeowners to refinance their existing interest-based mortgage with an Islamic mortgage; it has continued to emphasize refinancing over new home purchases. Ijara focused on first-time homebuyers but in 2003 began to branch out into the refinancing market. This points to Ijara's mission to reach Muslims who may have stayed out of the housing market altogether because of their views on Islam's prohibition of interest, and to Searchlight's strategy of reaching Muslims who already have an interest-based mortgage and are looking for a more sharia-compliant alternative.

Table 8.1   Loan Activity by State, 2002 and 2003

	Ijara		Searchlight	
	2002	2003	2002	2003
Alabama	0%	0.1%	0%	0%
Arizona	0	1	0	0
Arkansas	0	0.6	0	0
California	12	12	0	7
Colorado	1	0.8	0	0
Connecticut	0.6	2	0	0
D.C.	0	2	62	19
Florida	5	6	0	11
Georgia	4	7	0	0
Illinois	13	4	8	26
Indiana	1	1	0	0
Iowa	0.6	0.4	0	0
Kansas	0	0.3	0	0
Kentucky	0.3	0.3	0	0
Louisiana	0	0.4	0	0
Maryland	3	1	10	4
Massachusetts	1	4	0	0
Michigan	16	9	0	7
Minnesota	8	2	0	0
Missouri	0.3	2	0	0
Nebraska	0	0.1	0	0
New Jersey	1	7	19	14
New York	0	0	0	3
Nevada	0.3	0	0	0
North Carolina	1	3	0	0
Ohio	1	1	0	1
Oklahoma	1	0.6	0	0
Oregon	0.3	1	0	0
Pennsylvania	0	0.1	0	4
South Carolina	0	0.8	0	0
Tennessee	0	3	0	0
Texas	23	18	0	0
Virginia	0	0.1	0.6	0.6
Washington	1	3	0	0
Data not available	3	6	0	3

Source: Author's compilation from Home Mortgage Disclosure Act (HMDA) data, 2002 to 2003.

The gender and income profiles of applicants to each company differ, as well. Ijara's applicants tend to file their mortgage paperwork jointly, that is, each partner in a married couple signs the paperwork and is legally responsible for the contract. Searchlight's applicants are overwhelmingly more male. The differences are statistically significant. It is important here to note that the male and female applicants might either consist of single adults applying for loans and mortgages (who, with only one income, are more likely to be in the lower income ranges in their metropolitan statistical area), or married couples in which only the husband or only the wife (and probably the former) fills out the loan paperwork. Fair lending advocates have found that as income rises fewer women tend to apply for loans singly (for example, New Jersey Citizen Action 1997), representing a sort of marriage effect as more apply jointly with their husbands. In the case of Ijara and Searchlight, however, anecdotal information suggests that most loan applicants are married. It is not surprising that the gender category chosen by the applicant varies together with income level, whether the effect is due to the presence of two incomes in a household or, possibly, more progressive views on the marriage relationship correlated with higher socioeconomic status.

The data on race are tricky. A large proportion of applications are marked Other or Race Not Available. It is also difficult to interpret the HMDA racial categories. South Asian and Arab Americans might record themselves as Asian–Pacific Islander, Other, or white. Still, there are significant differences between the two companies and a weak relationship between race and choice of lender. Anecdotally, Ijara attracts more white converts than Searchlight, whose client base is more South Asian. Ijara is also thought to attract more Arabs than South Asians, though it is impossible to confirm this with HMDA data. If we assume that most people in the Asian–Pacific Islander category are South Asians, then it appears that the applicant pool for Islamic mortgages is overwhelming South Asian. There are few African American Muslims applying for Islamic mortgages. Karen Isaksen Leonard (2003, 4–5) summarizes various surveys of Muslim Americans by race; African Americans make up between 33 percent and 42 percent of all Muslim Americans in these surveys. They are not being served by these two companies, nor do they seem to be targeted by any of the other, smaller companies.

There is, of course, no HMDA data on sectarian allegiances such as Shi'a or Sunni. Leonard (2003, 34) reports that 15 to 20 percent of Muslim Americans are thought to be Shi'a. People who market Islamic mortgages say their primary market is Sunni Muslims but that Shi'a are drawn to them, as well. There are no Shi'a represented on the sharia supervisory boards of American Islamic mortgage companies, however.

There is a significant but very weak relationship between income level and choice of company. HMDA data reports income level in five ordinal categories based on the applicant's income as a percentage of the median income in their metropolitan statistical area. Searchlight's applicants tend to be poorer than Ijara's relative to those living around them. This may in part be an effect of Searchlight's concentration in urban areas where incomes are higher, although data from individual metropolitan statistical areas from which both companies have received applications suggests that Searchlight's applicants overall are less wealthy than Ijara's. This may also reflect the fact that, historically, Ijara has required higher downpayments (sometimes 20 percent) than Searchlight (usually, 5 to 10 percent), although in the years for which data is reported Ijara increasingly accepted lower downpayments in order to be competitive with Searchlight.

Searchlight's and Ijara's applicants can be compared to all mortgage and refinance loan applicants in the United States. Ijara is more similar to the aggregate data for all American lenders than Searchlight, which has far more male applicants. Ijara and Searchlight's applicants have slightly lower incomes than other American mortgagors. This may be an effect of their living in areas with higher median incomes, or it may be that, as anecdotally reported, truly wealthy Muslims prefer conventional (that is, non-Islamic) mortgages.

In summary, Ijara seems to be attracting applicants who tend to be wealthier and who tend to apply for mortgages jointly. Searchlight tends to be attracting poorer applicants who file as male rather than joint. Anecdotal evidence suggests that these applicants file singly even if they are married. There are a number of ways to explain the relationship between income and gender category. Married couples with two incomes are wealthier than single people with one. Yet many male Islamic mortgage applicants who apply singly are married. The wealthier couples may have more progressive views on marriage and finance, and take for granted that married couples would engage in financial activities like borrowing jointly. A more detailed statistical analysis (described in *Pious Property*) finds that Ijara's poorer joint applicants may also have more progressive views on marriage and finance than Searchlight's poorer single-filers. Ijara thus may have a more progressive client base overall than Searchlight, regardless of income level.

Why choose one mortgage replacement product over the other? People cited two factors, and these two factors usually worked in Searchlight's favor: perceived cost, and perceived level of sharia-compliance. Most people thought Ijara's mortgage alternative would end up costing them more than Searchlight's. "There really is no difference" between the two, one person said, "it's just that one is a little cheaper than the other." Speaking of Ijara, one person said, "I think the way it turned out was that our mortgage was like going to pretty much like double if we were going to go with them."

The issue of sharia-compliance came up quite a bit in discussions about the difference between the two companies. Those who had an opinion tended to think that Searchlight was more sharia-compliant than Ijara. Their reasons were at first confusing to me, because many of the same people who expressed doubts about Ijara also stated that its product was identical to Searchlight's. Of course, there are differences between the products. But it was not an assessment of the products themselves that led people to see Searchlight as more compliant. It was an assessment of the scholars and shaykhs who were believed to have endorsed each company, and an elision between the idea of endorsement and the idea of a universality or global reach that was afforded to Searchlight but not Ijara.

"We wanted to make sure we did something Muslim," one woman stated. "Ijara hasn't been approved by a lot of shaykhs." People cited Shaykh Taqi Usmani of Pakistan and the American Shaykh Yusuf Talal de Lorenzo. "Well, I mean, I don't know if they particularly *didn't* endorse Ijara, but they didn't, umm, it wasn't a public endorsement. But with Searchlight, like, all these scholars publicly endorsed it."

Searchlight's website and application packet contains copies of the fatwas issued by its Sharia Supervisory Board, the signatures of famous and well-respected sharia scholars and shaykhs prominently displayed. One couple explained:

A: Actually, even in our loan application—
B: There was like a written, ummm—
A: —yeah, there's like a page just with their endorsement—
B: —just saying it's part of the application.
A: Yeah, it's proof to the consumers that this is legit as far as we're concerned.

People were impressed with the caliber of the scholars who endorsed Searchlight's product. "He's like a world renowned faqih [jurisprude] and stuff, and he's like really hard line, like really hard line when it comes to things like riba."

People also relied on their friends for advice, especially friends who said they were against riba. Friends advised them to look for products with a lot of backing. Indeed, the word *backing* or other terms expressing an anterior warrant came up a lot in my informal conversations with Muslims in southern California. People said of Searchlight things like, "It's got good people behind it," or "It's really got a lot of backing." That anterior warrant translated into global reach. Almost everyone I talked to identified Ijara as a California company and Searchlight as national or as everywhere. This is despite Ijara's broader national reach. People had broad exposure to Searchlight's marketing materials; some had met representatives of the company at conferences. "They're, they're everywhere! Like, Searchlight is at every single conference, at every single event." Of Ijara, people said, "You don't really see them anywhere." Searchlight, by contrast, has "crossed the nation."

People also felt that Searchlight was more professional or more organized. People cited with approval the formality and professionalism of the paperwork they were required to fill out. "They even did credit checks!" "They looked at all our W2s." People were pleased that Searchlight did not trust them as potential clients, but required all the information a traditional lender would demand. Mortgage scholar Ann Burkhart (1999) laments that the nationalization and standardization of the mortgage business has led to ever-decreasing social connections—and therefore social obligations—between lenders and the communities in which they operate. Those I spoke with had exactly the opposite assessment of the quasi-anonymous quality of their relationship with Searchlight. They appreciated being catered to as Muslims. But they also appreciated being treated "like, as a real *client* or something," as one put it to me. Muslim companies, it was thought, were too lackadaisical or overly trusting of other Muslims. Not Searchlight. "It wasn't like traditional . . . Muslim companies, 'oh, it's OK, just let it go, whatever'." Professionalism here meant anonymity achieved through bureaucratic rationality. People preferred the formality of bureaucratic and market mechanisms that made them anonymous—and, indeed, that gave them no advantages even for being Muslim. If being Muslim meant getting a break from a Muslim company, such potential clients rejected the enterprise as suspect.

Ijara has essentially the same paperwork as Searchlight. With Freddie Mac involvement in the Islamic mortgage business, in fact, almost all Islamic home financing companies now use standard Freddie Mac mortgage application forms. Every company does credit checks; they all require W2s and other proof of income and continued employment. And, of course, considering the quantitative data, Searchlight has not in fact crossed the nation. Ijara has. Its distribution of clients, while not as deep in any particular area, is much wider than Searchlight's.

There has been a large and lengthy debate in Islamic banking and finance about the relative status of contracts like musharaka or partnership contracts compared to ijara (leasing) and mudarabah (profit and loss sharing). Scholars and practitioners often deride the former because they insulate the company from the risks of doing business. Ijara contracts are deemed more pure because they have a clearer exegetical basis, and mudarabah is deemed more equitable because it spreads the risk by sharing losses between company and client. Musharaka (and its close cousin, murabaha, a cost-plus contract) are seen as more efficient, but their theological status is in some doubt (see El Gamal 2000b; Saleh 1986). Islamic banking and finance scholars and professionals have agonized over the merits of these contractual forms; although many tend to feel better about leasing and profit-and-loss sharing than they do cost-plus or profit based contracts, many also recognize that the latter are simpler, more efficient, and more profitable in the long run. Because of this debate, and because Searchlight's profit payment is tied to an interest rate, I assumed at the start of my research that Ijara would attract more conservative Muslims who sought to adhere as closely as possible to the Qur'anic prohibition of riba, and that Searchlight would attract those willing to experiment, or those content with a sharia stamp of approval from known public figures even if the product looked like an interest-based mortgage from an end-user's perspective.

193

However, the people I interviewed who had detailed or even cursory knowledge of Ijara and Searchlight tended to claim that "Ijara is not really sharia" or "is not as sharia as Searchlight," as two interviewees put it. The latter comment is interesting because it understands sharia to involve levels of degree of quantity, not a difference in quality. People think Ijara is less sharia-compliant than Searchlight. Legal debates within Islamic banking for at least the past twenty years might suggest otherwise. So, too, might the end-user client's point of view, where what one sees on one's yearly statement looks like an amortization chart with columns indicating acquisition payments and profit payments that mirror precisely—down to the numbers and percentages—principal payments and interest payments.

When I began this research, I had expected Searchlight to be more pluralistic in its conception of Islamic law because its staff members had told me that its potential client base was more open to various interpretations, less rigid in their thinking, and even postmodern. One employee spoke of plans to set up operations in California specifically to capitalize on California Muslims' supposed greater flexibility in matters of religion. In contrast, people who work for Ijara speak of appealing to "puritans" who are concerned with the fundamentals of Islam. Throughout the course of my research, however, almost everyone who had some knowledge of Searchlight's product spoke of its greater religious or sharia weight than Ijara's.

The material presented in this chapter adds a layer of complexity to this apparent paradox, which I believe can be explained in terms of the changing status of Islamic legal traditions and practices in the United States. Khaled Abou El Fadl has noted that "in the United States the field of sharia is flooded with self-declared experts who inundate our discourses with self-indulgent babble and gibberish" (1998, 41). Leonard (2003) outlines the various efforts to create national-level fiqh councils in the United States, particularly the efforts of the Islamic Society of North America and the Islamic Circle of North America (see also DeLorenzo 1998). Some members of the resultant Fiqh Council of North America sit on the sharia supervisory board of Searchlight. Leonard cites Abou El Fadl's characterization of the current situation of Islamic knowledge in the United States as having "produced a landscape devoid of respect for the schools and methods of Islamic legal scholarship and for pluralism" (Leonard 2003, 63). She reports on Ihsan Bagby, Paul Perl, and Bryan Froehle's (2001) survey research indicating that imams and presidents of mosques in the United States cite the Qur'an (95 percent) and Sunnah (90 percent) as absolutely foundational and the various schools of Islamic law are seen as of little or no importance (52 percent) or only somewhat important (25 percent). Where do Searchlight and Ijara fit in this picture, and how can we square Searchlight's model with people's assertions that it is more sharia, with its postmodern aspirations? Likewise, how can we square Ijara's model with people's assertions that it is less sharia, with its so-called puritan aspirations?

Searchlight has a strong and persuasive marketing operation, as well as a Web presence that looks high-tech, savvy and professional. Its animated logo consists of the two words, *modern values,* juxtaposed to one another, and then separating apart as the words *finance* and *timeless* interject themselves to produce, *modern finance, timeless values.* It has a sharia supervisory board made up of truly prominent individuals, who have issued fatwas on Searchlight's products which are then posted on the company webpage for all to read (and to see the signatures of the jurists warranting the products). It is interesting, however, that the content of these fatwas seems less important than their form. They actually say very little, other than statements like, "After reviewing the mechanism as well as the agreements and documents, and after suggesting amendments that have been incorporated, the sharia supervisory board is of the view that given the circumstances prevailing in the United States, this arrangement conforms to the rules and principles of the sharia; and therefore, Muslims may avail themselves of this opportunity to acquire homes and properties by means of this method." There is no citing of authority or text or school of law. There is only the affirmation that the sharia supervisory board warrants the model.

Ijara, for its part (which has never had as snazzy a corporate marketing strategy but has relied more on the charisma and leadership of its founder) has gone on the attack, offering advice on how to select a home finance company that includes the following admonitions: "Please: Do not get overly impressed by intensive advertising that features 'Shariaa [sic] Boards' with religious rulings [or] 'fatwa'!" It also advises that clients ask of their finance professionals, "Is it a model that uses interest as a foundation for its calculations? If they immediately quote you a rate, this is nothing but interest." "Does the institution use intensive marketing concepts using religious slogans to 'sell' its services and operations?" "Does the company re-invest in the community?"

Often in the course of this research, I have been called upon to adjudicate the status of Ijara's versus Searchlight's models. I have resisted the call. Ijara's seems more correct, but only if what counts as sharia compliance is a literalist interpretation of religious texts, and only if the work of Islamic banking is understood to proceed from those texts, rather than to constitute, in itself, its own kind of religious or exegetical activity. This is a key point. My sense is that those who are intellectually captivated by Ijara's model will prefer it over Searchlight's. Indeed, Ijara makes an effort to engage the potential client (or interested researcher) in the exegetical act and the work of interpretation itself. It is fun and intellectually interesting to work out the legal-religious warrants of an ijara contract, to read hadith on leasing, and to ruminate on the market mechanism as a manifestation of the divine. Searchlight does not offer the same kind of hands-on relationship with its model. The model simply exists and is offered to potential clients as an already-worked-out, authorized contractual form. Its warrants are the fatwas. Their form trumps content and the mere fact of their existence underwrites the entire enterprise.

The determination of the choice between Ijara and Searchlight thus seems to have little to do with the actual product. People think the products are the same, and that they are both ijara contracts. It also has little to do with the interpretation of the product. People think ijara contracts are "really sharia" and mistakenly believe that Searchlight has a "really sharia" ijara-based product. But what makes many choose Searchlight over Ijara is not the product and not its sharia status, but the public backing of prominent scholars. This may explain the gender differences between applicants to each company. Those who choose Searchlight are not necessarily more conservative as much as they hold a particular understanding of Islamic law. Islamic law, for them, must look like law in the abstract sense. This interpretation, as requiring the public and formally bureaucratic backing of prominent scholars, may represent a transformation of sharia in the United States where charisma is actually becoming less important than bureaucratic rationality.

Achieving the backing of prominent scholars and thereby having the weight of an anterior warrant issued by such figures creates the illusion that Searchlight has a national presence. Scholars of global significance have endorsed the product, so the product must be of wider reach than Ijara. Wider reach translates into more sharia-compliant, given that sharia is supposed to be universally applicable. The illusion of national coverage also means formal anonymity—the anonymity of the nation-form itself, the anonymous horizontal solidarity of the "imagined community" Benedict Anderson (1983) characterized as having been forged through public print media such as newspapers. Here, the public print media are bureaucratically rendered, publicly available fatwas and standardized Freddie Mac application forms. Anonymity also translates into professionalism. Muslims debating mortgages are creating a world that brings into alignment standardized print media, public endorsements of prominent figures, and universal reach. It is something that resembles Islam itself: a standard, unalterable and untranslatable written text, chains of exegetical authority via hadith, and the universality of Islam expressed in the global horizontal solidarity of the umma, the global community of believers.

Furthermore, Islamic mortgages may be animated by a form of routinized charisma, but not necessarily in the Weberian sense. In making a fatwa look like an American legal document and concretizing it on paper, and in mobilizing Freddie Mac mortgage application packets for mortgage seekers and for international investors, Islamic home financing is routinizing people's preexisting understanding of law—not what it does or what it is, but what it looks like, how it appears on paper. Prominent shaykhs can now derive their authority and achieve greater prominence by publicly signing such pieces of paper. This is not the charisma of office so much as the charisma of form.

If Ijara represents sharia as a textualist endeavor backed by the intellectual activities of human beings talking and debating with one another as they assess the property's rental value, its living yield as a tangible asset, Searchlight represents sharia as a practical activity best understood as the working-out of their model and its form itself under the guidance of the esteemed fiqh scholars and experts who sit on its sharia supervisory board. "We do not change the math," Searchlight proclaims. The form is the same, and it is not the content that is different from a conventional mortgage so much as the form's own activity as it moves from fatwa to monthly payment.

This formalism dovetails with an American legal consciousness that places faith in formality and bureaucratic procedure—even if cynically so—to warrant any legal contract's legitimacy. If it looks like a legal document, it must be law. And it if is a legal document generated by an Islamic company, it must be Islamic law. In the context of the aftermath of 9/11, Muslim Americans may even be placing a renewed faith in the bureaucratic formality of liberal law and its guarantee of equality of opportunity, a promise that takes shape in the very textual bareness of the blank administrative form, in paperwork and documents in themselves rather than in their exegesis or interpretation. In doing so, Muslim Americans demonstrate both the durability of Islamic institutions in the United States, and the wide embrace of America itself.

I would like to thank Katherine Ewing and Stephanie Platz for their comments on earlier versions of this chapter.

NOTES

1. All quotations from the Qur'an are taken from the Dawood translation (2004).
2. Accessed at http://www.americanfinance.com/concepts.shtm.
3. Islamic banking and finance employs Arabic terms from classical jurisprudence for its contractual forms. I will set to one side here the interplay of Islamic jurisprudence and Arabic terms on the one hand and the dynamics of product positioning on the other (for a more complete discussion, see Maurer 2005).
4. The Federal Home Loan Mortgage Corporation was created by Congress in 1970 to provide liquidity to the real estate market by purchasing and securitizing mortgages, and selling the securities on the secondary market. The Federal National Mortgage Association, created in 1938, originally only purchased Federal Housing Authority loans but since 1968 has been allowed to purchase and resell any mortgages.
5. Freddie Mac Press Release, August 10, 2001, "Freddie Mac, Standard Federal Bank Announce New Islamic Home Financing Initiative for Michigan Families," accessed at http://www.freddiemac.com/news/archives2001/sohinitiative 0810.htm. See also *International Real Estate Digest,* "Freddie Mac provides lease-purchase mortgages for Muslims," September 4, 2001.

6. Edwin McDowell, "Financing Is Arranged for Observant Muslims," *The New York Times,* February 14, 2003, B8.
7. See *The Minaret,* "Islamic Home Financing Starting the Nation's Capital," July/August 2002, 19–20.
8. See Karen Dybis, "Banks Offer No-Interest Options for Muslims," *Detroit News,* December 21, 2004.
9. See Susan Sachs, "Pursuing an American Dream While Following the Koran," *The New York Times,* July 5, 2001.
10. Indeed, Freddie Mac's involvement with Islamic home finance came under the rubric of its "Summer of Homeownership" initiative which sought to bring greater access to underserved populations, particularly lower-income individuals and immigrants. According to some estimates less than 60 percent of Muslims in the United States are homeowners, compared to the American average of 69 percent (Thomas n.d., n9).
11. Unless otherwise indicated, all interviews conducted by the author 2002 to 2004, under conditions of anonymity.
12. I use pseudonyms here to protect the identities of the clients of these companies.
13. I discuss the exegetical basis of Searchlight's and Ijara's products in detail in *Pious Property.*
14. HMDA refers to primary mortgages as conventional loans and second mortgages or refinancings as refinancing loans. Although it may cause some confusion, since Islamic banking professionals refer to non-Islamic interest-based mortgages as "conventional loans," I maintain this terminology here.
15. California, Florida, Illinois, Maryland, Michigan, Minnesota, New Jersey, New York, Ohio, Pennsylvania, Virginia, and Washington, D.C.

REFERENCES

Abdul-Rahman, Yahia, and Mike Abdelaaty. 2000. "The Capitalization of Islamic (Lariba) Finance Institutions in America." Paper presented at the Fourth International Harvard Islamic Finance Information Program Conference, Cambridge, Mass., September 30, 2000.

Abdul-Rahman, Yahia, and Abdullah Tug. 1999. "Towards Lariba (Islamic) Mortgage Financing in the U.S.: Providing an Alternative to Traditional Mortgages." *International Journal of Islamic Financial Services* 1(2). Accessed at http://www.iiibf.org/journals/journal2/art3.pdf.

Abou El Fadl, Khaled. 1998. "Striking a Balance: Islamic Legal Discourse on Muslim Minorities." In *Muslims on the Americanization Path?* edited by Yvonne Haddad and John Esposito. Atlanta, Ga.: Scholars Press.

Anderson, Benedict. 1983. *Imagined Communities: Reflections on the Origin and Spread of Nationalism.* London: Verso.

Bagby, Ihsan, Paul Perl, and Bryan Froehle. 2001. *The Mosque in America: A National Portrait. A Report from the Mosque Study Project.* Washington: Council on American-Islamic Relations.

Bennett, Nicole, and Nikki Foster, with Margaret Tyndall. 2002. "Alternative Financing: Issues and Opportunities for Lenders and Interest-Averse Populations." *Community Dividend* 1. Accessed at http://minneapolisfed.org/pubs/cd/02-1.

Burkhart, Ann M. 1999. "Lenders and Land." *Missouri Law Review* 64(2): 249–315.

DeLorenzo, Yusuf Talal. 1998. "The Fiqh Councilor in North America." *In Muslims on the Americanization Path?*, edited by Yvonne Haddad and John Esposito. Atlanta, Ga.: Scholars Press.

Ebrahim, Muhammed Shahid, and Zafar Hasan. 1993. "Mortgage Financing for Muslim-Americans." *American Journal of Islamic Social Sciences* 10(1): 72–87.

El Gamal, Mahmoud. 2000a. "An Introduction to Modern Islamic Economics and Finance." In *Proceedings of the Fourth Harvard University Forum on Islamic Finance.* Cambridge, Mass.: Harvard Islamic Finance Information Program.

———. 2000b. "The Economics of 21st Century Islamic Jurisprudence." In *Proceedings of the Fourth Harvard University Forum on Islamic Finance.* Cambridge, Mass.: Harvard Islamic Finance Information Program.

Dawood, N. J., translator. 2004. *The Koran: With Parallel Arabic Text.* London: Penguin Books.

Leonard, Karen Isaksen. 2003. *Muslims in the United States: The State of the Research.* New York: The Russell Sage Foundation.

Maurer, Bill. 2005. *Mutual Life, Limited: Islamic Banking, Alternative Currencies, Lateral Reason.* Princeton, N.J.: Princeton University Press.

——— 2006. *Pious Property: Islamic Mortgages in the United States.* New York: Russell Sage Foundation.

Minnesota Housing Finance Authority. 2002. *State of Minnesota Analysis of Impediments to Fair Housing, Federal Fiscal Year 2002.* Minneapolis, Minn.: Minnesota Housing Finance Authority, Minnesota Department of Trade and Economic Development and Minnesota Department of Children, Families, and Learning.

Morris, Virginia B., and Abdulkader S. Thomas. 2002. *Guide to Understanding Islamic Home Finance in Accordance with Islamic Shari'ah.* New York: Lightbulb Press.

New Jersey Citizen Action. 1997. *Women's Access to Mortgage Lending in New Jersey.* Policy Report. Camden, N.J.: Rutgers University.

Saleh, Nabil A. 1986. *Unlawful Gain and Legitimate Profit in Islamic Law.* Cambridge: Cambridge University Press.

Thomas, Abdulkader Steven. n.d. "Methods of Islamic Home Finance in the United States: Beneficial Breakthroughs." *American Journal of Islamic Finance.* Accessed at http://www.nubank.com/islamic/.

Tyndall, Margaret. 2001. "Islamic Finance and the US Banking System." *Community Investments* 13(3): 17–19.

Vogel, Frank, and Samuel L. Hayes III. 1998. *Islamic Law and Finance: Religion, Risk, and Return.* The Hague: Kluwer Law International.

EPILOGUE

ON DISCIPLINE AND INCLUSION

ANDREW SHRYOCK

IT IS GOOD that this volume appears at a temporal remove from the events of September 11, 2001. The United States' reaction to the 9/11 attacks has included the invasion and military occupation of two (formerly) sovereign nation-states, a domestic security crackdown, new laws to justify the crack-down, and a reorganization of the federal agencies that execute and manage the global war on terror. Over the last six years, these developments have moved from the realm of the extraordinary to the realm of the commonplace. Though ominous, they now pervade our everyday lives, as if to verify Walter Benjamin's famous claim that "the state of exception in which we live is the rule." The essays in this book show how Arab and Muslim Americans are situated within this interplay of rule and exception, and the patterns revealed herein are not always the ones scholars (or community activists or media analysts or government officials) would have predicted in the early days of the post-9/11 era. Not only is there stark variation in how the backlash has been experienced in different Arab and Muslim populations across the United States, there is also a clear trend, in almost all the communities studied here, toward more assertive, tactically adaptive expressions of American identity.

These self-conscious acts of Americanization are rarely as new, in form or content, as they appear to be; still, they provide ideal locations in which to rethink current understandings of citizenship. It is important to take this con-cept apart, if only because it animates so many intellectual and political agen-das at once. As a rhetorical device, citizenship is used to facilitate (and block) the incorporation of immigrants, to expand (and contract) the limits of national belonging. As such, talk of citizenship has powerful, often contradictory effects. In discussing these essays, I focus on aspects of citizenship discourse that foster disciplinary inclusion. This idea is more complex, and much harder to assess, than disciplinary exclusion, the process realized in hate crimes, deportations, arrests, detentions, interrogations, profiling, and collective stigma. Without drawing attention away from these obvious forms of discrimination against Arabs and Muslims, the contributors to this volume have made deeper insights possible by pointing out unexpected ways in which inclusion, as policy and desire, is reshaping Arab and Muslim American communities in the post-9/11 era.

CITIZENSHIP, IN THEORY AND PRACTICE

The word *citizenship* surfaces repeatedly in this volume, but two essays make it central to their arguments in ways that are emblematic of larger trends. Sunaina Maira (chapter 2) examines modes of citizenship available to South Asian youth at a public high school in Wellford, a pseudonymous New England town. In making her case for three specific citizenship styles—flexible, polycultural, and dissenting—Maira puts forward a nuanced account of contemporary citizenship theory, building on the insight, now widespread in the literature, that legal citizenship does not ensure a sense of national belonging. This misfit between membership as an artifact of law and membership as a structure of feeling is the problem that citizenship theory is typically meant to address. Maira's high school students are clearly dealing with this issue in the heightened form it assumes for Muslims in the United States today. Indeed, local variations on this dilemma shape every essay in the volume. Maira's analysis of citizenship in theory, as theory, greatly enriched my reading of the other papers, even though, in her own study, the reach of her insights is limited by the peculiarities of her field site. The American high school is an incubator of citizens, and is designed to create them, but legal minors are not yet fully engaged in public life. Maira is fully aware of this fact, which should not be construed as a failing. Most of the essays in this volume deal with youth, specifically with students, a trend consistent with several themes I will discuss here. Maira's analysis tells us a great deal about how teachers and school administrators (who, in Wellford, are generally liberal and progressive) help immigrant children script alternative forms of American belonging, and how the students respond.

The power of Maira's presentation is amplified when it is read alongside Howell and Jamal's account (chapter 3) of the 9/11 backlash in Arab Detroit. This essay treats citizenship in practice, as practice, with the same analytical sharpness Maira brings to matters of theory. The landscape Howell and Jamal explore is (like high school) morally ambiguous and Byzantine. It is suffused with Maira's three citizenship styles, and, like good students and concerned teachers, we find that government agencies and Arab community leaders are equally committed to alternative forms of cultural citizenship. The ironic twist, however, is that liberals and progressives are not the only players on the Detroit stage, and conventionally politicized terms seem only to obscure a process that envelops politics of very diverse kinds. The FBI speaks the language of diversity fluently; the United States military is versed in the arts of flexible citizenship; local politicians, elected and appointed, join Arabs in multiple forms of dissent (but not in vociferous, public criticism of Zionism, an avoidance strategy many Arab community leaders in Detroit have adopted as well). Arab Americans, meanwhile, are busy reconfiguring their transnational networks in alignment with American geopolitical interests, using popular notions of multicultural pluralism to expand their institutions, and building coalitions with civil rights activists and other communities of color to oppose profiling and discrimination. The result, surprising to some, is an Arab community that has weathered the 9/11 backlash extremely well, only to find itself entangled in the very structures of surveillance and political discipline that continually place Arabs and Muslims at the limits of American identity.

If we fuse the approaches of Maira, Howell, and Jamal, the result is disciplinary inclusion, a citizenship style in which every act of recognition, every assertion of identity and belonging, entails (and is made against) a simultaneous message of Otherness and stigmatized difference. To the degree that it is oriented toward public opinion, or is responsive to images that circulate in public spheres, disciplinary inclusion engenders a politics of representation that is oddly collaborative, bringing members of Arab and Muslim communities into intimate contact with agencies and ideas easily portrayed as external to them. The dialogic quality of this process does not make the partners equal—it can, in fact, radically accentuate their inequalities—but it does mean that Others, even when reduced to the role of victim, are expected to take part in their own marginalization, or the marginalization of certain sectors of their communities, or certain aspects of personal identity. The result, visible in so many Arab and Muslim American communities, is seldom overt political opposition. Rather, disciplinary inclusion produces a regime in which people censor and police themselves in hopes of deflecting the gaze of external observers whom they imagine (with good reason) to wish them harm.

This conceptual vice is strong, but it is flexible as well, and the papers in this volume show how it operates across a wide spectrum of socioeconomic, national, religious, and ethnoracial locations. The professional, well-educated Bible Belt Muslims of Houston and Durham face challenges quite unlike those encountered by semi-skilled, semi-literate Rust Belt Muslims in Detroit and Hamtramck. Yet a larger context is palpable in both settings. Whatever their social position, Arabs and Muslims in the United States must contend with a mass mediated realm of endlessly updated imagery and knowledge about them that is highly unfavorable, at times hostile, and they must contend with the fact that their own government is at war with Arab and Muslim regimes and resistance movements, some of which are identified with immigrant homelands.

Against this hegemonic backdrop, Arab and Muslim Americans are easily associated with enemy aliens, and much of their citizenship work, as a result, is dedicated to altering this image, guarding against its repercussions, and coming to terms with American identification in spite of (or in relation to) these stigmatizing forces. Every essay in this book confronts the same hegemonic backdrop, showing how it colors everyday experience. The essays are at their best, however, when they show how local responses to marginalization vary, and how the resources individuals use to craft their responses are more American than they realize.

THE PECULIARITY
OF THE LOCAL RESPONSE

In most of this book's essays, authors and subjects alike are fully aware that the local climate for Arab and Muslim Americans—the conditions met in particular schools, mosques, neighborhoods, and metropolitan governments—can be quite different from (and often more sympathetic than) the harsh climate depicted in realms of mass mediation and geopolitics. There is a kind of surprise elicited (or assumed on behalf of the reader) by authors who must explain why, in their post-9/11 field site, new mosques are being built and Muslim outreach programs are expanding, why individuals who experience prejudice strongly identify with and as Americans, why large donations are being given to Arab and Muslim organizations by corporate and government funders, why Islamic banking has continued to flourish in a period when federal authorities have clamped down vigorously on Muslim charities and international money transfers, and why more Muslims have been appointed to public office. Local realities cannot, in any of these settings, be confused with the global, or even the national, because in each case Arab and Muslim identities are being shaped in opposition to images and assumptions that prevail in global and national publics. Not only do Arab and Muslim Americans change their local realities through critical engagement with these larger publics, they do so in collusion with local allies—not only political activists, but also the keepers of rather staid mainstream institutions—who stand ready to facilitate these efforts. The protective function of multicultural pluralism described by Joseph and colleagues (chapter 6) is perfectly real, but so is its disciplinary function, which makes protection and recognition available to Arabs and Muslims as Americans only in return for certain identity concessions.

The word *concessions* is perhaps not the best one. Even in a place like Detroit, where the Arab vote can make or break a candidate for public office, Arabs know that certain political views common in the Arab world cannot be freely expressed or enacted in the United States. Because people are aware of this silencing, and often criticize it among themselves, it is certainly fair to point out that mainstream Arab American identity politics is rife with tactical

203

concessions. Most identity shifts are not perceived as brute impositions, however, and suppler forces shape some of the most interesting material in this book. Ewing and Hoyler (chapter 4), for instance, examine the fascinating apparatus Muslim youth in Durham use to distinguish between culture and Islam. Islam, in their view, is universal—not to mention good, correct, and dignified—and it should not be confused with, or polluted by, aspects of Muslim practice and belief that are merely *cultural,* a term that often means *not really Islamic* and therefore open to criticism and change. It is hardly coincidence that many practices now deemed cultural are exactly those associated with immigrant parents and their so-called backward ways. It is also the case that "true Islam" very often enshrines values that are consistent with enlightened middle class American attitudes (on matters of gender, especially, but also on such topics as child-rearing, interracial marriage, and other contentious issues in Muslim American households).

If Americanization is rarely the expressed intent of these revaluations of values, it is routinely the outcome. Joseph and Riedel (chapter 7), in their study of an Islamic school in Chicago, find similar trends, in which a universal Islam is brought into line with key American values (or, just as often, American values are brought into line with a very particular, very Americanized experience of Islam as universal). At an even more implicit level, Maurer (chapter 8) notes the preference, among shari'a-conscious Muslims, for the physical appearance of American legal documents, an aesthetic choice that is changing the way fatwas should look if they are to be seen as Muslim and authoritative in the sense favored by a tradition of textual fetishism that is very American. It would be hard to convince Muslims in a Bridgeview classroom, or on an Islamic banking website, that they are partaking in a process of disciplinary inclusion, and this propensity to see choice instead of constraint (another American tendency) is no doubt why the process is so broadly effective.

Read's survey (chapter 5) of Arabs in Houston, focusing on a mosque and a church, captures with uncanny precision the source and directional flow of discipline, both that which is perceived as such, and that which operates in ways more covert or affectively internalized. Arab Christians, Read finds, experience less harassment than Muslims, feel less vulnerable in the United States, more readily identify as Americans, and are more likely to think other Americans see them as white. Indeed, in the Detroit Arab American Study (Baker et al. 2004), Christian Arabs were far more likely than Muslims to identify as white, a placement on the American ethnoracial landscape that says a great deal about their comparative sense of cultural belonging. These findings demonstrate, rather starkly, how the generic enemy status of Arabs in the United States and abroad is principally located in their status as Muslims. Hence, some of the most urgent culture work undertaken by Arab Christians, in Houston and Detroit alike, consists of asserting that they are not now, and have never been, Muslims.

REARTICULATING IMMEDIATE
AND MEDIATED WORLDS

I would like to conclude by noting some features shared by the essays in this book. I did not expect these commonalities, but they reinforce themes I have already discussed. The first is the overwhelming publicness of the essays. They are situated, with few exceptions, in spaces away from home, in spaces that are not quite private or intimate. I also notice the centrality of the interview and the survey. Several authors made use of participant observation as a method, but this technique appears not to have produced the bulk of evidence the authors collected and now analyze. In fact, participant observation seems primarily to have facilitated interviews and surveys, which in turn produced testimony, the principal form of data in this book. The result is a kind of polite distance appropriate to public and semipublic life. I was surprised throughout the book by the degree to which authors report events, and are told about things that happened to others, but rarely participate in events in ways that shape or figure centrally in the analysis. Generally, the researchers are not enveloped or immersed in the worlds they study, as they often are in more conventional ethnographic studies.

Although the papers tend to develop away from home, they are politically domestic in their orientation. They are located in spaces that are American, Americanized, and Americanizing. Active links to other countries, other homelands, are not explored in depth, although identification with these places, and presumed loyalties to them, receive attention in almost every essay, as does attention to what happens in countries of origin. The transnational consists, in most cases, of the logistics of visiting relatives and bringing them to the United States, or consuming media (popular and mass media) from South Asia or the Arab world. The negative consequences of connection to foreign places identified with enemies of the United States are vividly examined in several essays, and these negative consequences provide evidence for claims, put forward by Maira (chapter 2) and Howell and Jamal (chapter 3), that flexible citizenship of the sort enjoyed by Asian or Latino Americans has been effectively denied to Arabs and Muslims by the "war on terror."

Finally, more than half of the essays deal with young people, with college students, high school students, adolescents, or legal minors. This trend is linked to others by the fact that adolescents are moving out of domestic space and developing independent, public selves. Many of them, as Ewing and Hoyler (chapter 4) show, are constructing identities critical of those of their parents (whom they associate with the home and the homeland). The young subjects who appear in this book speak English and are mostly American-born; they are vexed by many of the identity issues that fascinate social scientists—gender, citizenship, religious beliefs, and values—so, as social types, youth are attractive to research.

If we combine these tendencies, it is apparent that the contributors to this volume have concentrated their efforts in zones of communal discipline, where citizenship is crafted and tested, where denial and bestowal of full citizenship can be measured and criticized, and where Americanization is likely to have its most discernible and publicly displayed effects. These zones (schools, houses of worship, community centers, markets, the political arena, the press) are important and worthy of our full attention. Of course, every concentration of research effort creates gaps and new possibilities for inquiry. In the present case, we are left to wonder how Arab and Muslim identity develops at home, in family life (both within and beyond the house), in languages other than English, in truly intimate spaces (of friendship, sexuality, worship, and political desire), in relation to other homelands, and at the margins of American citizenship. The authors take us to the very edge of this terrain, whose contours become visible, almost in the manner of a photographic negative, in contradistinction to the zones of public culture more fully explored here. I suspect, based on conversations with many colleagues, that research conducted at the threshold of the public and private—and certainly research that focuses on transnational ties—is widely construed, by IRB boards as well as by scholars and their subjects, as potentially harmful to Arab and Muslim Americans. This belief was less common in the pre-9/11 era, and it does not, even today, function as a block on fiction writers, filmmakers, and visual and spoken word artists, who currently provide our best, most illuminating access to "cultural intimacy" as Arab and Muslim Americans experience it.

Given these trends, it would appear that a future challenge, for research, is to study how the immediate and mediated worlds of Arab and Muslim Americans are articulated in everyday life. This agenda might have to wait until political conditions are friendlier to it, but it is now the road less traveled by, and exploring it will perhaps not make all the difference, but it will be proof that Arabs and Muslims are returning to the status of those we call normal people, or at least to the status of an immigrant and ethnic population. This shift has occurred before. It is part of a long history of identity formation through trauma—of political crisis, followed by political discipline, followed by new forms of political inclusion and identity—which gives the Arab Muslim experience in the United States much of its historical specificity. This volume, through its rigorous engagement with public and institutional settings in which Arabs and Muslims are "made American"—and treated as somehow less than American—sets the stage for new and important work.

REFERENCES

Baker, Wayne, Sally Howell, Amaney Jamal, Ann Lin, Andrew Shryock, Ron Stockton, and Mark Tessler. 2004. *The Detroit Arab American Study: Preliminary Findings and Technical Documentation.* Ann Arbor, Mich.: Institute for Social Research.

INDEX

Boldface numbers refer to figures and tables.